"It's a toss-up which will be first: England winning the World Cup a___in, or the UK winning Eurovision again. While you're waiting, this book is the perfect companion."
Tim Rice

"This book definitely gets douze points from me."
Mel Giedroyc, BBC TV presenter and former host of
The Great British Bake Off

_e_ always thought Eurovision was just a joke, but Chris West _ws_ how it has always been a mirror of cultural and political _ange._ He also thinks that as the most popular European _tion_, it can give lessons in transparency and accessibility to _e_ leaders of the EU. But he does give us some laughs too."
Robert Tombs, Professor of Modern History,
University of Cambridge

"For Europhiles, Europhobes and the Euro-cautious alike: witty, informed and insightful."
_n_ **Light, author of *Common People* and Senior Associate at Pembroke College, Oxford**

_t_ ever say that Eurovision isn't political. It is. Chris West's _k_ brings the colourful history of Europe to life through the _f_ the even more colourful Eurovision Song Contest. It is _pia_ of information, with everything I wanted to know about modern history and the contest."
Katrina Leskanich, Katrina & The Waves
(Eurovision winner, 1997)

Eurovision!

**A History of Modern Europe Through
the World's Greatest Song Contest**

Eurovision!

**A History of Modern Europe Through
the World's Greatest Song Contest**

Chris West

MELVILLE HOUSE UK

LONDON

Eurovision!

First published in 2017 by
Melville House UK
8 Blackstock Mews
Islington
London N4 2BT

mhpbooks.com   facebook.com/mhpbooks   @melvillehouse

First edition: April 2017

A CIP catalogue record for this book is available from the British Library

ISBN: 978-0-9934149-9-2

1 3 5 7 9 10 8 6 4 2

Printed and bound in Great Britain by Clays Ltd, St Ives plc
Design and typesetting by Roland Codd

Contents

List of Illustrations

1. **Beauty and the Box:** France's Jacqueline Joubert, presenter of the 1959 and 1961 contests.
2. **Vol – aaaa – re!** Domenico Modugno, Italy, 1958.
3. **Let it swing!** The UK's Sandie Shaw, 1967.
4. **Boom-Bang-a-Bad-Guys:** The UK's Lulu in front of Salvador Dalí's 1969 stage tribute to Franco and Mussolini.
5. **European Conquerors:** Sweden's Abba, 1974.
6. **A Little Peace:** Germany's Nicole, 1982.
7. **Viva la Diva!** Israel's Dana International, 1998.
8. **Eurovision heads East:** Turkey's Sertab Erener, 2003.
9. **Orange Revolution:** Ukrainian singer-songwriter Ruslana, 2004.
10. **Silver Revolution:** Ukraine's off-the-wall Verka Sedushka, 2007.
11. **Joyful and triumphant:** Norway's Alexander Rybak, 2009.
12. **A New Beauty?** Austria's Conchita Wurst, 2014.

All images © Getty Images

Introduction

Every May, 200 million people turn on their TVs or log on to the internet, not just to watch but to be part of the Eurovision Song Contest, an extravaganza of song, dance, stagecraft and politics.

Politics?

The European Broadcasting Union (EBU), who run the contest, insist it is non-political. They ban songs like Georgia's 2009 'We Don't Wanna Put In' ('put in' was sung 'poot-in' to make sure everyone got the point) to enforce this.

They are, I feel, right to do so: the pretence must be kept up. But the Eurovision Song Contest is political to its thigh-high, spangly boots. It is now and, as I plan to show in this book, it always has been.

There's politics in the songs. Not allowed through the front door, it sneaks in through the back. The winner of the 2016 contest, '1944', was a passionate denunciation of Stalin's deportation of the Crimean Tatars – and by extension, an equally passionate denunciation of Russia's annexation of the peninsula in 2014. In other years, we've had anti-colonialism, radical Socialism, Thatcherism, a marching song from Ukraine's *Euromaidan* movement . . . In the 1970s, a Eurovision* song even started a revolution.

There's politics in the voting, with blocs of nations supporting each other's songs. It drove Sir Terry Wogan to distraction, but most Eurovision fans love that moment when the Cypriot announcer says with a straight face, 'And our twelve points go to . . .' It's all part of the ritual. It also tells us something important about Europe.

---

* Yes, I know 'Eurovision' is technically not the correct name for the song contest. Eurovision is the TV arm of the EBU, who produce both the contest and a number of other programmes. But 200 million viewers call the show 'Eurovision'. Who am I to argue with them?

Behind this is the politics of belonging, not just to your bloc but to Europe as well. Eurovision asks, and always has asked, what it means to be 'European'. Estonia had no doubt in 2001, when it won the contest: it meant liberty. 'We freed ourselves from the Soviet empire through song,' said prime minister Mart Laar. 'Now we will sing our way into Europe!' Sixteen years on, ever more doubts are being expressed about our shared European identity. What will we find Eurovision telling us about that?

As well as providing insight into big national and international politics, the contest has also been a mirror for the subtler politics of gender, race and sexual orientation.

The contest has always reflected the changing role of Europe's women. As good a measure of this as any is the simple volume of female voices, from Corry Brokken quietly wishing her 1957 husband would put down his newspaper, to Céline Dion belting out 'Ne Partez Pas Sans Moi' in 1988.

The contest had to wait till 1964 for its first non-white entrant, the Netherlands' Anneke Grönloh, and till 2001 for the first black winner, Dave Benton. What does that tell us about Europe?

Eurovision is particularly loved in the gay community. Conchita Wurst's 2014 victory was applauded around most of Europe, not just as a good song well sung, but as a triumph for openness and personal authenticity. The contest's first openly gay contestant only appeared in 1997 – but go back to 1961, whose winner is often read as a song about a kind of love still forbidden at the time in many European countries. The contest means liberty here, too.

Eurovision has even had politics in its sets. In 1969, General Franco smuggled a Fascist emblem onto the stage. Moscow's lavish staging in 2009, which used 30 per cent of the LED screens in existence at the time, was a clear statement of intent – we want to be European!

Eurovision's very conception was political. It was the brainchild of Marcel Bezençon, a Swiss broadcaster who was a close friend of Jean

Eurovision!

Monnet, the man widely regarded as the founder of modern Europe. Like many of their generation, Bezençon and Monnet were haunted by the destruction of the Second World War, and were determined that Europeans should never fall on each other's throats with such viciousness again. They saw our mutual salvation in a United States of Europe – and a shared song contest as part of how we would get there.

Were they right? Eurovision might just have the answer.

The contest shows us other things, too. The more you watch it, the more you see it reflecting wider aspects of the continent's history, beyond politics. Morality, technology, fashion, economics, philosophy, faith – all these things have changed unimaginably in Europe in the last six decades, and they are *all* on display here.

Join me on an amazing journey through the history of a continent, told through the world's greatest song contest.

The
1950s

1955

Watch those recordings of early Eurovision Song Contests – they're almost all on YouTube – and you are back in a black-and-white world.

If you were watching at the time, your black-and-white TV would probably have had a screen not massively bigger than a modern tablet. You would have needed to turn it on a few minutes before, to let it warm up (at the end of this process, a little dot would appear in the middle of the screen, then expand to fill it with the new magic of broadcast images). You would have been lucky to have a TV at all. They cost more than a month's average wage. Despite this, your state-of-the-art consumer goodie might still lurk in a dark wooden exterior. Apart from a few spindly-legged modernist sets, televisions were expected to merge decorously with the other furniture in the living room.

That world was black and white in a subtler sense, too. Distinctions were clear: good guys and bad guys, men and women, adults and children, class, nationality. Not everyone accepted these, of course, but most people did.

In urban Europe, much work was repetitive – grey, perhaps, rather than black and white. It was like this in the home for most married women (or maybe via dull jobs in typing pools or shops) and on the factory floor or in stiff, hierarchical offices for men. In the country, there was the hard toil of tending the small family farm. People often worked Saturday mornings. For many, Sunday in Western Europe meant putting on formal clothes for church (attendance, which had been falling in the inter-war years, rose in the decade after 1945).

Duty mattered. Personal authenticity, truth to oneself, did not – though integrity was valued: honesty, reliability, truthfulness to a role. Many young European men were expected to learn this via National Service in their country's armed forces – despite the role of nationalism in the 1939–45 cataclysm, most people at that time were strongly patriotic.

Only the more raffish of Europe's youngsters would have sex before marrying. In many countries, they would have had little preparation: much sex education at the time was purely anatomical, often as much about flowers and rabbits as the slightly embarrassing fact that humans did this stuff too. If the woman got pregnant, she would face stigma and pressure to give up her child for adoption. The man could often just walk away. Or there might be a quick marriage, to ensure things stayed respectable. If, instead, the lovemaking had been with someone of the same sex, the participants would have been breaking the law in most European countries.

Some consumer goods were beginning to add colour to life in Western Europe. But in 1955 few families had fridges, washing machines, cars or TVs. Few enjoyed foreign holidays, or had any experience of a country other than their own, except for men who had seen 'abroad' as a battlefield. In the East, behind a vast barbed wire fence that split the continent in two, such luxuries were even rarer, despite the propaganda about happy workers and ever-booming production.

At its heart Europe, East and West, was still struggling with the legacy of war. Its cities were pockmarked with boarded-off bombsites. In its homes, photographs stood on mantelpieces showing sons, husbands, brothers, uncles or fathers who would never return from battlefields – or whole families who would never return from death camps. Men woke from troubled dreams of what they had seen or done. Europe's thinkers were wrestling with quite how this could have happened and what could be done to ensure it never happened again.

One answer was that of Marcel Bezençon and Jean Monnet: a united Europe.

It was not new. The vision – a Euro-vision, one could say – can be dated back to the Holy Roman Empire of Charlemagne. At the start of the seventeenth century, the Grand Design of France's King Henry of Navarre and his minister Sully had envisaged a 'High Christian Republic' encompassing all Catholic and Protestant Europe. With its six regional councils and one overarching one, this was a sophisticated intergovernmental system based on culturally linked sub-units which the modern EU could do well to revisit. Henry was assassinated before he could turn this vision into reality.

In the nineteenth century, Victor Hugo, author of *Les Misérables*, argued passionately for a united Europe. At the Paris Peace Conference of August 1849, he spoke of the day when 'bullets and bombs will be replaced by votes, [and by] . . . the venerable arbitration of a great sovereign senate, which will be to Europe what parliament is to England'.

After the First World War, the Pan-European Union was founded by Count Richard Nikolaus von Coudenhove-Kalergi, to promote a single European state based on liberalism, Christianity and social responsibility. Eminent individuals such as Albert Einstein, Fridtjof Nansen and Sigmund Freud became members.

In September 1946, Winston Churchill made a speech in Zurich, where he advocated a 'sort of United States of Europe'. At the heart of his Euro-vision lay a co-operating France and Germany, but not Britain. In his model there would be four great powers: the United States of America, the Soviet Union, the British Commonwealth and Europe.

By 1949, full-on Euro-visions had become complicated by the lowering of the 'Iron Curtain', but the idea of a united *Western* Europe (maybe, just maybe, joined by the East at some time in the remote future) lived on. That year, the former French prime minister Robert Schuman spoke of a community of nations that would comprise those that possessed 'the European spirit'. He defined this as a consciousness of 'belonging to a cultural family and having a willingness to serve that [family] in the spirit of total mutuality, without any hidden motives of hegemony or the selfish exploitation of others'.

By 1949, there was action, too. The Council of Europe (a human rights organization, nothing to do with the modern EU) and NATO were set up in that year. The EBU first met in 1950, at a hotel in Torquay. Two years later, 1952 saw the formation of the European Coal and Steel Community (ECSC): six nations – Germany, France, Italy, the Netherlands, Belgium and Luxembourg – agreed to hand over national control of these sectors, both key to waging war, to a transnational 'High Authority'. The authority's first president was Jean Monnet.

Such was the Europe in which the Eurovision Song Contest was conceived. The actual date was 20 January 1955, when Marcel Bezençon suggested the idea to an EBU meeting in Monaco. Later that year, the EBU formally decided to go ahead with it the following May. The show would be called *Le Grand-Prix Eurovision de la Chanson Européenne*. It would be held in Lugano, Switzerland. If it was a success, they might even consider having another one.

What sort of music would it feature?

In 1955, there was a wide gulf between Europe's 'serious' music, essentially the western classical tradition, and its popular music, which was all part of that post-war rush to untroubling conformity: the world of German *schlager*, Italian *musico leggera*, Dutch *levenslied* or Britain's BBC Light Programme, of artistes like Freddy Quinn, Johnny Jordaan or Alma Cogan. In between these two sat jazz and a number of local musical traditions, such as the francophone *chanson*, where singers like Georges Brassens and Édith Piaf took on darker subjects: failed love, social alienation, existential disillusion.

However, a new music was beginning to make itself heard with ever-increasing insistency from across the Atlantic, on records imported to port cities like Liverpool, or broadcast by American Forces Radio or the freewheeling private Radio Luxembourg.

There was nothing in the EBU brief for the new contest to exclude rhythm and blues or rock 'n' roll, but somehow this music found itself off limits. Why? It could have been that it was deemed not European enough, but my own suspicion is that it was simply about numbers. The *Grand-Prix* was aimed at a middle-class family audience because the EBU thought that would attract the most viewers. Given the profile of TV ownership at the time, they were probably right. Oma, Mama, Papa and the younger kids would all watch it; if their stroppy seventeen-year-old wanted to sneak up to their room and listen to Alan Freed on their new transistor radio, well, let them. They'd soon grow out of it.

The contest has never quite got away from this early bias. That's part of its quirky charm. But it is also what makes it such a good mirror of its times – by not seeking always to present 'cutting edge' developments in music (often a minority interest), it allows itself to reflect wider social trends instead.

1956

Date: 24 May
Venue: Teatro Kursaal, Lugano, Switzerland
Debuts: Belgium, France, West Germany, Italy, Luxembourg, Netherlands, Switzerland
Winner: Lys Assia, Switzerland
Winning Song: 'Refrain'

There are no video recordings of the first Eurovision Song Contest, except for the winner's reprise. I find this oddly apt.

1956 was a watershed year in the history of modern Europe. It was the year of the Suez crisis, when Europe's two biggest colonial powers, Britain and France, suddenly found out how little clout they had in the post-war global order. Their attempt to forcibly recapture the Suez Canal, newly nationalized by Egypt's President Gamal Abdel Nasser, was halted in its tracks by condemnation from the new 'Third World', from Russia, and above all from the United States, which threatened to bankrupt Britain if it continued the adventure. So much for Churchill's 1946 vision of 'four great powers'. It was also the year that Russian tanks steamrollered into Hungary, killing over two thousand people and, with them, any hopes that with the death of Stalin the Iron Curtain would quietly rust away.

But both these events happened in the autumn of '56. The first, lost Eurovision had been held in the spring of that year. It comes to us from a simpler, vanished world.

We have no film of it, but we do have sound. The first ever Eurovision song was the feather-light 'De Vogels Van Holland' (the Birds Of Holland). 'Toodle-oodle-oo' go Holland's birds – more musically than any other nation's, of course. Nothing is quite as it seems in

Eurovision, however. The singer, Jetty Paerl, came from a Jewish family that had had to flee Holland in 1940. Paerl's friends and more distant relatives had not been so fortunate: the Netherlands' Jewish population had been 140,000 in 1939; by 1947 it was just 14,000. Most of those missing 126,000 had perished in Auschwitz or Sobibor, just over ten years before the Lugano contest. (It's worth remembering that the Holocaust was closer in time to 24 May 1956 than 9/11 is to us today.)

The songs that followed (two from each nation, the only time such a format has been used in the contest) were either *chansons* – Belgium's Fud Leclerc felt like joining 'Messieurs Les Noyés Dans La Seine' (Gentlemen Drowned In The Seine) – or further light entertainment. Germany's nautical Freddy Quinn added a little swing. After they'd been sung, it was time to decide the winner. Eurovision wouldn't be Eurovision without controversial judging. There were more Swiss judges than those of any other nation, because Luxembourg had balked at the cost of sending judges to Lugano and, with touching faith in pan-Europeanism, had asked two Swiss to stand in for them.

Guess which nation won (reputedly by one vote).

'Refrain' was a pleasant, reflective ballad about lost love. No other places were announced, though it is rumoured that two *chansons* came second and third: second, the other German entry, 'Im Wartesaal Des Grossen Gluck' (In The Waiting Room For Good Luck) (it's a *chanson*: we've got a long wait), and third Fud Leclerc.

Half the fourteen songs sung at Lugano in 1956 were in French. Watching Eurovision now, we are used to songs in English (except from France) and results announced in English (except by France), but in 1956 French dominated.

Nobody was surprised. In 1956 it was France and Frenchmen like Robert Schuman and Jean Monnet (and French-speakers like Marcel Bezençon) who were driving European integration. French was the language of the new European institutions, including the original EBU brief for the *Grand-Prix Eurovision de la Chanson Européenne*.

More significant still is the list of Lugano participants. Apart from the Swiss hosts, the competitors are the six members of the 1952 European Coal and Steel Community. ECSC outsiders Britain, Austria and Denmark had applied to participate, but for various reasons did not end up on the Kursaal stage. (Britain had an entrant ready, zither-playing Australian singer Shirley Abicair, with a song called 'Little Ship', but she never made it to Lugano. It is not clear why, though it might have been because Britain suddenly decided it didn't want to be represented by a non-Brit. Australia in Eurovision? What an extraordinary idea!)

Six decades later, these six countries remain the ones where the European flame burns most brightly. If Europe becomes 'two-speed', it is the Europe of Lugano 1956 (minus Switzerland) that will be at its heart.

Looking back not decades but centuries, the list of Lugano competitors also maps with spooky neatness onto the Holy Roman Empire at its height, when Charlemagne was crowned its emperor on Christmas Day in 800 AD. Add Austria and Bohemia (the western half of the modern Czech Republic) and remove Southern Italy, and the Lugano list *is* 'Europe' as conceived 1,156 years earlier. Charlemagne's empire lasted, in name anyway, until 1806, though it kept changing shape over that time (it lost large chunks of what is now France pretty quickly and ended up as a kind of proto-Germany). But if the great emperor's ghost had been watching the contest on 24 May 1956, he would have felt totally at home with its geographical extent. This, he would have thought, is civilization.

Almost exactly a month after the contest, on 26 June, representatives of 'Lugano Europe' met in Brussels to discuss a report from former Belgian prime minister Paul-Henri Spaak, which proposed they form a Customs Union, a free trade area with common external tariffs (for

Chris West

a more detailed explanation of these terms, see Appendix A). This is arguably the moment that the European Economic Community (EEC), which later became the European Union (EU), was conceived. The EU and the Eurovision Song Contest may not quite be twins, but they are born from the same stock and have a very narrow age difference.

1957

Date: 3 March
Venue: Hessische Rundfunk, Frankfurt, West Germany
Debuts: Austria, Denmark, UK
Winner: Corry Brokken, Netherlands
Winning Song: 'Net Als Toen' (Just Like Then)

As Charlemagne's former empire planned its new, members-only future, Eurovision opened itself to newcomers. The three applicants who missed out on Lugano got to participate this time. The 1957 contest featured ten songs in six different languages (seven if you count Flemish). The presenter, Anaid Iplicjian, had been born in Armenia. Eurovision was reaching out to a wider Europe.

The show loosened up, too. It was more fun. Singers entered down a flight of stairs. Props were used. Germany's Margot Hielscher sang into a chunky Bakelite telephone (revealing her song character to be one of her country's better-off citizens: only 7.6 per cent of West Germans owned telephones at that time). Italy and the Netherlands had musicians accompany the singers on stage. Dutch violinist Sem Nijveen played a particularly attractive, jazzy solo, which helped the song romp to victory ('Net Als Toen' got nearly half as many votes again as France's 'La Belle Amour', which came second). Nijveen was another Dutch survivor of the horrors of 1939–45; born Samuel Moses, he had spent much of the Nazi occupation of the Netherlands in hiding.

The theatrical performance of the evening came from Denmark's Birthe Wilke and Gustav Winckler: dressed for the part, they sang their song, 'Skibet Skal Sejle I Nat' (The Ship Must Sail Tonight), about a naval officer – not an ordinary seaman – about to leave his new love, then concluded with a kiss that was both long (thirteen seconds) and passionate.

Perhaps theatrical isn't the right word. Their kiss was cinematic – Hollywood cinematic: think Ingrid Bergman and Cary Grant in Alfred Hitchcock's *Notorious*. In 1957 Western Europeans were getting much of their cultural input from across the Atlantic. The great musicals of Rodgers and Hammerstein – *Carousel, The King and I, Oklahoma* – had made it onto the silver screen in the mid-fifties (*South Pacific* would follow in 1958). In 1957, two lads called John Lennon and Paul McCartney met at a fete in a Liverpool suburb, and found they shared a passion for music – not *chansons, levenslied* or *schlagers* but American rhythm and blues.

In political Europe, the time between the first and second Eurovision contests had been filled with diplomatic activity. 'Lugano Europe' had accepted Spaak's report, and then had to thrash out the details of exactly what form the new supra-national entity would take. This was not easy, as members differed both in overall vision and specific national interests. In essence, the Netherlands and Germany wanted a more market-focused system, while France and Italy sought more social protection and regional aid. Luxembourg and Belgium stood in the middle, pressing for compromise to ensure a successful outcome.

At one point, the Dutch were on the point of quitting. Their cars, outside the Castle of Val Duchesse where the negotiations were taking place, had their engines running (cars needed to warm up before you drove them in 1957). But they stayed. After six months of wrangling, agreement was reached. Three weeks after the 1957 song contest, the Treaty of Rome was signed.

The treaty created the European Economic Community. This involved Spaak's planned Customs Union, but signatories agreed to take their unity further and pursue common policies in transport and agriculture. Perhaps most significant of all, the document began with the assertion that the leaders of The Six were 'DETERMINED to lay the foundations of an ever-closer union among the peoples of Europe' – surely a deliberate echo of the Constitution of the USA, with its desire 'to form a more perfect Union'.

On 1 January 1958, the EEC became a reality. Various bodies came into being along with it. These are in essence still the main bodies of Europe-level government today.

At the heart of the new community was its Commission, a kind of civil service with former politicians from community members in charge: an overall president, Germany's Walter Hallstein, plus three vice-presidents and five other commissioners with specific responsibilities such as transport, competition, social affairs and agriculture.

I say 'kind of' civil service, as its power was greater than that, with a unique role in the creation of Europe-level law as well as its implementation. Hallstein was much more visible and influential than any civil servant, so much so that he annoyed national leaders, who thought he was setting himself up as their equal. They were right: Hallstein was a passionate federalist* who saw his job as laying the foundations for a European political state. In such a state, the Commission president would be the equal of any national leader, and maybe their superior.

However, the Commission was not the omnipotent behemoth portrayed by Eurosceptics. Its power was to be balanced by two other institutions, both consisting of politicians elected by their national electorates. First of these was the Council of Ministers, consisting of ministers from member states. The second was the European Parliamentary Assembly, forerunner of the modern European Parliament (the name changed in 1962). This was a gathering of MPs from member states' legislative assemblies: members were not directly elected to the Parliament until 1979.

---

* For an explanation of this term, and others denoting an individual's opinion of political Europe, see Appendix B.

The European Court of Justice had the job of ensuring that the rulings of these new entities were put into practice in member nations.

Since 1958, the main addition to these four has been the European Council, where heads of state meet and set Europe's overall political direction and agenda. This was formed in 1974, with the sound of Abba echoing in Europe's ears.

In 2017, there are seven formal 'institutions of the European Union'. These are the five above, plus the Court of Auditors, founded in 1977, which has the unenviable job of monitoring EU expenditure, and the European Central Bank (ECB), founded in 1998 to oversee the new economy created by the introduction of the euro.

European political bodies were proliferating. Luckily, there was still only one Eurovision Song Contest, pure (apart, perhaps, from Birthe and Gustav) and simple.

1958

Date: 12 March
Venue: Netherlands TV Service Studio, Hilversum
Debut: Sweden
Winner: André Claveau, France
Winning Song: 'Dors, Mon Amour' (Sleep, My Love)

The 1958 contest was opened by Italian *cantautore* (singer/songwriter) Domenico Modugno. After a slow, rather operatic intro to his song, which had the unmemorable title of 'Nel Blu Dipinto Di Blu' (In The Blue Painted In Blue), he suddenly flung out his huge goalkeeper-like hands and launched into its refrain. Eurovision had taken wings.

The song, retitled 'Volare', became a global hit. Modugno's words were translated into English by New York lyricist Mitchell Parish, and Dean Martin took the song to number one in the US. 'Volare' has been regularly covered ever since – by Ella Fitzgerald, Oscar Peterson, David Bowie, the Gypsy Kings and even Frank Zappa. It has found its way onto football terraces. Interestingly, when translating, Parish kept part of the song in Italian. While the elite in late 1950s Europe worried about Elvis and creeping Americanization, elite America still looked to Europe, especially France and Italy, for sophistication.

All this was to come, however; at the time, the Eurovision judges placed this classic – in a '50 Years of Eurovision' poll in 2005 it was voted the second greatest Eurovision song ever – third. The contest winner was a very Gallic ballad sung by the even more Gallic André Claveau, and second was a piece of light opera called 'Giorgio'.

'Volare' pointed a bright way forward for Eurovision, towards making it a showcase for fresh European songwriting/performing talent that did not reject America but embraced its influences with flair and originality. 'Giorgio' suggested another future, that of formulaic lowest common denominator Euro-ditties, with a dollop of la-ing and lyrics full of words recognizable all round the continent: place-names, wine, well-known dishes. 'Giorgio' got twenty-four votes; 'Volare' thirteen. The dinging and donging start here.

Luckily for its growth prospects, Western Europe's economy was following the example of 'Volare', combining the best of America and Europe: US corporate organization, mass production and marketing; European taste and design. As the 1950s matured, the half-continent saw ever more consumer goods becoming available at prices ever more of its people could afford. Among these were TVs on which to watch Eurovision. In 1953, there had been one set in France for every 1,000 citizens; by 1958, this figure was over twenty per thousand, and a couple of years later, it would be forty. The year's debutant, Sweden, for whom Alice Babs sang the cute 'Lilla Stjärna' (Little Stars) in national dress,* showed even more dramatic growth, with less than 1 television per 1,000 inhabitants in 1953 but around 150 by 1960.

For Germany, Margot Hielscher returned to Eurovision in 1958 as 'Miss Juke Box', hymning the delights of music you could get for two *Groschen* (cents). Her nation was the economic superstar of the 1950s, with its economy growing at 8 per cent a year. By 1958 that economy had become bigger than Britain's.

There were various reasons for this: the generosity of the USA's postwar Marshall Aid, the industriousness of German workers, but most of all the nation's consensus political system, the 'Social Market Economy' championed by Chancellor Konrad Adenauer and his finance minister Ludwig Erhard. In this model, private, not state, ownership of enterprises was preferred, and competition between them encouraged. The market, not the state, determined the direction of the economy: no

---

* Alice might have played it cute for Eurovision, but she was not uncontroversial in her home country. As a young jazz singer she had upset more conservative Swedes with movies like *Swing it, Teacher*. She later worked with, and was much admired by, Duke Ellington.

grand planning. But the state was not inactive. A strong central bank was committed to fighting inflation – older Germans still remembered the hyperinflation of 1923. Taxes were high; the government spent them on socially useful projects such as schools, hospitals and roads, as well as welfare. In return for this expenditure, trades unions were expected to work with employers' organizations to set pay levels, not just go on strike.* And in return, enterprises were expected to invest for the future rather than pay out big immediate dividends.

This is now seen as the standard 'European way', but it was radical in 1958. France still preferred top-down state planning, countered by a stiff dose of anarchy on the shop floor. Italy had the shop-floor anarchy without the dirigisme. Britain encouraged the free market but its labour relations were class-obsessed and confrontational. All over Europe, intellectually fashionable Socialist and Communist parties (the latter shrinking after the Soviet invasion of Hungary, but still influential in France and Italy) continued to talk of state ownership of 'the means of production' – i.e. of all enterprise. Behind the Iron Curtain (except in Yugoslavia), such monopoly was a fact. The nearest approach to Germany's Social Market Economy was that of the Nordic countries, with their long tradition of social democracy (*Folkhemmet* in Sweden: society as a large family), though these involved higher levels of state spending.

All European economies, however they were run, were benefiting from advances in technology – though this didn't always deliver flawlessly. There are few things that true aficionados of Eurovision love more than a voting cock-up, and 1958 was a vintage year, thanks to hostess Hannie Lips' battles with lagging, half-audible phone lines and a hand-operated scoreboard that looked like it had been borrowed from an English village cricket ground.

---

* In the 1950s Britain and France lost around 2 million working days a year through strikes. Germany's annual average loss was around 100,000 days.

1959

Date: 11 March
Venue: Palais des Festivals, Cannes, France
Debut: Monaco
Winner: Teddy Scholten, Netherlands
Winning Song: 'Een Beetje' (A Little Bit)

The relative performances of 'Giorgio' and 'Volare' in 1958 did not augur well for Eurovision, and that showed in the next year's poor contest – well, that's my view anyway: other Eurovision fans will no doubt differ.

What cannot be denied is that France put on a fine show. It chose an elegant venue – coverage of the evening begins with a shot of the Mediterranean, then pans along Cannes' palm-lined Promenade de la Croisette. The staging inside the Palais des Festivals was adventurous. There were three ornate carousels – Eurovision meets Louis XIV – which were divided into quarters, and spun round to reveal each artist against a national backdrop.

The backdrops were amusingly stereotypical: a windmill for the Netherlands' Teddy Scholten; Big Ben for Britain's Pearl Carr and Teddy Johnson; the canals of Venice for Domenico Modugno, who returned with another song, 'Piove' (It's Raining), that didn't do well in the contest but went on to become a global hit. The backdrops reflect the traditional vision of Europe as a continent of distinct nations.

This might seem strange coming from the home of Robert Schuman and Jean Monnet, but by March 1959, France had undergone a change of leader. In May 1958 the former wartime head of the Free French, General Charles de Gaulle, had become president. De Gaulle was a keen European, but he had no time for federalism;

instead he was what Europe scholars call an intergovernmentalist. He did not want ever-closer union, but ever closer co-operation between independent nation states. The General talked of *une Europe des patries* (the usual translation, 'a Europe of nations', doesn't capture the Gaullist passion of the word *patrie*).

For him, of course, one *patrie* was supposed to have more power than any other. As he once told a minister, 'Europe is the chance for France to become what she has ceased to be since Waterloo: the first in the world . . . Italy is not serious . . . The English console themselves for their decline by saying that they share in the American hegemony. Germany has had her backbone broken.'

What had brought de Gaulle to office was the crisis across the Med from the Palais des Festivals. Algeria had been the most bizarre of all European imperialist ventures. It was not just a colony but a part of France (and thus part of the new EEC). Its four *départements* were supposed to be as French as Pas-de-Calais or Lot-et-Garonne. Indigenous resistance to this had been building since 1945, coalescing into the National Liberation Front (FLN) in 1954, which fought an escalating guerrilla war against the colonial power.

In May 1958, European *'pied noir'* settlers, afraid that the Paris government was planning to admit defeat and grant Algeria independence, took to the streets of Algiers and seized government buildings. The colonial French army joined them. Paratroopers landed in Corsica, and had plans to launch a coup in France itself – which were only cancelled when de Gaulle was made president: the army thought he would support the cause of *Algérie Française*. De Gaulle quickly visited the colony, bravely walking among the crowds and telling the *pieds noirs* that he had 'understood' them. Order was restored, but it was fragile and everyone knew it.

Unfazed, Eurovision sang on. The 1959 winner was the pert Teddy Scholten, who told her overeager admirer she would be faithful 'a little bit' too (until they got engaged, of course). It's a neat lyric that works best in its original Dutch, as it plays with that language's compulsion to stick the playful diminutive *je* on the end of every noun.

Britain came second. The UK's first entry to Eurovision, back in 1957, had been a dud. The operatic 'All' misjudged the feel of the contest. (The song was also extremely short – it still holds the record for the briefest Eurovision entry ever – and its conductor Eric Robinson did not get on with singer Patricia Bredin: he brought the orchestra in before she was ready.) As a consequence of its poor result, Britain had gone into a Euro-sulk in 1958 and not entered. The following year saw it come back with a classic piece of camp and begin a long run of high placings.

As in Eurovision, so in political Europe. At the start, Britain failed to get the point of the new EEC. One UK diplomat reportedly told delegates at a conference in 1955, where the new entity was being planned: 'Gentlemen, you are trying to negotiate something you will never be able to negotiate. But, if negotiated, it will not be ratified. And if ratified, it will not work.' Soon, however, it would be eager to join.

Third was France's 'Oui, Oui, Oui, Oui' (I shan't bother to translate this one). Sweden's Brita Borg asked her mother not to wait up for her as she went out on a date: she was twenty-two now, and could look after herself. Most memorable of all, perhaps, was Austria's Ferry Graf, who produced the contest's first full-on novelty number. 'Der K Und K Calypso Aus Wien' (The Imperial And Royal Calypso From Vienna) featured calypso, swing and yodelling. The song is the first of a string of magnificently plumed turkeys that have strutted across the Eurovision stage over the years, usually to come last, some with that ultimate so-bad-it's-good Eurovision accolade of *nul points.**

---

* No Eurovision judge has ever actually announced 'X-land, *nul points*'. It doesn't make grammatical sense in any European language, and even if it did, it would not be said: if you don't get any points, you just don't get mentioned. But who cares? The phrase has entered the mythology of the contest, and I shall enjoy using it.

The
1960s

1960

Date: 29 March
Venue: Royal Festival Hall, London, UK
Debut: Norway
Winner: Jacqueline Boyer, France
Winning Song: 'Tom Pillibi'

Watching Eurovision in 1960, one would have had no sense that the coming decade would end up being regarded as one of unparalleled radicalism in Europe. If anything, the competition had become more sedate than, say, 1957. In '57, most male singers had worn lounge suits; in 1960 standard masculine wear was a dinner jacket and black bow tie. The theatricality of the late-fifties contest had given way to simply standing up and singing. Lightness had conquered originality and depth. The first act on stage, Britain's Bryan Johnson, sounded like a scoutmaster trying to jolly along laggards on a cross-country hike, though his song purported to be about a man dying for love. The winner was a jaunty little piece about a boy who makes up fantasies about himself, sung by a girl who sees through them but loves him anyway (some people thought the song was about a rich show-off, but that misses its gentle irony). The most creative, experimental entry, sung in local dialect by Luxembourg's Camillo Felgen, came last.

But Eurovision is a sign of its times. Was this what 1960 wanted? Among the young, the great rock 'n' roll revolution had lost its oomph the day Elvis was drafted into the US army.* It never really recovered.

---

* Elvis was actually discharged in 1960, but switched to recording mainly ballads and making movies, most of them dreadful.

Looking round Europe's seats of power on 29 March 1960, the atmosphere is one of slightly exhausted conservatism. *Le Général* was in charge in France, Adenauer's Christian Democrats in Germany, the bloodhound-jowled Harold Macmillan in Britain, a centre-right coalition in the Netherlands, Christian Democrats in Italy. Scandinavia did differently, with Social Democrat or Labour leaders – but this was traditional for that part of Europe. Norway had voted Labour since 1935. With a couple of brief breaks, Denmark had been Social Democrat since 1929. Sweden's Tage Erlander had been prime minister since 1946.

If there was political change, it was in Europe's colonies. De Gaulle had slowly come to the conclusion that to retain Algeria was, after all, impossible, and on 16 September 1959 made a U-turn, announcing on television that its people could choose their own fate in a referendum once four years of peace had passed. This satisfied neither the FLN, who wanted independence sooner, nor the *pieds noirs*, who took to the streets again in January 1960. The violence would continue, but there was now only one realistic outcome to the struggle.

France divested itself of most of its sub-Saharan African empire in 1960. February of that year saw Harold Macmillan give speeches in Accra and Cape Town, where he talked of 'the wind of change blowing through this continent'. In June, Belgium, terrified by what it saw happening in Algeria, hastily gave independence to the vast Congo basin it had so viciously misruled since 1885 (the new nation collapsed into anarchy almost at once). Only Spain and Portugal, still outside the charmed circle of Eurovision in 1960, seemed immune to the new mood of decolonization.

1961

Date: 18 March
Venue: Palais des Festivals, Cannes, France
Debuts: Finland, Spain, Yugoslavia
Winner: Jean-Claude Pascal, Luxembourg
Winning Song: 'Nous Les Amoureux' (We, The Lovers)

A wind of change blew through Eurovision in 1961. It did so literally: on the day of the contest, the *mistral* suddenly descended on Cannes, filling the usually placid sea with white horses. It did so figuratively: inside the Palais des Festivals, three new participants joined the show, which had been quietly expanding since 1956 and now featured sixteen European nations. Among these debutants was Yugoslavia. Eurovision had breached the Iron Curtain.

Yugoslavia was not a standard member of the eastern bloc. Its president, former partisan leader Marshal Josip Broz Tito, had no intention of letting Moscow tell him what to do. (After Stalin's death, a note was found in his papers from Tito. It read: 'Stop sending people to kill me. We've already captured five of them, one of them with a bomb and another with a rifle . . . If you don't stop sending killers, I'll send a very fast-working one to Moscow and I certainly won't have to send another.' There is even a theory that Tito put his threat into action and poisoned the Soviet dictator.)

In some ways, Yugoslavia shared the sinister features of Soviet empire nations – elections were rigged and it had a ruthless secret police force – but in other ways it looked west. Many factories were controlled by workers and managers, not state planners, and were encouraged to compete commercially with rivals rather than just meeting artificial, centrally imposed targets. Culturally, Ljiljana

Petrović looked perfectly at home in Cannes, singing her ballad of lost love, 'Neke Davne Zvezde' (Some Distant Stars).

There was a wider range of songs on offer than in 1960, too. Several – from the Netherlands and Sweden, for example – swung. A few others tried to. Italy produced a powerful ballad. Like 'Volare', 'Al Di Là' (Beyond) failed to win Eurovision then went on to be a global hit. Britain's entry, The Allisons, sounded dangerously like the kind of American-influenced music youngsters were listening to. Full-on rock 'n' roll might have died with Elvis's conscription and Buddy Holly's air crash, but there were still acts like the Everly Brothers, who were the models for 'Are You Sure?'

Even more subversive – so subversive that hardly anyone noticed it at the time – was the winner. 'Nous Les Amoureux', sung by Parisian actor Jean-Claude Pascal, is about love that is forbidden by religion and frowned on by society, though one day, the singer hopes, he and his lover will be able to carry on their relationship without controversy. The song is, surely, about a gay love affair.

At the time, sexual activity between men was illegal in nearly half the countries participating in Eurovision that year, including Austria, Britain, Germany and (another '61 debutant) Spain. Britain had seen attempts to change this law blocked. The Wolfenden report, back in 1957, had recommended decriminalizing sex between men, but the Conservative cabinet had not followed the recommendation. In these countries, blackmail was an ever-present threat to gay people, as two films made in 1961, *Victim* and *The Loudest Whisper*, made clear.

Ljiljana Petrović might have breached the Iron Curtain in Eurovision, but 1961 is best known as the year that the Curtain became not just Iron but Concrete. There had been barbed wire between East and West Germany since 1952, but Eastern citizens could cross to the West via Berlin, which, though deep in Eastern territory, was partially occupied by the USA, Britain and France. As the Western economy began to take off, more and more Easterners took advantage of this escape route. By 1961, a sixth of the population of the Soviet-occupied German Democratic Republic (GDR) had headed west. Booming West Germany had found jobs for almost all of them.

On the night of Sunday 13 August, GDR workmen began encircling West Berlin with barbed wire barriers. A few days later, concrete walls followed. On 24 August, the first individual was killed trying to cross this barrier: Gunter Litfin, a 24-year-old tailor, was shot by GDR border guards as he tried to swim across a canal in Spandau. Other deaths followed, including that of Peter Fechter, a bricklayer who took an hour to bleed to death in no man's land. For much of that hour Fechter screamed out for help. The West couldn't rescue him and the East wouldn't.

In October, a trivial dispute about diplomatic passports escalated into a situation where American and Soviet tanks were facing each other across Checkpoint Charlie – armed, ready to fight, and with back-up plans involving a quick escalation to nuclear weapons. If one soldier had panicked and fired . . . The US and Soviet leaders, John F. Kennedy and Nikita Khrushchev, communicated via a Soviet agent in Washington, and the tanks inched back. Some historians argue that Berlin, in October 1961, was the closest that the Cold War ever came to turning into a nuclear conflict: more dangerous, even, than the Cuban missile crisis that followed a few months later, or than the events of 1983 which will be described later.

For Europeans, this was a terrifying time but also a humiliating one. The Berlin standoff was essentially between the two super-powers. Europe was just the setting. Like Suez back in 1956, it was a sign of the new impotence of European nations that had, two and a half decades before, confidently ruled vast global empires. Whether it liked it or not, Europe was now dancing to a new 'K And K Calypso', Kennedy and Khrushchev.

1962

Date: 18 March
Venue: Grand Auditorium de RTL, Luxembourg
Debuts: None
Winner: Isabelle Aubret, France
Winning Song: 'Un Premier Amour' (First Love)

For lovers of Eurovision, 1962 is most notable as the first year where entries got *nul points*. It had been theoretically possible for a song to score zero under the old voting system, but nobody had.* In 1962, a change in the voting method, whereby national juries could only award points to three songs, made such an eventuality more likely. Four entries, including one from Eurovision veteran Fud Leclerc, ended up suffering that fate. Fortunately Leclerc didn't throw himself into the Seine as a result.

Yugoslavia continued to distance itself from the enormities taking place in Berlin and entered a sophisticated love song. 'Don't Turn The Lights On At Twilight' – *Ne Pali Svetla U Sumrak* – sang Lola Novaković. Instead just let our two cigarette ends burn in the darkness (in 1962, cigarettes were cool). It came fourth. The top three places were occupied by entries in French, the runaway winner coming from France itself. 'Un Premier Amour' was haunting and passionate, a classic of Eurovision's black-and-white era.

France finally separated from Algeria on 5 July. Estimates of the death toll in the independence struggle vary wildly: historian Alistair Horne settles on 700,000. Violence continued after independence,

---

* Several had come close, with *un point*, including Corry Brokken in 1958, trying to follow up her 1957 victory. She is still the only artist both to win the competition and to come last.

with vicious Algerian reprisals on *harkis* (collaborators) and a far-right assassination attempt on de Gaulle in the south-west of Paris in August.

On 30 July 1962 the EEC's Common Agricultural Policy (CAP) was introduced. Part of the 1957 Treaty of Rome, the policy had its origins in the immediate post-war years: treaty signatories could remember hungry times, and wanted to ensure a healthy and developing EEC agricultural sector. But by 1962, it was already an anachronism. The idea was that the CAP would agree prices for basic products then manipulate the market to ensure those prices prevailed, putting tariffs on imports and buying up domestic produce if demand was too slack. This soon led to overproduction. A bizarre new European landscape of wine lakes and butter mountains appeared. Food prices to EEC consumers were kept artificially high. Third world producers were unable to sell to relatively rich Europe. All around 'Lugano Europe', environmental damage would be caused by overfarming to produce unwanted products. Eurosceptics point to the CAP as the classic example of Brussels misgovernment, not just for its unwisdom but for the fact that, once in place, it proved incredibly hard to reform.

France was the main beneficiary, and – just as it still dominated Eurovision – France had the loudest voice in the Community. De Gaulle worked tirelessly to keep it that way, most importantly by fostering Franco-German relations. He and Chancellor Adenauer had regular meetings; at one, in 1962, in Reims, they posed for pictures in the cathedral where Charlemagne's son Ludwig had been crowned Holy Roman Emperor in 816. Early in 1963, they would sign a treaty agreeing to consult one another on all major policy decisions.

Outside the EEC, seven other countries had teamed up to form EFTA, a free-trade area with no aspirations to further political unity. However, EFTA was geographically disparate, consisting of states dotted around the edges of Charlemagne's old empire. It was smaller than the EEC (its population was 92 million, compared to the EEC's

170 million) and less developed industrially. EFTA was always going to have its work cut out if it wanted to outperform its populous rival in Europe's industrial heartland.

Britain was one of the EFTA countries, along with Austria, Denmark, Norway, Portugal, Sweden and Switzerland. Eurovision viewers wouldn't have guessed it from its 1962 entry, 'Ring-a-ding Girl', but things were stirring in the UK's musical life. In February 1963, 'Please Please Me' became The Beatles' first number one single. The record company had wanted the four Liverpool lads to cover a *schlager* called 'How Do You Do It?', but they refused and insisted on putting out their own song.

This was a radical break from the 'Tin Pan Alley' model of popular music production, whereby professional writers wrote for passive performers (Eurovision still often follows this model, despite the fact that many of its best songs – 'Volare' and 'Waterloo' for example – have been written by their performers). The Beatles set a trend for individual empowerment that resonated through Western Europe – and, wherever it could, through Eastern Europe. All around the continent, a new generation was stepping up to the plate, less deferential than their war-haunted parents.

1963

Date: 23 March
Venue: BBC Television Centre, London, UK
Debuts: None
Winner: Grethe and Jørgen Ingmann, Denmark
Winning Song: 'Dansevise' (Dance Song)

TV coverage of the 1963 contest begins with the usual stirring *Te Deum*. Then violins swirl and the camera pans down through a dramatic evening sky to . . . a 1960s office block.

Nowadays we regard these things as spectacularly ugly, but in 1963, the new BBC Television Centre represented modernity and progress, two magic words at the time. Later that year, the leader of the British Labour Party, Harold Wilson, would paint a picture of his nation 'reforged' in the 'white heat' of a technological revolution – and the year after that he would be elected to power. Wilson's vision, shared by many elite figures in Europe, was technocratic; a tidy, planned, hi-tech future imposed top-down by men (and the occasional woman) in suits, working for large bureaucratic organizations like Wilson's new Ministry of Technology, which was given the Orwellian abbreviation 'Mintech'.

Europe's relationship with technocracy would soon sour. Just over five years later, students would be ripping up the cobbles of Parisian streets in furious protest at it. But this was 1963, and at the time it looked like the way forward. Perhaps an inkling of its ultimately unsatisfactory nature came from this contest, where, in the name of efficiency, songs were performed in a special studio cut off from the audience, who watched in a separate part of the building. This gave the opportunity for imaginative sets which were varied, artist to artist, but took away any sense of occasion. No applause greeted the performers. Rumours persist that some or all the performances were pre-recorded – this is still denied, but it's hard to see how the sets could have been changed quickly enough between songs for it not to have been the case.

The winning entry captured the year's 'early-sixties-modern' mood perfectly. In front of a backdrop of revolving op-art circles, Jørgen Ingmann accompanied his wife Grethe on jazzy guitar; there's something rather icy about the piece (until the last bar) that is both refreshing and slightly sinister.

'Dansevise' nearly didn't win at all. 1963 is another vintage year for connoisseurs of Eurovision voting disasters. Norway, announcing its results fifth, initially gave Denmark two votes and Switzerland three, but did not present the results in the correct format, so was asked to resubmit them after everyone else had voted. The contest soon became a race between Denmark and Switzerland. At the end, when Norway resubmitted its results, they had changed. Denmark now had four votes and Switzerland just one, giving victory to Norway's neighbour. A ripple of surprise ran round the audience. Hostess 'Miss Catherine Boyle' rang Monaco to check a vote that had initially included too many points (cue another wonky phone line), then announced 'Dansevise' as the winner.

In a final moment of comedy, an award was announced for the song's composers. The cameras cut to the stairway down which the winners would appear; the BBC orchestra played a fanfare; and . . . nobody appeared. 'They're not here to receive the prize,' said the quick-thinking prize presenter, BBC Controller – what a techno-cratic title! – Stuart Hood.

Hood then went on to give a short speech about the amazing achievement that was the broadcast, and how good it was that viewers were able to enjoy the results of modern science without 'that chill of fear which so often accompanies the miracles of technology today'. He was no doubt alluding to the terrible weapons of destruction being built on both sides of the Iron Curtain.

Shortly after the Checkpoint Charlie face-off in 1961, the Soviet Union had tested the 'King of Bombs', a hydrogen bomb almost 2,500 times more powerful than the devices that had obliterated Hiroshima and Nagasaki.* This was, presumably, for use in Europe. West of the Curtain, Britain and France were working on smaller but still monstrous versions of similar weapons, and sporadically testing them in remote Pacific islands or in the deserts of Australia or Algeria. The previous year, 1962, had been a record year for such tests, with 140, almost 100 by the USA alone. Later in 1963, the US, USSR and Britain (but not France) signed a treaty banning tests above ground. But the horrific threat of these weapons did not go away.

This 'white heat of technology' Eurovision is now best known for very human failings: bloc voting, the comic non-appearance of the winning composers. The very next day, The Beatles' first album came out, recorded in one day on relatively simple equipment but bursting with raw human emotion and rebellious energy. Maybe that was the moment Europe's technocratic dream began to die.

Away from the contest, Britain and Denmark had decided to abandon EFTA and had applied to join the EEC. Ireland was filing an application at the same time. The initial noises from Brussels had been welcoming, and officials had begun working on the terms of entry. All three applicants had substantial agricultural sectors and their entry into the EEC club would upset the existing CAP. But if 'Europe' were to expand, such issues needed sorting.

By the start of 1963, it looked as if the door was about to open. Then on 14 January General de Gaulle announced out of the blue that he was vetoing Britain's application. He came up with a range

---

* The test took place in the Arctic archipelago of Novaya Zemlya. A village thirty-five miles away was totally destroyed, and windows were shattered in Finland and Norway.

of reasons, the most oft-repeated being that Britain was too close to America. There was some wisdom to his arguments – Britain was clearly less committed to the European project than The Six – but de Gaulle sceptics argue that he was much more concerned about protecting France's interests than those of Europe as a whole. Whatever the General's motive, Denmark and Ireland backed out at the same time, afraid that they would soon find themselves being bullied in a similar manner. Political Europe remained the world of Lugano 1956, and would do so for a decade.

Meanwhile, the USA – which had no desire to subvert the EEC via Britain – was busy trying to protect Europe from the Soviet Union. On 26 June, President Kennedy made a speech at the Town Hall in the Berlin district of Schöneberg, where he told hundreds of thousands of people cramming the surrounding streets, '*Ich bin ein Berliner.*' If one is being pedantic, this does mean 'I am a doughnut': technically, he should have just said '*Ich bin Berliner.*' But everybody knew what he meant, and felt a surge of reassurance that he would protect them from the Soviets. Maybe some kind of lasting peace would result from his determination . . .

Five months later, the President was dead. The Cold War calypso played on.

1964

Date: 21 March
Venue: Tivoli Concert Hall, Copenhagen, Denmark
Debut: Portugal
Winner: Gigliola Cinquetti, Italy
Winning Song: 'Non Ho l'Eta' (I Am Too Young)

Key themes of the European 1960s bubbled to the surface in this contest. One was youth. A sixteen-year-old singer won by a record margin. The song, however, was a gentle ballad and not a standard-bearer for the teen-driven sexual revolution of the second half of the decade. Instead, lyricist Nicola 'Nisa' Salerno had Gigliola Cinquetti ask to be allowed to start playing the adult game of love in her own time.

Salerno was one of Italy's leading lyricists, noted for his creation in song of well-observed characters, especially the young. Other favourites include a wealthy young man who craves everything American in 'Tu Vuò Fà L'Americano' and 'Guaglione', another youngster on the verge of adult emotion, this time a boy in love with a woman who ignores him because he's still just a kid. Critics of Eurovision often overlook the heritage of quality lyrics lurking in among the contest's dings and dongs, diggi-loos and diggi-leys.

Other young Europeans were developing their own music and styles, too. Britain was swept by Beatlemania. France, Spain and Italy took the Fab Four on board indirectly: youngsters borrowed the chorus from 'She Loves You' and launched their own style, calling themselves 'yé-yés'. Yé-yé music was melodic and rock 'n' rollish, its lyrics simple statements about love and sexual attraction. The Beatles would soon move on, ditching their suits and haircuts for kaftans and long hair, but the yé-yés were happy to look and stay chic: the girls (who drove the movement) kittenish, the men suave and rugged.

A second theme to emerge in Eurovision 1964 was political activism. After the third-from-last entry had been performed, a man who had sneaked backstage pretending to be a stagehand burst onto the podium and unfurled a banner that read 'Boycott Franco and Salazar'. The cameras panned away to the scoreboard; he was hustled off stage; the show went on – though maybe the judges were influenced, as Spain and Portugal between them gathered one point.

General Francisco Franco had come to power in 1939 after Spain's infamous civil war. Dr Antonio Salazar had ruled Portugal even longer, since 1932. In many ways, the two Iberian dictators were very different. Salazar was a quiet intellectual with much less blood on his hands than Franco. His regime, known as the *Estado Novo*, had leant towards the Allies in the war, unlike his neighbour. But both used secret police and media control, and neither allowed elections or democratic parties. Though this was not the emerging European way, the two dictatorships were tolerated in mid-sixties Europe – and in Eurovision – because the real enemy lay across the Iron Curtain. The two regimes would last another decade: the song contest would offer its usual insights into their story at that time.

A third new theme was race. Up till then, the contest had been a whites-only affair. The Netherlands' Anneke Grönloh broke this mould, singing the poppy 'Jij Bent Mijn Leven' (You Are My Life), which ended up mid-table, although she was second to sing.*

Grönloh had been born in a small Indonesian village. Her parents had come to Holland after the war and settled in Eindhoven. In the 1950s and 1960s many former subjects of Europe's old empires made similar journeys, as the economies of the old parent countries began to

---

* Second is a hexed position in Eurovision. Nobody has ever won from that slot, and three acts singing second have got *nul points*. The curse lives on: in 2016 Gabriela Gunčíková of the Czech Republic sang second and got no televotes at all.

Eurovision!

take off and extra hands were needed. Algerians and Moroccans came to France; Jamaicans, Indians and Pakistanis to Britain; Indonesians like Anneke Grönloh to the Netherlands. Germany, with no old empire to tap for labour, started inviting workers from poorer countries, at first from Southern Europe then, after 1961, from Turkey. In September 1964 Germany's millionth 'guest worker', Armando Rodrigues de Sá from Portugal, was officially given a motorbike by the government.

Anneke Grönloh made a huge success of her adopted home: in 2000 she was voted her country's 'Singer of the Century'. Many – I believe most – other new arrivals in Europe have essentially happy stories to tell, too, of challenges met, friendships made and new opportunities taken. But they could also encounter prejudice and sometimes outright hostility. Britain's 1964 election was notorious for racism: in one seat, Smethwick in the West Midlands, Conservative Party supporters came up with the slogan, 'if you want a nigger for your neighbour, vote Labour'. While not adopting the slogan, the aspirant Tory MP refused to condemn it. The Labour Party seized the moral high ground, until it was revealed that the Smethwick Labour Party club had a 'whites only' membership policy. Non-white Eurovision entrants were rarities for a long time after 1964, and it took until the new century before a black singer stepped up onto the winner's podium.

Arguably, a fourth theme of the contest was religion: Bosnian singer Sabahudin Kurt was the first Muslim to sing in Eurovision. However, this does not resonate with the era, the way the other themes above do. Religion in the 1960s was not seen as a major issue. Wasn't it a bit old hat? It was certainly a private matter, with little political relevance.

In other ways, Eurovision 1964 was more traditional. France fielded an attractive young woman with a plaintive song (whatever happened to Rachel?) Britain's Matt Monro came second – was this becoming a habit? And there was a clutch of *nul pointe*rs, mainly from peripheral countries. But things were about to change.

1965

Date: 20 March
Venue: Sala di Concerto della RAI, Napoli, Italy
Debut: Ireland
Winner: France Gall, Luxembourg
Winning Song: 'Poupée De Cire, Poupée De Son' (Wax Doll, Sawdust Doll)

The 1965 contest, the tenth, felt a need to modernize, but wasn't quite sure how to. The route chosen by many entrants was to add Latin percussion to their orchestrations: the bongo player in the RAI house orchestra must have had weary fingers by the end of the evening. A more radical route was chosen by Luxembourg. As usual, the Grand Duchy headed over the border in search of French artistes to create its entry, but this time it called in yé-yé guru Serge Gainsbourg. Cue seventeen-year-old France Gall, rasping Gainsbourg's dig at young singers manufactured by the music biz who sing about love but don't know anything about it. 'Poupée De Cire, Poupée De Son' is rocky, slightly discordant and totally teenage – Gall is both energetic and vulnerable.*

An even more modern lyric came from Denmark. In 'For Din Skyld' (For Your Sake), Birgit Brüel sings of how she is getting fed up with her partner pushing her into a stereotypical feminine role; she wants 'to love in friendship', as an equal; she wants this for herself, but also for him, as it will make him more human, less of a gender stereotype himself. And if he doesn't listen, she'll be off . . .

---

* Gall's vulnerability was genuine. The following year, she recorded another song for Gainsbourg. 'Les Sucettes' (Lollipops) is full of double entendres about oral sex. Despite a comically obvious video, when she recorded the song, Gall did not understand these, and she was mortified when she later found out.

Betty Friedan's book *The Feminine Mystique* had appeared in America in 1963, kicking off a new wave of feminist thought that took the topic deeper into private life and social pressure (earlier feminism had been more about legal equality and getting the vote). Its message, nicely expressed in this song, was still a minority one in Europe in 1965. It was to stay that way for a long time. Even those ultra-radical students from 1968 can sound extraordinarily sexist to modern ears, and in the 1970s men were men and wore the medallions to prove it. If anything gave Europe's women more freedom in 1965, it was not changing attitudes, fresh ideas or even Eurovision songs, but the contraceptive pill, which had been available in Britain and Germany from 1961 (take-up in these countries had been slow, but by 1965 its use was common). However, this in itself did little to change stereotypes.

Alongside the bongos, Eurovision 1965 had its quota of ballads. Ireland, one day to dominate the contest, made its debut with Butch Moore's fifties-style 'I'm Walking The Streets In The Rain'. The UK's entry, Kathy Kirby's 'I Belong', can be seen as having political overtones: an appeal to The Six, or at least The Five over the head of *le Général,* to be allowed to join them (it had no effect, but came second in the contest).

Eurovision 1965 was the first to be broadcast to Iron Curtain countries other than Yugoslavia. This was a sign of a thawing in relations across the Wall. Would it last?

One final feature of the 1965 show is notable: Sweden's 'Absent Friend' was sung in English. Despite Britain's absence from the EEC, English was becoming ever more widely spoken around Europe – largely due to American influence, but also thanks to British popular music. French remained the language of international diplomacy and, of course, of the EEC – but in France itself, the Académie Française was gearing up to do battle with *le weekend, le parking* and (my favourite) *le talkie-walkie.*

Eurovision!

After the 1965 contest, the EBU responded with a new rule that all songs had to be in a native language of the country. Was this an idealistic move to protect authentic European cultures from Americanization? Or was it a move by a francophone bloc to preserve its linguistic hegemony? Five nations (France, Belgium, Switzerland, Monaco, Luxembourg) could sing in French. Luxembourg and Monaco often used French performers, lyricists, composers and conductors. Songs in French had won six of the first ten competitions, despite less than a third of Western Europe's population being francophone.

France was certainly doing its best to keep control of political Europe. In the same month as France Gall's win, the EEC was brought to a legislative halt by the Empty Chair Crisis. The long-serving Commission president, Walter Hallstein, had come up with a set of reforms that included the replacement of the old voting system in the Council of Ministers, which had insisted on unanimity, with a more streamlined one where some measures could be passed by a majority. General de Gaulle disliked Hallstein anyway, both because of the latter's federalist ambitions and because Hallstein regarded himself on a par with national leaders. Hallstein's reforms were the final straw for the General; when the five other EEC members backed them, de Gaulle forbade French participation in the Council. As it was France's turn to chair it, European-level government effectively stopped.

The General stuck to his guns through the rest of 1965. However, in the domestic presidential election that December he fared less well than he had hoped: his brinkmanship had clearly rattled French voters, who feared it would cause the EEC to collapse, something neither French industrialists nor French farmers wanted. He returned to the negotiating table, and the Luxembourg Compromise was signed on 26 January 1966. Unanimity was retained for votes where 'vital national interests' were at stake. Exactly how these interests were to be defined – or by whom – was never made clear.

De Gaulle had the last laugh, though. Under French pressure, Hallstein asked not to be nominated for a third term as Commission president, and was replaced in 1967 by Belgian lawyer Jean Rey.

The crisis and the confusion caused by the Compromise stalled attempts to build workable Europe-wide institutions for the next decade or more – a period known as the time of 'Eurosclerosis'. During that era, EEC decisions would largely be made bilaterally and informally by the leaders of France and Germany.

1966

Date: 20 March
Venue: Grand Auditorium de RTL, Luxembourg
Debuts: None (there would be no new entrants till 1971)
Winner: Udo Jürgens, Austria
Winning Song: 'Merci, Chérie' (Thank You, My Love)

Given the new language rule, it was ironic that the 1966 contest was won by an Austrian song with a title in French. But balladeer Udo Jürgens had paid his Eurovision dues, coming sixth and fourth in previous contests.

There were more interesting entries, however. For Norway, Åse Kleveland came onstage in a trouser suit rather than the standard long dress, carrying a guitar which she then played, with the orchestra providing (by the standards of the competition at the time) minimal accompaniment. Her performance of 'Inter Er Nytt Under Solen' (Nothing Is New Under The Sun) was intense and honest, the lyrics poetic and the tune catchy. She came third. Kleveland went on to serve as Norway's minister for culture under Gro Harlem Brundtland from 1990 to 1996, and to chair Norway's influential Humanist and Ethical Association: no passive feminine stereotypes for her. If Serge Gainsbourg and France Gall tried to push Eurovision towards mainstream pop, Åse Kleveland led it towards deeper, quirkier places: intelligent, sensitive, accompanying herself on guitar, she was the nearest the contest has ever got to Joni Mitchell.

The Netherlands continued its chipping away at racial barriers by fielding Milly Scott, the first black singer to perform in Eurovision. Unfortunately she was given a weak novelty song, 'Fernando En Fillipo', and collected only two votes.

France's entry, 'Chez Nous' (Where We Live), was all about a young man who has captured the heart of an American visitor – after which, he says, she should stay in France, as life is much better there. Dominique Walter had a point. In 1966 America was escalating its war in Vietnam and beginning to plunge into interracial violence. Vietnam would soon start having effects in Europe. No Western European nation took part in the fighting (Britain's Harold Wilson withstood strong US pressure to do so), but US spending on the conflict began to create an inflation which, initially domestic, soon became global. Vietnam also inflamed a new mood of European radicalism. Between them, these forces would begin to undercut the old economic and political models that had fuelled Western Europe's growth since 1945.

Despite these interesting entries, Eurovision 1966 is largely remembered for its bloc voting. The most blatant example came from the Nordic countries. Sweden, who fielded an arch novelty song about a 'hip' pig breeder, came second – all its votes bar one came from Denmark, Norway and Finland. Portugal and Spain swapped maximum points (neither entry collected more than one vote from the rest of Europe put together). Austria gave neighbours Switzerland maximum points; Switzerland gave Germany maximum and Austria the next best possible. Britain's Kenneth McKellar sang in a kilt and got most of his votes from fellow Celts across the Irish Sea. The Luxembourgeois audience grew restless, then laughed, then whistled as another bloc vote came in.

This neatly parallels the shenanigans in the Council of Ministers the year before, where national self-interest lurked behind the talk of greater Europe-wide concern. Robert Schuman's 1949 'European spirit' seemed a distant dream.

Away from Eurovision, popular music was changing fast. American influence was to the fore, thanks to writer/performers like Bob Dylan and Frank Zappa, but British acts were pushing the boundaries too: albums like The Beatles' *Revolver* or *Fresh Cream* by Cream (Eric Clapton, Jack Bruce and Ginger Baker), and singles like the Kinks' 'Sunny Afternoon' were genuinely original. Change – and a whiff of strange-smelling cigarettes – was in the air.

1967

Date: 8 April
Venue: Hofburg Palace, Vienna
Winner: Sandie Shaw, UK
Winning Song: 'Puppet On A String'

The heart of anyone who had taken *Revolver*, *Fresh Cream* or 'Sunny Afternoon' off their turntable and turned their TV on for Eurovision 1967 must have sunk when Thérèse Steinmetz opened the show with 'Ringe-Dinge'. However 'L'Amour Est Bleu' (Love Is Blue) from Luxembourg followed. Singing second probably spelt doom for the song's chances of victory, but it went on to sell shedloads and has become bracketed with 'Volare' as the outstanding Eurovision songs that didn't win. After Vicky's classic came the usual mixture. France's 'Il Doit Faire Beau Là-bas' (The Weather Must Be Good There) is rather nice (I know, these judgements are subjective). I can't watch the Belgian entry without getting the giggles. Monaco's 'Boum Badaboum' is Serge Gainsbourg's take on the Cold War: give me some time to love before we all get blown up, sings Minouche Barelli (a French singer who eventually moved to Monaco). It is arguably the most interesting lyric in the contest, and certainly the ugliest tune.

Portugal was represented by Angolan singer Eduardo Nascimento, with 'O Vento Mudou' (The Wind Changed). Reputedly Dr Salazar selected him to show how happy the citizens of Portuguese colonies were. But did the propaganda backfire? Couldn't the title be construed as a reference to Harold Macmillan's speech back in 1960? Portuguese songwriters became the masters of using the contest to make political points: the tradition probably started here.

Unlike Europe's other former imperialist powers, Portugal still had no intention of dissolving its empire. The nation soon found itself embroiled in colonial wars, against guerrillas who were increasingly well armed (by the Soviet Union) and well organized. In 1967, all young Portuguese men were required to serve four years in the army, at least two of which would be in its African colonies: Angola, Mozambique or Guinea. Portugal thus found itself on the front line of a new Cold War, where the Soviet bloc battled the West for influence in the non-aligned world. Despite its own ruthless imperialism east of the Iron Curtain, the Soviet Union managed to portray itself as a purveyor of liberation. Dr Salazar, pretending that the wind was never going to change, played straight into its hands.

The Eurovision winner often captures the mood of a moment in Europe's history with beautiful clarity. 1967 has to be one such year. Shoeless and mini-skirted, Sandie Shaw was a representative of Swinging London, the new cultural revolution that was sweeping a city once the global capital of the 'stiff upper lip'. Along with its music, British fashion, design and photography suddenly led the continent, and even the world.

'Puppet On A String' went on to top charts around Europe, the first time a Eurovision winner had enjoyed such success (previous ones had all struggled to do well outside their core language markets). That also makes it a pivotal song in the history of the competition.

It was hardly radical, however. Its singer reportedly hated its 'cuckoo-clock tune' and 'sexist lyrics'. I imagine the contest's *chanson-* and ballad-loving founders disliked it too. Music critics and fans of the new 'serious' rock certainly did. But so what? Instead, 'Puppet On A String' marched off and created its own new territory: Europop. Europe's citizens loved it, defying their cultural elders and betters and buying over a million copies of the vinyl 45 rpm single. No previous winner had sold so well.

Eurovision!

There was never a doubt just who was pulling the strings in the EEC. A month after the 1967 contest, Britain, Denmark and Ireland reapplied to join the Community. In November General de Gaulle vetoed their applications again.

Instead of expanding, 'Lugano Europe' looked inwards and concentrated on tightening its inner workings. A couple of months after de Gaulle's *non*, a Merger Treaty united the three entities to which The Six belonged – the old Coal and Steel Community, the EEC and Euratom (an attempt at uniting atomic energy policy which never achieved much). These entities were now institutions of a new, higher institution, the European Communities (EC). This name would live on till 1992 and the arrival of the modern term European Union (EU).

The EEC was by far the most important of these three entities, and the change created confusion in the general public and the media, who never took to the term EC and kept on talking about the EEC for all levels of European government. For example in 1973 Britain applied to join the EC, not just the EEC, but the media talked only about the latter. As with Eurovision, so with political Europe: I shall ignore the technicalities and follow the man and woman in the European street. I shall talk about the EEC from now until 1992, when the EC, EEC and Euratom all became part of the new EU.

Other European boundaries were tightening in 1967, too. In September the GDR began construction of a stronger fortified wall along its western border. Concrete watchtowers replaced wooden ones; special roads were built to make patrolling easier; tripwires and electronic sensors were put in place; mines were laid. Escapes from the East fell by a factor of ten. Escapes *to* the East remained constant, of course, at zero. The division of Europe was starker than ever.

1968

Date: 6 April
Venue: Albert Hall, London
Winner: Massiel, Spain
Winning Song: 'La, La, La'

The story of the 1968 winner is bizarre, even by Eurovision standards. Massiel, a yé-yé star, was not the first choice for the role. The verses – which, unlike the chorus that gave the song its title, had proper words – were originally to be sung in Catalan by Joan Manuel Serrat. Serrat was a leading performer in the Catalan *Nova Cançó* style - songs in the north-eastern language, often critical of the Madrid government. General Franco, who just about tolerated *Nova Cançó* at home, would not allow such subversive regionalists to represent the country abroad, and insisted the song be sung in Castilian, the official Spanish language. Serrat refused, and Massiel was brought in at the last moment. The irony that a row should take place about the language a song called 'La, La, La' should be sung in is delightfully Eurovision, with its apparent triviality but, behind that, the serious issue of a nation's politics and identity.

There is also a perpetually humming rumour that Franco bribed juries to vote for the song. This has been strenuously denied, but who knows the truth? 'La, La, La' is cheerful and catchy, and most of the other entries were mediocre ('Stress' by Norway's Odd Børre was a quirky exception, but hardly winner material). Perhaps Massiel won because she deserved to.

'La, La, La' didn't exactly cover the contest with glory, but 1968 is still a memorable Eurovision, as it was the first to be broadcast in colour. Britain had been the first Western European nation to broadcast colour TV, in July 1967. West Germany, the Netherlands and France soon followed. (However, we Europeans mustn't be complacent here. America had had colour TV since the 1950s and Japan since 1960. Iraq started colour broadcasts in 1968, ahead of most European countries.)

Most of the artists made full use of the new technology. Dresses were day-glo yellow, turquoise or lime green. Some of the men went colourful, too, especially Switzerland's Gianni Mascolo with his ill-fitting orange suit, and two brightly clad medieval minstrels from Yugoslavia (who were one of the first Eurovision acts to employ that staple of later contests, the key change two-thirds of the way through the song). Even more sedately dressed male competitors began to ditch black ties, some for nylon polo-neck shirts or, in the case of Britain's Cliff Richard, for a Regency dandy's ruff exploding out of the front of his jacket.

Colour was entering European – especially Northern European – life in other ways, too. More and more northerners were heading south for holidays in bright, sun-soaked Portugal, Greece or, most popular of all, Massiel's homeland Spain, which welcomed around 17 million visitors in 1968 (the figure in 1960 had been about 5 million). Ironically, these destinations were now all dictatorships, Greece having joined the club thanks to a military coup in April 1967. Returning home to their prosperous democracies, these visitors could stay international by eating out at ever more affordable ethnic restaurants: many post-war immigrants had found this business to be a lucrative one. Younger Western Europeans could tune in to 'pirate' radio stations, like Radio Caroline, Radio London and Radio Veronica – which offered an alternative to stuffy, cautious government-run broadcasters.

Even more challenging alternative media were on offer in northern capital cities – and especially London, where underground magazines like *IT* and *Oz* began to promote the full-on hippie lifestyle: sexual experimentation, drug use and radical politics.

Eurovision!

Outside these capital cities, sexual morality changed more slowly: historians are still arguing about how swinging the late sixties were in Clermont-Ferrand, Duisburg, Karlstad, Stoke-on-Trent or Zwolle. But there was clearly change in the air. Homosexual intercourse, long legal in Belgium, France, Luxembourg and the Netherlands, had been legalized in England and Wales in 1967. Germany followed suit in 1968 and 1969, East Germany passing its law ahead of West.

In reaction to the new era, 1968 saw the papal encyclical *Humanae Vitae*, which forbade contraception and reaffirmed the church's view that marriage was the only place for sexual activity.

France's 1968 Eurovision entry was 'La Source' (The Spring), sung (beautifully, of course) by 1962 winner Isabelle Aubret. It's a very strange song, about a place in a wood haunted by the victim of a gang-rape. But 1968 was a very strange year in France's history.

The events of May 1968 began with student protests about student issues: overcrowded classes, aloof academics and sleeping arrangements in dormitories. But behind them was a deep new radicalism. The students, who became known as '*soixante-huitards*', argued that Europe's growing prosperity – and, even worse, that of America – had been bought at the price of sterile conformity and the exploitation of poorer nations and of the natural world. The whole system was rotten, they argued; it needed to be ripped up and power put back in the hands of the people (or at least those people who agreed with the *soixante-huitards*).

On 6 May, a huge demonstration marched through the French capital and erupted into violence; demonstrators hurled cobblestones at the CRS riot police, who responded with tear gas. On 10 May, barricades appeared in the Quartier Latin; the police charged in and arrested anyone they thought responsible. Public sympathy for the students rose; a general strike was called for 13 May. Wildcat strikes and factory occupations followed – anyone passing the Berliet truck factory in Lyon would have found the sign outside respelt as

Liberte. By 18 May, two million workers were out. A week later this had risen to ten million. On 27 May, a deal was struck between employers and the official trades unions, but nobody was listening to them any longer. France looked about to collapse into anarchy.

Then General de Gaulle disappeared. Riots in the streets, the economy in free fall, and no president.

He had flown in secret to see the chief of the French forces in Germany.* Apparently de Gaulle's first words to General Jacques Massu were '*C'est foutu*' (it's fucked). Massu assured him of the military's support, promising the president he would again be able to have his breakfast on the Boulevard Saint-Germain. De Gaulle flew back to Paris, announced fresh elections and probably treated himself to a croissant and some proper coffee. Students returned to college and strikers to work, and when the elections took place on 23 and 30 June, the result was an overwhelming victory for the right. Later that year, the new French government did about the least *soixante-huitard* thing it could do, test a hydrogen bomb.

The wind of change in 1968 soon wafted through lands unable to participate in Eurovision. Soviet-occupied Czechoslovakia had been particularly slow to cleanse itself of the legacy of Stalin. Even the Russians had concluded that change was necessary, and in January a new party secretary had been appointed. Alexander Dubcek was not a freewheeling sixties radical but a loyal party man who thought the party should do a better job. This meant liberalizing Czechoslovak life, giving people more freedoms, curtailing the powers of the secret police, abolishing press censorship and turning over more of the economy to consumer goods. He talked of elections, which he was convinced the Party would win: what could be better than 'Socialism with a human face'? Press censorship was abolished.

---

* The formal occupation of Germany had ended in 1955, but French forces remained there until after the fall of the Berlin Wall, when numbers were cut back substantially. A small French force would remain in the small town of Donaueschingen until 2014.

Eurovision!

Western Europe watched with admiration. Eurovision did its bit: Austria asked Czech singer Karel Gott to represent it. Support for this quiet revolution didn't extend to giving 'Tausend Fenster' (A Thousand Windows) many votes, however. He came twelfth.

Perhaps the judges knew what was going to happen. On the night of 20–21 August, Czechoslovakia was invaded by 250,000 troops from Russia, Poland, Hungary and Bulgaria. It was a much less grisly affair than Hungary 1956. Dubcek told people not to resist; a few did, and eighty-two of them died. The subsequent clampdown was gradual. Dubcek remained in office, though now with little power; when he was finally sacked he didn't suffer the fate of Hungary's 1956 leaders, execution, but was given a job as a forestry official. Some people were allowed to leave the country. But the statues of Stalin remained – and the building work continued along the wall between the two Europes.

A third European conflict area in 1968 was Northern Ireland – a topic which will soon find its way onto the Eurovision stage, courtesy of Dana in 1970, and so will be discussed there.

Even in Brussels, 1968 saw calls for change. On 21 December, Sicco Mansholt, a former Dutch resistance fighter now EEC Commissioner for Agriculture, filed a report highly critical of the Common Agricultural Policy, which was now guzzling 90 per cent of the Community's budget. He suggested that rather than endlessly subsidising inefficient agriculture, the EEC should pay small farmers to quit the industry.

Mansholt had been one of the original designers of the policy; his courage in changing his mind is rare in politics. But it was in vain. His new ideas did not go down well with farmers of any size, who in 1968 style took to the streets. Mansholt had to be protected with an armed guard when they came to Brussels. His report would be watered down into three minor directives in 1972, while both the CAP budget and the lakes and mountains of unwanted produce would continue to grow for the next two decades.

This remarkable year ended on a breathtaking note as American astronauts left Earth's orbit for the first time, flew to the moon, took pictures of a fragile, lonely planet, then came home again. Europe watched, entranced – but was also quietly reminded which nation now held the dominant global position that Britain, France and, later, Germany had once fought to hold.

1969

Date: 20 March
Venue: Teatro Real Opera House, Madrid, Spain
Joint Winners: Salome, Spain; Lulu, UK; Lenny Kuhr, Netherlands;
Frida Boccara, France
Winning Songs: 'Vivo Cantando' (I Live Singing); 'Boom Bang-a-Bang';
'De Troubadour' (The Troubadour); 'Un Jour, Un Enfant' (One Day, A Child)

As if in a deliberate snub to the *soixante-huitards*, the stage of
Eurovision 1969 was dominated by a giant silver object unpleasantly
reminiscent of the symbol of General Franco's Falangist party, which
in turn looked very like the old Roman fasces used as a symbol by
Mussolini. The piece was designed by Salvador Dalí, which raises
intriguing questions. Was he pressured into designing it the way he
did? Was it supposed to be some kind of ironic comment? Or did he
miss the likeness and just think it looked nice? (An interesting idea,
given Dalí's usual insight into the human unconscious.)

However it got there, it was a final piece of grandstanding from
the old dictatorship. In July, Franco would announce that when
he died, Spain's legitimate king, Juan Carlos, would become head
of state. The rural/traditionalist model favoured by both Iberian
dictators had been fading for a while, anyway: Spain had begun to
modernize its economy; its politics would follow. A better symbol
of Spain's future than the onstage fasces was the interval act, which
took the form of a psychedelic travelogue based round the theme
of the Four Elements, to the most discordant music ever heard on
Eurovision (until Jemini took to the stage in 2003, anyway).

Eurovision 1969 is largely Europop, with bouncy root-fifth bass
lines, but the songs are fun and some of the lyrics are original

– though not Britain's 'Boom Bang-a-Bang'. From Portugal, Simone de Oliveira sang 'Desfolhada Portuguesa',* a passionate, sensual poem by Ary dos Santos, a committed opponent of the *Estado Novo* regime.

That regime had lost its former leader late in 1968, when Dr Salazar suffered a brain haemorrhage, after which his deputy Marcelo Caetano took over. Salazar was expected to die quickly, but lived on for two more years, during which time nobody dared tell him he had been replaced. He was surrounded by people who pretended to him that he was still running the country.

Portugal has never won Eurovision, but in a way has got more out of it than any other nation, as the contest became a mouthpiece for the opposition before the fall of the old regime. As we shall see in 1974, it also played a key role in that fall.

Sweden's Tommy Körberg sang a song to Judy, his friend, in 'Judy, Min Vän' (lyrics by Roger Wallis and Britt Lindeborg), saying he didn't want to be her partner. She loved material things ('house, TV and car' – goods that few Europeans had owned in 1956 but which by 1969 had become widely available and affordable). He wanted freedom, connection to nature and emotional intensity. Judy was a child of Europe's early sixties; he was one of its late sixties.

Judy's friend was no *soixante-huitard*, however. He was expressing a personal view of how he wanted to live, not a political one about how the world should be. These sentiments were more in line with what most people felt in Western Europe in 1969 than the opinions of the Parisian students. The far-left dreams of the Rive Gauche never became reality in Europe, but the coming decade would see many young Europeans quietly step off the rungs of the established career ladder, the way the singer wants to in this song, and 'do their own thing'.

---

* This title is hard to translate. Literally it means Portuguese Maize-Threshing. The poem compares human love to love of the land.

Eurovision!

Sadly Eurovision 1969 is now best remembered for its farcical result. In rehearsal, presenter Laurita Valenzuela had asked EBU scrutineer Clifford Brown what would happen in case of a tie, and had been told that it had never happened before and never would. But as the votes came in, such an outcome looked more and more likely. Then it happened, not only with two songs but four. Valenzuela turned to Brown (who was rather bizarrely seated onstage) and asked what to do next; he brusquely told her there were four winners. She was so taken aback that she asked again, and got the same answer.

Austria, Finland, Norway, Portugal and Sweden decided not to re-enter next year. The four-way win was the major reason, though some of 1969's more thoughtful entries had come from among these countries, who perhaps didn't fancy being in a Europop competition. Was Eurovision heading for the end of the line?

There was no doubt that 28 April was the end of the line for General de Gaulle, who stepped down after losing a referendum. His successor, Georges Pompidou, was a technocrat who is now best known for initiating France's TGV (high speed rail) system and the modernist art museum in the Marais that bears his name. Pompidou was also keen on other nations joining The Six: Charlemagne's empire was about to expand.

West Germany also acquired a new leader in 1969. Willy Brandt belonged to a new generation. Previous German leaders, while fundamentally liberal in politics, had been personally rather starchy and formal; Brandt was warmer and more open. He had a fresh vision for dealing with his divided nation, replacing the old doctrine, whereby the Federal Republic broke diplomatic relations with any country that recognized the GDR, with a more pragmatic approach which became known as *Ostpolitik*.

Another mould-breaking leader elected in 1969 was Sweden's Olof Palme, a fierce critic of colonialism, apartheid and both America and the Soviet Union. At home, he passed a series of measures to promote gender equality, increased already high taxation and spending on the nation's welfare system, and rewrote the constitution to take all remaining power from the monarchy.

Western European life seemed to be heading in interesting new directions. But at the same time, a sinister new kind of politics was emerging: terrorism. Northern Ireland was drifting towards sectarian anarchy. In Italy in December 1969, a bomb exploded at the HQ of the National Agrarian Bank in Milan, killing seventeen people. This was the beginning of the *Anni di Piombo* (Years of Lead – lead as in bullets), which lasted into the mid-1980s. The late 1960s also saw the first deaths caused by Basque terrorists in Spain, though ETA would keep its worst atrocities for the early 1980s.

So, like Eurovision, Western Europe ended a decade which had looked to be heading for a jolly, liberated party in a more nuanced, troubled mood. Eurovision through the 1960s shows us an efflorescence of individuality and colour. Off with the bow ties and ball gowns; on with the polo-necks and mini-skirts! But what next?

What most young Western Europeans, like Judy's friend, wanted was less 1956-style 'order' and duty, and more authenticity: more individuality, more freedom to buy what they chose, wear what they chose, live as they chose. More colour. Older commentators, whose values belonged to the old black-and-white world, questioned where these freedoms would take the half-continent: towards uplifting personal liberation or destructive selfishness?

East of the Iron Curtain, meanwhile, Europeans' problems were different: too little change, state violence an everyday fact of life, the future grey and static rather than colourful but uncertain.

The
1970s

1970

Date: 21 March
Venue: RAI Congrescentrum, Amsterdam
Winner: Dana, Ireland
Winning Song: 'All Kinds Of Everything'

Because of the low number of entrants – twelve: there hadn't been so few since 1959 – the first contest of the new decade was padded out with 'postcards', those little clips that come before each entry, and which are now an essential part of Eurovision. These stressed local rather than European identity, just as Cannes' carousels (strangely, also back in 1959) had done. General de Gaulle would have approved.

The 1970 contest also marked the debut of set designer Roland de Groot, who in 1976, 1980 and 1984 was to produce a string of imaginative stagings, with his trademark shifting geometrical shapes and blocks of colour. This year's set featured shiny spheres and floating semi-circular platforms, rearranged for each artist. Different-coloured lighting bounced off the spheres to create a perpetually changing effect. Even if its songs aren't exactly cutting-edge, Eurovision has always showcased a range of supporting skills, in lighting, in stage design, in broadcast technology, which are exactly that. De Groot has as much a place in the Eurovision Hall of Fame as presenters like Katie Boyle or Lill Lindfors, composers like Ralf Siegel/Bernd Meinunger, Rolf Løvland or Thomas G:son, or even Abba or *Riverdance*.

Male inconstancy, admitted by the singer, was the theme of Henri Dès' bouncy, ironic 'Retour' (Return). Italy's Gianni Morandi wasn't in it for the long haul, either: tears and apologies from him will be the end of the passionate affair, he is suggesting (not that, from his singing delivery, he seems too upset about this). Back in

1963, another Italian, Emilio Pericoli, had jokily sung about how he charmed various glamorous females. One senses he never got far, but Morandi sees the sun in his love's eyes first thing in the morning. One can assume it isn't just because he's brought her a cup of tea.

Relationship patterns were changing. 'Serial monogamy' was becoming ever more popular around Europe. Divorce rates in Europe had fallen in the 1950s, but began to accelerate after about 1965, Britain and Scandinavia leading the trend. In France they would take off a few years later, in the mid-1970s. In Italy they were still low: the character in Morandi's song would be expected to marry at some point and stay that way once he had done so.

The winner, by contrast to all this permissive-society philandering, was a young girl of radiant wholesomeness: Dana. Behind this (there is almost always a 'behind this' in Eurovision) lurked the terrible unfolding of events in Northern Ireland. Dana came from Bogside in Derry (or Londonderry, depending on your political allegiance).* In the previous August this estate had seen a battle between largely Protestant police and its Catholic residents. This had led to the British Army being sent into the province. Initially the army had been welcomed, but it had not taken long for feelings to sour. A month after Dana's win, rioters fought a gun battle with the new arrivals. In June, six men – five Protestant, one Catholic – were murdered by terrorists.

Dana wanted to show that there was another side to life in the province, and did, briefly, though events overtook her. In the long run, the winsome eighteen-year-old would grow into a strong woman. In 1997 she stood for president of Ireland and came third in the vote. Two years after that she was elected as a Euro MP for Connacht-Ulster, a job previously held by Ray MacSharry, of whom more later.

---

* Despite living in Northern Ireland, Dana had always pursued her musical career south of the border. At sixteen she was singing in Dublin folk clubs and had signed to an Irish record label. She won the right to represent Ireland at Eurovision by winning that nation's annual National Song Contest.

Eurovision!

Second came Britain's Mary Hopkin, who tried winsome too, with 'Knock Knock (Who's There?)' but didn't really pull it off. Germany's Katja Ebstein, a distant third, didn't try winsome. It's not her style. The success of 'Wunder Gibt Es Immer Wieder' (Miracles Always Happen) was Germany's best result in the competition so far, and a sign of that nation's continuing post-war rehabilitation.

The process continued when, later in the year, Willy Brandt visited Warsaw to sign a treaty recognizing post-1945 borders. Part of his itinerary took him to a memorial commemorating the inhabitants of the infamous ghetto, where a quarter of a million Jews had been herded into a small part of the city by the SS and murdered. Brandt laid a wreath as planned, then, unscripted, fell to his knees and remained there in silence. While it's easy to be sceptical about any 'spontaneous' gesture by a politician, Brandt seems to have been genuinely overcome by the moment. 'I did what people do when words fail them,' he said later. This gesture, which became known as the *Warschauer Kniefall*, was of great significance in Eastern and Central Europe, and helped create an impression of Germany as a modern state genuinely eager both to acknowledge and to move on from its horrific past.

The 1970 song contest was a success. The winner was a hit all round Western Europe, a sure sign that despite continual critical tutting, Eurovision had found its niche and was entertaining people across the half-continent. It also launched the career of a global superstar. Spain's Julio Iglesias had been a goalkeeper at Real Madrid, but his sporting career was cut short by a car accident; while recovering, he began to compose songs. The bright blue suit and (nearly) matching tie he wore to perform 'Gwendolyne' is probably not the best outfit he has appeared in – but his career got under way, and he is since estimated to have sold 300 million records.

Despite the *Europe des patries* message of Eurovision 1970's postcards, federalists kept the flame of a United States of Europe alight. October of that year saw the publication of a report by Pierre Werner,

Luxembourg's minister of finance, which presented a road map towards 'irrevocable fixing of parity rates' between EEC currencies. Werner's idea was that the separate currencies would continue to exist but be completely interchangeable, the way banknotes in Scotland issued by different banks are equivalent. The aim was to have this system in place by 1980. The French, despite de Gaulle's departure, still thought it too integrationist.

The timing was not right, either. The world's currencies were becoming less and less stable, due to dollar inflation induced by the Vietnam war and the subsequent collapse of the post-war Bretton Woods monetary agreement, which had effectively linked the world's major currencies to that of the USA. Werner's plan was quietly shelved. The seeds of European Monetary Union had nevertheless been sown.

1971

Date: 21 March
Venue: Gaiety Theatre, Dublin
Debutant: Malta
Winner: Séverine, Monaco
Winning Song: 'Un Banc, Un Arbre, Une Rue' (A Bench, A Tree, A Street)

In 1971 everyone wanted to be back in Eurovision. Eighteen nations took to the stage, including new arrivals Malta (who came last: new arrivals often take a while to adjust to the contest). TV audience numbers kept rising. Estimates for 1971 are as high as 250 million. There was another fine set, this time with a vaguely Celtic feel – Roland de Groot had raised the bar. The only weak point was the wavering organ music over the postcards, which sounded like it had been relayed live from the local funeral parlour.

A change in the rules allowed groups, which brought in harmony vocals and countermelodies. Some of the best harmonies came from Sweden, who fielded a quartet: two female lead vocalists (one dark-haired, one fair), backed by two bearded men playing guitars. In other words . . .

The Family Four. They came sixth. Five places above them, 'Un Banc, Un Arbre, Une Rue' used countermelodies to great effect. The entry was officially from Monaco, though its singer was French, as were its writers and the orchestra's conductor. Séverine claimed never to have visited the principality before the contest, and was not invited to do so after winning. It's a fine song, however, and sold well round Europe. It even made it into the UK Top Ten, in its original French. The lyric bemoans the selfishness that overcomes us as we leave childhood and start competing in the adult world: a dig from France – sorry, Monaco – at the evils of the Anglo-Saxon economic model.

After Derry-based Dana's win for Ireland in 1970, Britain chose a Northern Irish singer for 1971. Clodagh Rogers, from Ballymena in County Antrim, received death threats from the Irish Republican Army (IRA); her bravery in defying these deserved a better song than 'Jack In The Box'. (After 1967, Britain spent years trying to redo 'Puppet On A String', but never quite managed it.)

Meanwhile order in her home province was collapsing. In February 1971, the first soldier was shot dead in Belfast. In March, three off-duty soldiers were murdered. Later in the year, internment without trial was introduced, and in December Protestant paramilitaries let off a bomb in a Belfast bar that killed fifteen people. January 1972 saw 'Bloody Sunday', when troops fired on a protest march in Londonderry, killing fourteen Catholics. Was a part of Europe about to collapse into civil war?

For Germany, Katja Ebstein sang again. Her song, 'Diese Welt' (This World), had an environmental message. Influenced by the Apollo 8 mission, it sings of how the world is just a 'speck of dust' in space, but it's the only home we've got. Right now, we're not looking after it properly. The topic is now staple fare in Eurovision, but it wasn't in 1971: 'Diese Welt' blazed the trail.

Modern environmentalism tends to date itself from US author Rachel Carson's *Silent Spring*, a book about the overuse of pesticides published in 1962, but the European response at that time was to ignore it, considering it an American problem. As the 1960s drew to a close, our confidence began to diminish. Trees in Scandinavia and Germany's Black Forest began to lose leaves or needles, as if struck by a mysterious illness. The oil tanker *Torrey Canyon* foundered on a reef and spewed thousands of gallons of oil onto British and French beaches – an event referenced in the lyrics of 'Diese Welt'.*

---

* They were by Fred Jay, an Austrian-born writer who fled Hitler in 1938 and ended up in America: an early example of American involvement in Eurovision.

Eurovision!

In 1971, Friends of the Earth was founded by groups in France, Sweden, Britain and the USA. Greenpeace, originally Canadian but nowadays based in Amsterdam, was formed the same year. In 1972 the Club of Rome, an independent 'think tank' founded by industrialist Aurelio Peccei and Alexander King, scientific adviser to the Office of Economic Cooperation and Development (OECD), would publish *The Limits to Growth*. The book painted a gloomy picture of the future, with population rising, pollution increasing and ever more strain being placed on the earth's finite resources.

That year would also see the UN hold a conference on the environment in Stockholm. Environmental issues would finally be taken seriously by EEC leaders when they gathered for a 'summit meeting' (the forerunner of the modern European Council) in October of that year. But that was 1972: Eurovision got there before the politicians.

Eurovision 1971 was the biggest yet. The same year political Europe at last began to consider expanding to match it. Two months after the competition, Britain's new Europhile prime minister, Edward Heath, met Georges Pompidou to discuss British membership of the EEC (no other European leader was present at the discussion). Denmark, Norway and Ireland also began similar talks. The new applicants would have to pay a price for admission, however. Politically, the EEC might have had noble ambitions, but financially it was all about one thing, agricultural subsidy. Changing that was not up for discussion. The new arrivals – especially Britain and Denmark, with their small but efficient agricultural sectors – were going to have to pay a substantial and continuing entry fee.

1972

Date: 25 March
Venue: Usher Hall, Edinburgh, UK
Debuts: None
Winner: Vicky Leandros, Luxembourg
Winning Song: 'Après Toi' (After You)

The most notable thing about Eurovision 1972 was the fashion, especially for men. Hair had been getting slightly longer over the last few contests. This was the year it broke free, cascading over necklines and suddenly matching that of female contestants for length. Lapels blossomed in sympathy; clothes began to sport glittery motifs; sleeves and trouser legs started to flare ever wider – rising to a sartorial crescendo with the last entry, Serge from the Netherlands, who also wore various shades of poster-paint lime green. The decade that taste forgot had hit its stride (not that 'taste' and 'Eurovision' have ever precisely coincided).

The winner of the contest was an international co-operation: a Greek singer, French, Greek and German lyricist/composers, and a German conductor. The tuba player's cousin had once been to Luxembourg. 'Après Toi' was a powerful ballad that went on to sell very well around Europe, keeping up the traditions of winners since 1967.

Ireland and Malta sang in local languages, Gaelic and Maltese. Neither met success, coming fifteenth and last respectively (Malta's his 'n' hers pink polka-dot outfits probably didn't help). This reflected a new sensibility in Europe. Activists were beginning to fight to save the continent's threatened minority languages, especially on the western Celtic fringe. Welsh-speaking schools had been set up in 1971. The Gaelscoileanna, Ikastola and Diwan movements in Eire, the Basque country and Brittany respectively, would soon follow suit. Regionalist political parties began to attract votes: in 1974, the Scottish Nationalists would return eleven members to London's Westminster Parliament.

Eurovision did little to follow this trend. Regional cultures added colour and interest to the competition, but, as Ireland and Malta found, were not rewarded by judges. Instead, the results reflected the overwhelming linguistic trend of the era, the continuing march of English (or, more accurately, American). It was decided that for the next Eurovision, entrants would be allowed to sing in whatever language they wanted. This could be seen as a defeat for less populous cultures, another sign of their being swamped by 'big' languages. Performers from smaller countries were delighted, however. Singing in English, surely, would heighten their chances of victory.

The language debate at this time highlights the issue of the conflict between Europe's centre and its periphery. There are various ways of dividing the continent. East/west was the obvious one before 1989. Nowadays, people talk of the 'olive line', a north/south division below which long, blazing summers make life move at a slower pace and where membership of the euro is causing appalling hardship. But a divide between centre and periphery seems the most lasting and instructive. There are various ramifications, but the simplest version places the old Lugano 1956 core at Europe's centre and the rest on the periphery – to start with, anyway; subtleties will emerge as this story develops. Up to 1973, Eurovision winners had largely been in the languages of 'centre' countries: French mainly, plus Dutch, Italian and German (in 1967 English managed to sneak in). Would the new rule allow peripheral Europe to sing in one of these languages and start winning?

In 1972, Norway established its position as peripheral and proud of it by voting not to proceed with its application for EEC membership. Yet the country had been, and would continue to be, an enthusiastic participant in Eurovision – one of the most interesting ones, with a fascinating variety of contributions in its fifty-five years, though 1972's 'Småting' (Small Things) was not one of their finest.

By contrast, on 1 January 1973 the European centre opened its gates to Britain, Denmark and Ireland (two of the three had been unsuccessful applicants to sing at Lugano back in '56), via EEC membership. However, even these early joiners have since proven to be independently minded. They have never cuddled into the EEC/EU system the way the original Six did. Denmark has not joined the euro. Ireland has voted against two major EU treaties in the 2000s. And Britain – well, more of that later.

1973

Date: 7 April
Venue: Nouveau Théâtre, Luxembourg
Debut: Israel
Winner: Anne-Marie David, Luxembourg
Winning Song: 'Tu Te Reconnaîtras' (You Will Recognize Yourself)

Along with the removal of the language rule, the 1973 contest saw another significant change, the arrival of Israel. People often ask why this non-European country is allowed into Eurovision. One suggested answer is that it was a way of testing potential military communications technology with the West's main ally in the Middle East. The truth is simpler and boringly technical. The contest is open to all nations who are in the EBU, and eligibility for the EBU is determined by geography. You can join if your territory, or part of it, lies within an area bounded to the west by the Atlantic Ocean, to the east by the meridian 40 degrees E, and to the south by the parallel 30 degrees N. North African and Middle Eastern countries, all EBU members, could have decided to sing in Eurovision, but Israel got there first, since when those countries have mostly declined to exercise their right to participate.

The previous year, eleven Israeli athletes had been murdered at the Munich Olympics: security at the Nouveau Théâtre was tight. Terry Wogan, on his second gig commentating for Britain, later recalled seeing armoured cars and machine guns. The audience was told not to stand up and applaud any songs, as they might get shot.

The presentation began with a display of modern broadcast technology: modern in 1973, that is, with not a computer or a microprocessor in sight. Some modern (also in 1973) fashions were then displayed by Belgium's Nicole and Hugo, who both sported platform shoes, purple bellbottom trousers, and purple tops with huge rhine-stone-encrusted lapels and flapping, flared sleeves.

By contrast, Portugal once again produced a serious song with hidden political barbs. Ary dos Santos' 'Tourada' (Bullfight) was a satire on the *Estado Novo* regime as a cavalcade of fools and crooks. Marcelo Caetano had tried to liberalize the system a little bit – his reforms had included rebranding the secret police by giving them a new name – but, like the Russians in Czechoslovakia, he then panicked and was now trying to revert to authoritarian rule.

Both Sweden and Israel used female conductors in Eurovision 1973. Up to this point, the contest podium had been a male preserve. Such exclusivity was a mirror of European life generally. In 1973 the European Parliament was 95 per cent male, and there were no women among the fourteen EEC Commissioners.

But things were changing. Women were entering the workforce in ever greater numbers, especially in Britain and Scandinavia, where for a woman to have a career became more the rule than the exception (in Southern Europe, women still tended to work until marriage, after which many returned to the home). However, these careers were usually halted by a 'glass ceiling' of male power – though not always: in Britain, Margaret Hilda Thatcher, a 48-year-old former Oxford chemistry student, was already Secretary of State for Education and had her eye on even greater things.

Sociologists began talking of the 'feminization' of European society. In 1973 the number of Europeans working in the service sector surpassed those working in industry for the first time, and it was argued that these new jobs required more 'emotional intelligence', an arguably female quality, than the old muscular industrial ones.

Eurovision's new language rule actually did little to change the contest, except produce some poor songs in English by non-native speakers. The winner was a powerful ballad in French that went on to sell well round Europe. A song in Spanish, 'Eres Tú' (You Are), came second and sold even better, thus joining the elite band of classic non-winners. It has been covered by such acts as Bing Crosby, Acker Bilk and Eydie Gormé, as well as being recreated in steel-band and punk versions. A British *schlager* came third, bouncily celebrating that nation's new EEC membership: 'Power To All Our Friends', sang Cliff Richard. So it was Eurovision business as usual.

It looked like business as usual in 1973 for Western Europe's economy, too, despite the questions asked by the *soixante-huitards* and the Club of Rome.* Inflation might have been creeping up, but unemployment remained under 3 per cent, a level that most economists consider to be 'full employment' and which had been pretty constant since before this story began. Western Europe, by adopting – or at least adapting – the German Social Market model, seemed to have found the formula for socially balanced prosperity, steering a middle course between the obsession with market forces across the Atlantic and the grim totalitarianism behind the Iron Curtain.

On 6 October, Yom Kippur, the holiest day in the Jewish calendar, Egypt and Syria launched surprise attacks on Eurovision's latest participant country with the aim of getting back lands lost in the 1967 Six Day War. The move was so successful that within three days Israel was contemplating using tactical nuclear weapons. This panicked the Americans into launching an airlift of military hardware to its ally. On 14 October, a massive tank battle turned the tide. By 22 October, Israeli forces were 100 kilometres from Cairo, at which point a cease-fire was brokered.

The Arab world was furious at what they saw as the West's meddling in a war which they reckoned they should have won – though in fact Europe had done very little meddling: America had requested permission to use its European bases for its airlift, but only Portugal

---

* German-born, British-based economist E.F. Schumacher added his voice to the questioning in 1973 with his book *Small is Beautiful*.

and the Netherlands had said yes. On 17 October, the Arab-dominated Organization of Petroleum Exporting Countries (OPEC) cut oil production and raised prices by 70 per cent. In December, they doubled the price again, to $11.65 per barrel (at the start of October, the price had been $3). Countries seen as too 'pro-Israel', such as the Netherlands, were denied access to their oil at any price. (The Netherlands suggested that, in the name of European unity, EEC oil supplies be pooled. This did not happen.)

The effect was immediate. Western Europe plummeted into recession. Car-free Sundays were enforced on the public roads of Britain, Germany, Italy, the Netherlands, Norway and Switzerland. In early 1974, Britain began working a three-day week. Its stock market went into free-fall, and electricity shortages became a part of national life. 'Power To All Our Friends'? The nation didn't even have enough power for itself.

In every Western European country unemployment started rising. Inflation rose with it, confounding economists, whose theories had previously insisted that the two phenomena should be inversely correlated. A fresh concept had to be invented for this new world of inflating currencies and economic stagnation: stagflation.

Boom bang-a-bang! This wasn't just a 'recession' but the end of an era, the end of a system that had driven the world's advanced economies since Pattillo Higgins and Anthony F. Lucas had struck black gold in Texas in 1901. The cheap oil economy was dead.

The words of the Club of Rome suddenly looked frighteningly prescient. Europe had boomed since 1945. It had got used to booming; it had come to assume that growth was automatic if governments kept to a reasonably sensible set of rules. But supposing this wasn't the case? Supposing the *trente glorieuses* (as the French came to call the era from 1945 to 1973: it sounds snappier than *vingt-huit glorieuses*) was an exception, a lucky break based on cheap oil and the importation of American business methods? What was in store for Europe now that this lucky break was over?

1974

Date: 6 April
Venue: The Dome, Brighton, UK
Debut: Greece
Winner: Abba, Sweden
Winning Song: 'Waterloo'

We all needed cheering up. Could Eurovision 1974 manage that?

The contest nearly didn't take place at all, because of a terrorist threat from the IRA. Only after a thorough search of the venue was the event allowed to run, and security remained tight throughout the proceedings. Once it did start, the material seemed uninspiring. Spain (flamenco-type guitar) and debutant Greece (bouzouki) provided some interesting ethnic flourishes but were short on melody. Things weren't looking too good . . .

Eighth to sing was Sweden. We got a short postcard to the tune of Hugo Alfven's 'Swedish Rhapsody': viewers were probably wondering already if that was going to be the only decent tune they'd hear all evening. Conductor Sven-Olof Walldoff walked onto the podium dressed as Napoleon. Oh, God, not a novelty song . . . Then Anni-Frid Lyngstad and Agnetha Fältskog, the latter in a blue catsuit, glitter and silver platforms, bounded down onto the stage, and the contest changed for ever.

'Waterloo' is still regarded as the definitive Eurovision song – it romped to victory in the 2005 'best of the best' poll, and rightly so. It brought a new energy to the competition: finally rock rhythms and instrumentation had found their way in alongside the ballads and the Europop (actually, 'Waterloo' reinvented Europop, killing the old format). It was also a groundbreaking victory for Europe's periphery over its centre – no previous winner had been as far-flung as Sweden. Europe was a bigger place on 7 April 1974.

Lyrically, 'Waterloo' was precision-engineered for the contest, with its instantly recognizable, one-word title sold enthusiastically throughout the song. British viewers no doubt also enjoyed the reference to the defeat of France in 1815: especially apt in the year that English became Eurovision's *de facto* language. But I find some other Eurovision 1974 lyrics more intriguing.

Yugoslavia, which was beginning to recant its earlier, half-western political models and to turn more hard-line,* reflected on the effect of war on 'Generacija '42' (The Generation Of '42). Belgium lamented the loss of late sixties idealism with 'Fleur De Liberté' (Flower Of Freedom). Best of all, perhaps, was lyricist Michel Jourdan's meditation on romantic break-ups, 'Celui Qui Reste Et Celui Qui S'en Va' (The One Who Stays And The One Who Leaves), sung by Romuald for Monaco. The francophone countries had a tradition of producing quality words. Was this tradition about to meet its Waterloo? Eurovision would surely be the poorer if it did.

Politically, the most significant song came once more from Portugal. On 24 April at 10.55 p.m., the Lisbon radio station Emissores Associados de Lisboa broadcast the nation's Eurovision entry, 'E Depois Do Adeus' (After Goodbye). This was a secret signal for a group of young army officers to launch a *coup d'état*. Early next morning, key locations – the local military HQ, TV and radio stations, and Lisbon airport – were occupied, and other institutions, such as City Hall, the national bank and the defence ministry, were surrounded. A few high-ranking old-guard loyalists escaped from the last of these and set up a rival HQ – but hardly any servicemen

---

* Sixties Eurovision entrant Vice Vukov found himself banned from singing in the 1970s, due to his support for greater Croatian independence. His records were removed from all shops. After 1989, he went into politics and in 2003 was elected to the Croatian parliament, representing the centre-left Social Democratic Party.

obeyed their orders. Instead, crowds came out onto the streets and started handing red carnations, in flower and in plentiful supply at the time, to soldiers. By the end of the day it was 'after goodbye' to the *Estado Novo*; Portugal had a new government, committed to 'three ds': democracy, decolonization and development. The change had been brought about with minimal violence (four people were shot by the secret police). This was a model example of people power – the modern European way of bringing about regime change.

Europe was still not without violence, of course. There was the threat of terrorism, so bravely defied by Eurovision in 1973 and 1974 (Brighton would be the scene of a brutal bombing a decade later). And two months after making its debut in Eurovision, Greece found itself in a virtual war with Turkey over Cyprus. Conflict between Greek and Turkish Cypriots had been escalating ever since Britain had granted the island independence in 1960. On 15 July 1974, a military coup removed its moderate government, replacing it with one determined on *enosis*, unity with Greece. Turkey responded by invading five days later, capturing a small corridor of land between Kyrenia and Nicosia. The Greek government then collapsed. Peace talks began, but these did not progress: on 14 August, Turkey launched a second invasion, and this time took over the north-western third of the country – territory that it still holds today, though most nations do not recognize the occupation. When Cyprus entered Eurovision in 1981, it would be its Greek sector that did so, as all but the most unaware Eurovision watcher will know from its voting. Northern Cyprus would have to wait till 2013 to take part in a song contest – but that's for later.

If Abba changed Eurovision for ever, 1974 also saw a major change in political Europe, with its leaders agreeing to have their previously irregular 'summit meetings' – there had been seven since 1961 – on a regular and more frequent basis. There would be three a year (it soon became four), and there would be a system of rotating presidency.

In theory this would now be the place where the big pan-European decisions were made: Commission, Parliament and Council of Ministers were supposed to follow its essential direction. In practice, of course, the big nations still held all the cards, as the Dutch already knew after their ill-fated appeal for oil-sharing the previous year.

This body would later become known as the European Council – confusing, given the already existing (non-EEC) Council of Europe and the EEC's own Council of Ministers, which was often known as the 'Council of the EEC'. However, historians now backdate the name 'European Council' to the 1974 decision: lists of Council meetings tend to begin with the first of the new, formal, regular get-togethers, in January 1975.

1975

Date: 22 March
Venue: Stockholm International Fairs and Congress Centre, Sweden
Debut: Turkey
Winner: Teach-in, The Netherlands
Winning Song: 'Ding Dinge Dong'

After the best Eurovision winner ever, the contest looked poised to move up a gear and show that new-generation Europop could be genuinely original. What amazing new Abbas would emerge this time round? First to rise to the challenge was a group from the Netherlands. A blip, no doubt: their clothes were ridiculous and their song had lyrics that made 'La, La, La' sound deep. Never mind, something better would come along . . .

Many of the entries that followed had the new, post-Abba rockier feel. 'Let Me Be The One' by Britain's The Shadows featured three electric guitars. Germany's Joy Fleming looked across the Berlin Wall and sang the blues in 'Ein Lied Kann Ein Brücke Sein' (A Song Can Be A Bridge). Not rocky but lyrically intriguing was Switzerland's 'Mikado'. Behind a suddenly outdated *schlager* beat, singer/songwriter Simone Drexel came up with a neat image for the selfish new age she feared was dawning. In the game Mikado (alias pick-up-sticks, jackstraws or spillikins) you mustn't show your feelings. If someone else makes a mistake, well that's their tough luck: don't get involved.

By contrast, Portugal unashamedly celebrated its Carnation Revolution with 'Madrugada' (Dawn). Singer Duarte Mendes was a captain at the national artillery training school; he wanted to perform the song in army uniform but had to be content with a red carnation in his buttonhole. However, like many revolutions, the events of 1974 had been less conclusive than Mendes was telling the Eurovision audience: while he hymned his victory in Stockholm, factions were struggling for power back home, and it was still not clear who would end up the winner. On 25 November 1975, a coup would be launched by Communist paratroopers. A counter-coup would follow the same day, which finally ended the jostling for power; elections would be held in 1976. Across Portugal's border, General Franco died five days before the two November coups. King Juan Carlos became head of the Spanish state, and set in train a cautious but ultimately effective process of reform.

After listening to this selection of interesting entries, the judges considered their options, then chose the song they considered the summit of songwriting achievement for Western Europe in the year 1975.

Oops!

Perhaps what the judges liked about the winning song was its daftness. 'Ding Dinge Dong' looked longingly back at the sixties and tried to recapture some of that era's lost fizz and innocence. (The song uses the word *uptight* in the old jazz-slang sense of 'good', the sense Stevie Wonder had used back in 1965 in his song 'Uptight (Everything's Alright)'. Ten years on, this was already retro: the meaning had changed to its current one, frustrated and over-controlling.)

But the sixties were gone. The old economic model was collapsing. Inflation was rising, stirring horrific memories in Germany. Nobody knew what would replace the old economy – or whether anything would.

Maybe the *soixante-huitards* had been right after all. Dump the system; it had failed. Eurovision 1975 was accompanied by far-left protests on Stockholm's streets against the amount of money being spent on staging the contest, and, more generally, the poor quality of capitalist 'commercial' music. An *Alternativfestival* was set up, where anyone could come, sing and parody Eurovision at its worst – though could anyone have done a better job than Teach-in?

Eurovision!

(Intriguingly, the anti-Eurovision argument was later to cross the political divide, and would be heard from the right, when it was the amount of *public* money being spent on the contest that came in for criticism. The moral, perhaps, is that aspirant political elites like to set themselves up as aesthetic elites, too, and that distancing yourself from Eurovision is one way of doing this. Instead, why not be a *true* revolutionary? Enjoy Eurovision and be proud of it!)

Far-left politics of a more violent nature raised its head too, with yet another terrorist threat to Eurovision, this time from Germany's Red Army Faction (RAF). It did not materialize, but a month after the Stockholm contest, members of the faction seized the West German embassy in the city and murdered the military and economic attachés.

At the other end of the Eurovision table from the triumphant dinging and donging, with three votes, was debutant Turkey. One can't help feeling that prejudice was responsible for this, as their song was a pleasant, well-sung ballad, 'Seninle Bir Dakika' (A Minute With You), that didn't deserve this fate.

Turkey had been knocking on Europe's door since joining the Council of Europe in 1949 and NATO in 1952 (where it soon became a key player: it was the presence of US missiles on Turkish soil that had prompted the Soviet Union to build bases in Cuba). In 1963 it had signed an agreement with the EEC that created a road-map to its accession. Since then, the map had not been followed – and has not been to this day. Various reasons were cited in 1975, and still resurface. Cyprus is one (Greece boycotted Eurovision 1975 due to Turkish participation). Turkey's human rights record is another.[*] It has still to admit its role in the 1915 Armenian genocide. Geographically, only 3 per cent of the country is in Europe. Is it too big? In 1975, its population was around 40 million; now that figure is 75 million and

---

[*] The Economist Intelligence Unit produces an annual 'democracy index'. In the most recent one, Scandinavia tops the bill, with most Western European countries looking good. The lowest EU nation is Romania (59th), while Turkey is 97th.

it is poised to overtake Germany, Europe's most populous country, by the end of the 2010s if current growth rates in the two countries persist. Is it too different? Many Europeans feel that the country really isn't European culturally – a feeling hotly contested by many educated Turks. Rather than get into a debate about that here, we shall follow Turkey's Eurovision career and see what light it sheds.

Across the Gulf of Bothnia from the 1975 contest venue, a truly pan-European 'Conference on Security and Co-operation in Europe' which had been running since 1973 reached its climax. On 1 August, the Helsinki Accords were signed by leaders of Europe, east and west – including Turkey – and of the US and the Soviet Union.

The Accords had three principal aspects, oddly referred to as 'baskets'. One accepted existing boundaries in Europe, not good news for the three Baltic states of Estonia, Latvia and Lithuania annexed by Stalin in 1940. West Germany's new Chancellor, Helmut Schmidt – he had replaced Willy Brandt in 1974 – commented that though 'frontiers are inviolable', one 'must be able to change them by peaceful means and agreement'. East Germany's Erich Honecker was less keen on change, reminding everyone that Europe's two twentieth-century wars had been started by 'disregard for the sovereignty and territorial integrity of other states'. *Touché.*

The Accords' second basket encouraged trade, cultural and scientific links between the two blocs. The third dealt with human rights and 'free circulation of ideas and information'. The Soviet Union saw the Accords as a win, thanks to basket one, but over time the third would become a thorn in its imperial side.

1976

Date: 6 April
Venue: Congresgebouw, Den Haag, Netherlands
Debuts: None (no new entrants till 1980)
Winner: Brotherhood of Man, UK
Winning Song: 'Save Your Kisses For Me'

Eurovision 1976 saw victory for a song so middle-of-the-road that you could put cats' eyes in it. But before one sneers, 'Save Your Kisses For Me' then sold millions of singles around Europe, more than any other winner before or since, even 'Waterloo'. The four singers, already popular in Europe, continued to enjoy success for the rest of the decade. It's also interesting that, after the previous year's lyrical inanities, the 1976 contest was won by a song whose effect relies on its lyric. Everything about the winner seems ridiculously trite until the last line reveals its audience to be a three-year-old child, after which it's quite cute.

The winning nation was having less good fortune with its economy. Britain's inflation level was the worst in Europe, though Italy ran it a close second. The same month as it won the contest, its currency began to collapse on world markets. By December, Chancellor Denis Healey was forced to go to the International Monetary Fund, a global pot of cash set aside to rescue failing third-world economies, and beg for a bailout, a humiliation that some commentators put on the same level as Suez two decades before. 'Goodbye, Great Britain' said America's *Wall Street Journal*.

Meanwhile in London's suburbs, an angry new music was beginning to make itself heard, about as different to 'Save Your Kisses For Me' as could be imagined. Punk.

The other entries to Eurovision 1976 ran the usual gamut from the comical (try keeping a straight face while watching Finland's mountainous Freddi telling us to let our hips go 'Hippety Pump Pump') to thoughtful but not very melodic entries from Spain and Belgium. Greece bemoaned the refugees, ruins and dead bodies in Cyprus (the Greek Cypriot ones, anyway).

Nonsense titles came from Switzerland, Germany – and France, though the French managed to do nonsense in style, Catherine Ferry putting pert hedonism into 'Un, Deux, Trois'. Life, she pointed out, is not a novel by Kafka. The judges agreed – the song came second. At the other end of the table, Norway's Anne-Karine Strøm sabotaged a catchy entry about superspy Mata Hari by putting on some ludicrous sunglasses halfway through. It is as if she felt 'I'm winning here: I'd better do something about that'. She is the only artist to have come last twice in Eurovision, but Norwegians don't seem to give a damn. Or do they? Such is the perpetual enigma of the land of Grieg, Munch and Ibsen.

A topic that did not get covered was the environment. After 'Diese Welt' back in 1971, the subject had been ignored in the contest – as it had been in Europe's media: people were more concerned about stagflation. But 1976 put it right back on the public agenda. In July, six tonnes of TCCP, a gas containing deadly dioxins, escaped from a factory in Seveso, northern Italy. In the end, no human life was lost, but images went deep into Europe's consciousness, of forcibly abandoned villages surrounded by barbed wire, behind which men in what looked like spacesuits cleared up thousands of tons of poisoned earth. In January 1977, it was announced that the Acropolis in Athens was under threat from pollutants, largely from car exhausts. This all went to add to the worrying, seventies sense of 'game over' for the Western way of getting and spending that had served Europe so well.

1977

Date: 7 May
Venue: Wembley Conference Centre, London
Winner: Marie Myriam, France
Winning Song: 'L'Oiseau Et l'Enfant' (The Bird And The Child)

Eurovision 1977 was due to be broadcast in April. The host, however, was London, and the UK plus the 1970s meant strikes, in this case by BBC cameramen and technicians, so it ended up being postponed till May.

A Soviet empire version of the contest was launched in the same year, on time and with no similar problems. Song festivals had long been popular in Eastern Europe, for example the Golden Stag and Golden Orpheus Festivals in Bulgaria or the Lyre Festival in Bratislava. There had been one at Sopot near Gdansk, Poland, since 1961 (the first three had actually been held in the Gdansk shipyard, after which the venue was moved to the nearby Forest Opera amphitheatre). In 1977, the Sopot Festival was rebranded as the Intervision Song Contest and broadcast all round the Soviet bloc.

Intervision competitors came from the Warsaw Pact nations,* plus Cuba, Finland and, for some reason, Spain, to vie for first prize, the Amber Nightingale. The organizers developed an imaginative system of public voting: if you liked a song, you turned all your lights on; if you disliked it, you turned all your lights out. The electricity distributor in each country measured the change in usage during each song. The Nightingale went to the one that used the most. In 1977 this was Helena

---

* The Treaty of 'Friendship, Co-operation and Mutual Assistance' had been signed by Albania, Bulgaria, Czechoslovakia, East Germany, Hungary, Poland, Romania and the Soviet Union in Warsaw in 1955. Albania left the group in 1968.

Vondráčková from Czechoslovakia with 'Malovaný Džbánku' (Painted Jug). The middle of the Marxist-Leninist road looks and sounds remarkably like the middle of the capitalist one.

Sadly, similar tastes in popular entertainment did not stop the two camps threatening to obliterate each other. While Helena Vondráčková was collecting her Amber Nightingale, Russia's military was deploying a new weapon, the RSD-10 Pioneer missile (known to the West as the SS-20). These could be fired quickly and easily from mobile launchers: the RSD-10 was powered by solid fuel, whereas previous Soviet missiles had to be slowly and riskily filled with liquid propellant at the point of firing. They were reliable and accurate: they could be used tactically, to nuke Europe's airfields and military bases rather than to obliterate whole cities – a move away from total madness, one might think, but a change which experts thought made war more likely.

Russia was doing well in 1977. It hadn't suffered in the oil crisis, having plenty of black gold of its own. Its ideology was proving attractive to the third world, where Soviet-backed guerrilla fighters were filling the power gaps left by the last departing imperialists.

Unsurprisingly, the ideology was less attractive in Eastern Europe. The 'Charter 77' movement, founded in Czechoslovakia, was dedicated to reminding the authorities of their human rights obligations under the Helsinki Accords. Karel Gott, who had sung in Eurovision back in 1968, recorded a song about Jan Palach, a Czech student who had committed suicide in 1969 in protest at the Soviet invasion.

The authorities clamped down on these protests. Several Charter 77 members – including Vaclav Havel, who later became the first president of post-Communist Czechoslovakia – ended up in prison. Gott was told that this was the end of his singing career unless he signed a document criticizing the Charter. He obeyed.

In many Western European countries, Communist parties were growing again – though this was perhaps only partially pleasing to

Moscow, as they were doing so on the back of a reformed ideology which became known as Eurocommunism, where parties no longer automatically followed the Soviet line. Italy's Communist Party was the second biggest in the nation's parliament, having won 34.4 per cent of the vote in the previous year's election.

The year also saw more terrorist activity in the West – no doubt to the delight of the Soviets, who probably supported it financially (exactly how far this went remains open to debate: one source claims that the Soviet Union was spending around $200 million a year on training and arming terrorists around this time, but this figure comes from the US government, which might not be the most objective observer).

The Red Army Faction certainly received help from the Stasi, the East German secret police, as was discovered after 1989. In 1977 the faction reached the climax of its activities. Germany's prosecutor general was murdered in April. Banker Jürgen Ponto suffered the same fate in July. In October, Lufthansa Flight 181 from Mallorca to Frankfurt was hijacked by Palestinian terrorists demanding the release of RAF prisoners. The aircraft ended up in Mogadishu, where the terrorists poured duty-free spirits over the hostages ready to burn them alive. But instead the plane was stormed by an elite German anti-terror squad, GSG9. Three members of the RAF subsequently committed suicide. The insanity was over – in Germany, anyway, though in Italy, further horrors, courtesy of left and right, were to follow, as were ETA atrocities in Spain.

All this was symptomatic of a troubled Europe. What was the best way out of the mid-seventies economic mess? Sharp left? Turn right? Muddle along?

Austria's 1977 Eurovision entrants, Schmetterlinge, supported the first option. Their previous work had been an opera entitled *The Passion of the Proletariat* ('passion' as in suffering, as in the Passion of Christ), which took listeners through events like the Paris Commune of 1871 and the 1917 Russian Revolution. 'Boom Boom

Boomerang' was both a parody of Eurovision and an attack on the music industry as a whole, as a purveyor of mind-numbing but money-making pap.* (The song's critique extended to blues, rock 'n' roll, reggae and soul, which leaves one wondering what sort of music we would be allowed to listen to in Schmetterlinge's ideal world.)

The second option was suggested by Britain's Lynsey de Paul and Mike Moran, who lamented the economic state of their country with 'Rock Bottom', suggesting we 'rub out' the old system and start it again. Schmetterlinge might have approved of this, but not of the UK duo's intended rebuild. De Paul was an admirer of Margaret Thatcher, who was now leader of Britain's Conservative Party. Still in opposition, Mrs Thatcher was eager to introduce a strong dose of what would later be called 'neo-liberalism' into British political life. She intended to curb the power of trades unions, cut both taxes and government spending, deregulate markets, sell state assets to private buyers and encourage entrepreneurship.

Muddle along? That year's voting was particularly shambolic, with half the scores on the board at the end of the evening being incorrect (luckily, this didn't make any difference to the actual positions).

Maybe we should just forget politics, and boogie. Eurovision 1977 saw a number of entries go disco, with sixteenth beats and quacking wah-wah guitars. Germany brought in Silver Convention, a successful act in this new genre, then gave them a poor song, 'Telegram'. A deliberate homage to Margot Hielscher's 'Telefon', twenty years earlier? Probably not.

Two interesting songs looked at the role of women in the new Europe. Again, different options were presented. Italy's Mia Martini sang 'Libera', a celebration of being a modern woman, free to live life however she chooses. Belgium's 'A Million In One, Two, Three' sang of a less liberated choice, reminiscent of Abba's 'Money, Money, Money'.

---

* The title is, surely, a dig at Abba's 'Bang-a-boomerang', a chirpy *schlager* which had featured in Sweden's Eurovision elimination contest in 1975, sung by duo Svenne and Lotta, and on Abba's third album.

Eurovision!

There was also some national quirkiness on offer. The Swiss entry featured an alphorn, and Finland's 'Lapponia' recreated a folk tale but spoilt a potentially haunting piece with too conventional an arrangement: Eurovision would learn how to do Celtic/Norse in the 1990s.

In the end, the winner was neither political, nor disco, nor about female roles, nor quirkily ethnic, but a ballad, on the tried and tested Eurovision theme of the value of innocence and love in a potentially cruel world. It was, perhaps, a dull choice given the intriguing alternatives, more in tune with the *zeitgeist*, on offer, but Marie Myriam put in a fine performance which included singing the first verse unaccompanied. The song, though, did not sell well afterwards, ending the run of winners from 1967 that had become hits around Europe. From then on, such breakouts would be rare.

The old rule that entries had to be in the native language (or *a* native language) of a competitor was reintroduced for this contest, and would last two decades. The problem with the rule became apparent the moment the results were announced. The table splits into two. Numbers one to eight are almost all in English or French; numbers nine to eighteen are almost all in other languages (there's one francophone entry down there, which had been poorly sung). The native language rule encouraged colour and diversity. But given the judges' obvious preference for familiar languages, it narrowed the pool of potential winners.

Political Europe's own issues are mirrored in this dilemma. How do you strike a balance between on the one hand local accountability, relevance and autonomy, and on the other the centralization of power, which should create efficiency and is the only way to address Europe-wide issues?

1978

Date: 22 April
Venue: Palais des Congrès, Paris
Winner: Izhar Cohen and Alpha Beta, Israel
Winning Song: 'A-Ba-Ni-Bi'

The 1978 song contest is now probably best remembered for one of Eurovision's classic *nul points* entries: 'Mil Etter Mil' (Mile After Mile) from Norway's Jahn Teigen. The modern system of points allocation (or something very like it) had begun in 1975, which meant that getting none at all would be a rare event. So far nobody had endured this embarrassment. So far . . .

Teigen did not get off to a good start: he was allocated the dreaded number two singing slot. Then he had a very public accident on his way to perform. Instead of between-the-acts postcards, French TV showed pictures of the artists behind the scenes. Over 100 million viewers saw the Norwegian singer head for the stage and, too busy waving at a camera, walk into a wall. Things didn't get much better during his performance – Teigen ended up twanging his braces like a nineteenth-century dignitary giving an after-dinner speech.

But was his song *that* much worse than some other clunkers from 1978? Than Luxembourg's cringe-making attempt to suck up to France, 'Parlez-vous Français'? Than Britain's clichéd 'The Bad Old Days'? No. Teigen got *nul points* because he was from a peripheral country, singing in an obscure language. OK, the braces didn't help . . .

Nordic neighbour Bjorn Skifs decided on a different route: he'd defy the language rule and sing 'Det Blir Alltid Värre Framåt Natten' in English (as 'It Always Gets Worse At Night'). But he chickened out at the last moment, and ended up forgetting his Swedish lyrics.

As in 1977, the winning entries ended up largely in French and English, the bottom ones 'the rest'. Some of the latter tried language-independent titles like 'Boom Boom', 'Dai-Li-Dou', or an Austrian song about a witch-turned-sex-goddess, 'Mrs Caroline Robinson', but to no avail.

Of course, the winner bucked this trend by cleverly choosing a nonsense title/hook. Israel's victory created all sorts of problems for other Middle Eastern and North African broadcasters, as they did not recognize the country's existence. Most had a commercial break during Cohen's performance, and many simply stopped the broadcast when it became clear who was going to win. Jordanian TV, needing to fill the time, showed a bunch of daffodils.

Eurovision 1978 wasn't a vintage edition. Arguably the best thing about it – apart from Jahn Teigen's braces – was the interval act, where France showed its cultural credentials by giving us Oscar Peterson, Stéphane Grappelli and Yehudi Menuhin. Perhaps we'd have had more fun watching Intervision, where the 1978 Amber Nightingale went to Russia's Alla Pugacheva, despite her making the sign of the cross at the end of her song 'Vsyo Mogut Koroli' (Kings Can Do Anything), to loud applause from the audience. Compère Jacek Bromski indulged in some anti-Soviet jokes, too. When the line to get Moscow's vote went dead, he told them to 'wake up'. When the line stayed down, he added, 'Better let them sleep' – a comment that was cut out of the actual broadcast.

Pugacheva was Intervision's Abba: she is reputed to have sold 250 million records in her career, which is still flourishing. She had some of the French *chanteuse* about her, but no self-pity; she had some of the German cabaret artiste, but no creepiness. Ebullient, sexy, emotional, unafraid to speak her mind, Pugacheva was a true people's heroine during the grey Soviet era. After that era she launched her own branded clothing, perfume and shoes, as well as potato crisps and a radio station, Radio Alla.

Eurovision!

As 1978 turned into 1979, relationships between the homes of Intervision and Eurovision grew ever more sour. In January, German and British leaders agreed to have American Pershing II ballistic missiles and Gryphon cruise missiles stationed on their territory, in response to the RSD-10s. Was Europe heading towards Berlin 1961 again?

We were certainly headed for more economic difficulties. The Shah of Iran was overthrown in a revolution in February 1979. Oil output from the country plummeted and the price duly took off again, reaching $34 per barrel (remember, it had cost $3 per barrel in September 1973). This price was, of course, the one paid by the US and Western Europe. Behind the Iron Curtain, oil remained cheap. The Soviet Union just kept on whistling the latest Alla Pugacheva hit and producing all the oil that it and its empire needed (plus some more for export).

1979

Date: 31 March
Venue: Binyanei Ha-ouma Convention Centre, Jerusalem
Winner: Gali Atari, with Milk and Honey, Israel
Winning Song: 'Hallelujah'

Despite the missiles and the oil price, Eurovision 1979 took place in an atmosphere of optimism, because five days before the event, the hosts Israel had signed a treaty with Egypt based on 'Accords' reached at Camp David in the USA the year before. The Sinai Peninsula was to be demilitarized; autonomous Palestinian authorities would be set up on the West Bank and in Gaza; Israel's existence was formally recognized by Egypt. Peace in the Middle East at last!

The contest's opening travelogue stayed true to this optimism, showing Israel as a modern nation where different faiths coexisted. Dov Ben David's stage set reinforced this message with its futuristic, shifting steel circles: let's leave the past and move into the future. The postcards reappeared, as witty mimes having contemporary fun with outdated stereotypical national images. And then there was the winning song, building like the peace process itself, from a solo voice to four-part harmony and full orchestra, singing of simple gratitude for life itself.

It only just won: the voting was among the most exciting ever. Spain's super-catchy, cute 'Su Canción' (Your Song), sung by graceful Peruvian-born Betty Missiego plus four children, led going into the last vote – from Spain itself, who awarded Israel the points that gave it victory. In third place was former winner Anne-Marie David with the enigmatic 'Je Suis l'Enfant Soleil' (I Am The Sun-Child), a fine lyric put across with her usual skill. And then fourth . . .

It didn't seem the most tactful thing for Germany to enter a contest in Israel with a song about Genghis Khan. But that's what they did – and the audience gave Ralph Siegel and Bernd Meinunger's classic Eurovision romp a hearty round of applause. That shows the mood of the time: a robust determination to move forward, not to get mired in affront, however unspeakable the sins of the past.

All these four songs were outstanding in their own Eurovision ways. Britain's entry, 'Mary Anne' by Black Lace, was rather less outstanding. It had been chosen by juries listening to tapes, because the televised event to select the entry had been cancelled due to another industrial dispute, this time about which trades union the person operating the electronic scoreboard should belong to. Winter 1978 saw the nation plunged into disorder by waves of strikes, often 'wildcat' ones called at short notice. Britain's voters decided this really was Rock Bottom, and a month after Eurovision 1979 voted for Margaret Thatcher.

The rest of Western Europe was watching, and a new tone of respect for the commercial marketplace and distrust of national deals between organized labour and organized capital began to enter political discourse all round the half-continent.

In 1979 the first direct elections to the European Parliament were also held. Back in 1957 (the year from which we have those first black-and-white videos of Corry Brokken and Sem Nijveen), the Treaty of Rome had stated that members of the European Parliament should be directly elected to their seats by the voters of the EEC. However, this hadn't happened. Instead, the body still consisted of members appointed by their countries' individual parliaments. Finally, in a bizarre piece of Euro-politics, the Parliament threatened to take the Council of Ministers to the European Court of Justice to get the Council to allow it to have proper Europe-wide elections.

Turnout varied across Europe. In the world of Lugano 1956 it was high, as it was in Ireland. In the more sceptical Denmark it was below 50 per cent. Sulky Britain only managed 34 per cent. The result was a balanced house: the largest party was the Party of European Socialists (PES), but two conservative groupings came second and third, the European People's Party (EPP) and the more Eurosceptic European Democrats. The PES and the EPP are still the main players in the European Parliament today; the European Democrats fell apart in the late 1980s.

The new Parliament held its first session on 11 July. Maybe inspired by Margaret Thatcher's victory, it elected a woman president, French Holocaust survivor Simone Veil. Veil came from a small party, the Liberals. This is the European way: compromise, rather than simply putting the biggest beast in the biggest party in charge.

East of the Iron Curtain, people didn't bother with this messy democracy business – but at least they had Intervision. The 1979 contest took place from 22 to 25 August, and again came up with a winner who was both eminent and independently minded. Poland's Czeslaw Niemen had written protest songs in 1968. After the clampdown, he switched to progressive rock. The main track from his 1969 album *Enigmatic* was based on a nineteenth-century work by the bohemian Romantic poet Cyprian Norwid. Later he recorded with members of John McLaughlin's Mahavishnu Orchestra – as well as singing and composing, Niemen was a fine keyboard player. There is now a statue of him in the Polish city of Kielce. I can't think of any Eurovision winners from this era with similar credentials (Teach-in's plans to record with Karlheinz Stockhausen never came to anything). There was much less division between high and low culture in Eastern Europe. Even the bouncy Alla Pugacheva made a hit record out of Shakespeare's Sonnet 90.

The 1970s looked to be ending on a loud, proud note for the boss nation of Intervision. Oil-rich, admired in the third world while keeping its own empire quiet – what could go wrong for the Soviet Union?

On 27 December, Russian special forces stormed the Tajbeg Palace in Kabul and captured the Afghan president Hafizullah Amin, who had only recently ousted a pro-Soviet incumbent, Nur Muhammad Taraki. The aim of Operation Storm 333 was to remove Amin, put a new, pro-Soviet man in his place, then retreat. It would all be over by Karl Marx's birthday.

The intervention would turn into a dirty war that lasted nearly a decade: Russia's Vietnam. The Afghan campaign would sap the resources and morale of the invading nation. It would inject further poison into already deteriorating relationships between East and West, once again raising the threat of nuclear conflict in Europe. In the even longer run, it would both radicalize and arm men like Osama bin Laden: the horrific mid-2000s terror attacks in Madrid and London had their genesis on 27 December 1979.

The hopes of the Eurovision audience in the Binyanei Ha-ouma Convention Centre would be dashed by these events, too. Instead of drawing together slowly towards a modern, amicable solution, the Middle East would split apart again as old hatreds and fanaticisms, apparently extinguished in 1979, reignited.

The
1980s

1980

Date: 19 April
Venue: Congresgebouw, Den Haag, Netherlands
Debut: Morocco
Winner: Johnny Logan, Ireland
Winning Song: 'What's Another Year?'

The grim economic climate brought about by the second oil price shock of 1979 meant that no one really wanted to host Eurovision 1980. The Dutch ended up volunteering. They have been reliable, undemonstrative supporters of things European since the start, despite not getting any special goodies out of the EEC. One can argue that France got the power and the agricultural subsidies, Belgium and Luxembourg got the economic boost from the new institutions that were sited within their borders and Germany and Italy got forgiveness for the war, but it's harder to see what special benefits the Dutch got – apart, perhaps, from a nice warm feeling of *gezelligheid*.

The year's most interesting Eurovision songs came from peripheral nations. Turkey's entry began with tabla drums and Middle Eastern scales, and stayed that way. The singer, Adja Pekkan, talked of a difficult, love-hate relationship with her lover, 'Pet'r Oil'. The francophone nations, usually chief suppliers of intelligent lyrics, came up with nothing to match this. Morocco made its debut – Israel did not enter in 1980, as the date clashed with *Yom HaZikaron*, the nation's military Remembrance Day, so the North African nation felt able to participate. Samira Saïd sang a rather standard Eurovision entry, 'Love Card'. Neither Pekkan nor Saïd did very well in the contest, but both have gone on to be superstars in their own cultures.

After the poor performance of 'Love Card' (it came second last), Morocco withdrew from the contest and has never ventured into Eurovision since.

Norway, as often, provided the most unusual entry: 'Samiid Aednan' (Land Of The Sami), based on a Sami yoik chant. The Sami, sometimes referred to as the Lapps, are the semi-nomadic inhabitants of Norway's northern regions, and the song was linked to protests about plans to build a dam and flood part of these traditional lands. The protests had come to a head with a hunger strike by activists in front of the Norwegian parliament in autumn 1979.

Behind the protests was a deeper, older discontent. At the time, Oslo was still carrying out the sinister-sounding policy of 'Norwegianization', an attempt to assimilate the Sami into the national mainstream that had started early in the century. At the height of this policy, back in the 1930s, Sami had been unable to buy land, and even in 1970 children were not allowed to speak the language in schools (even at playtime). The new decade would see the policy abandoned, and in 1997 Norway's King Harald V would apologize to the Sami for its ever having been carried out.

And then there was Ireland: 1980 was another triumph for the periphery as Johnny Logan won with his ballad (ably assisted by fellow Celt, Scottish saxophonist Colin Tully). 'What's Another Year?' sold well around Europe.

The centre's contribution to the proceedings was mostly lightweight, except as a barometer of fashion and musical trends. The Netherlands' Maggie MacNeal introduced us to the decade's big hair and big make-up, and Belgium's Kraftwerk-inspired Telex put synthesizers centre stage: a new development for the contest. 'Synthpop' would become a major aspect of 1980s popular music, taking the focus away from the electric guitar for the first time since 1963.

An exception to the centre's poor showing was Germany. Katja Ebstein sang 'Theater', another camp classic from Ralf Siegel and

Eurovision!

Bernd Meinunger, whose second place inched Europe's economic leader one notch nearer the Eurovision winners' podium.

Siegel and Meinunger also wrote Luxembourg's 1980 entry, 'Papa Pingouin', which was a classic in a different, so-bad-it's-good Eurovision way. The song never recovered any dignity it might have had when a backing singer in a giant penguin outfit tripped over a stair eleven bars into it. So was 'Papa Pingouin' a dismal failure? It went on to sell a million copies in France. However, virtually none of the proceeds went to the two young singers, Sophie and Magaly Gilles. Life did not turn out well for the pretty, chirpy Parisienne sisters. Sophie contracted HIV in the late 1980s, and died in 1996, after which Magaly became a recluse.

AIDS, which would overshadow the new decade, was unheard-of in 1980. In 1981, the first abnormal cluster of otherwise healthy men contracting a rare form of pneumonia was noted by doctors in Los Angeles. The condition would acquire its name in 1982, and the virus responsible would be isolated by scientists at the Pasteur Institute in Paris in 1983. Public knowledge, however, would lag behind: Britain was the first European nation to prioritize AIDS awareness, with TV advertising, but this wasn't until 1986. France, Italy and Spain were slower to react – would Sophie Gilles have lived had they moved faster? Those countries still have higher levels of HIV in their populations than the UK. Being diagnosed as HIV positive would remain a virtual death sentence until 1997, when the 'triple cocktail' of drugs known as Highly Active Anti-Retroviral Therapy (HAART) began to prove successful in halting the development of 'full-blown' AIDS. That was a year too late for Sophie.

Third place in Eurovision 1980 went to the UK's Prima Donna (a group put together specially for the contest) with 'Love Enough For Two'. The country's new premier did not feel that way about Europe's budget, however. Britain's per capita GDP was lower than that of most other EEC members, but, because the budgetary rules were skewed by the CAP, it had to make the second highest contribution to the EEC pot. The battle over this would come to a climax in 1984, and rumble on for years afterwards.

East of the Iron Curtain, the fourth Intervision Song Contest took place in August 1980. It was won by Finland's Marion Rung, who had entered two weak songs for Eurovision in 1962 and 1973, but produced a much better one here, the ballad 'Hyvästi Yö' (Goodbye Night). Finland had a unique position in Cold War politics (mirrored, perhaps, by Yugoslavia). After a bitter war with Stalin, the Nordic nation had signed its own treaty with Russia in 1948. It did not accept post-war US Marshall Aid or join NATO; there were close economic ties between it and its imperialist neighbour. But it retained political and economic freedom, and acted as a bridge between East and West – it's no accident that the 1975 Accords had been signed in Helsinki. Until the collapse of Communism, Finland continued to have to look both ways politically, hence its participation in both song contests. (Talking of Yugoslavia, which had not entered Eurovision since 1976, 4 May 1980 saw the death of its leader, Tito, a ruthless man but one around whom the country had unified. With his death, the slow countdown to the horrors of the mid-1990s began.)

Intervision 1980 was the last one. The reason could not have been more significant: the breakup of the Soviet empire started just down the road from Sopot, on 14 August, when workers at Gdansk's Lenin shipyard went on strike.

Unrest had been bubbling in Poland (and especially on its Baltic coast) since riots about food prices in 1970 and 1976. In 1979, the newly elected Polish pope had visited the country and given its people a new rallying point, a reminder that there were older, deeper ethical codes than those of Communism.

On 7 August 1980, Anna Walentynowicz, a former shipyard 'model worker' turned activist, was dismissed for belonging to a then illegal trades union, the WZZ. Her colleagues went on strike. This soon grew into a wider protest about many issues. On 31 August, the government agreed to implement a charter featuring twenty-one demands, including freedom of speech, an improved healthcare system and recognition for the union as an entity independent of the Communist Party. But it dragged its heels putting these into practice. Public unrest continued, including a brief but effective nationwide strike in March 1981, by which time the Solidarity union, which had been formed in the aftermath of the 1980 strike, had millions of members all over Poland. It was as a result of this unrest that Intervision 1981 was cancelled.

Later in the year, the country's new leader, General Wojciech Jaruzelski, declared martial law; his defenders argue this was in order to prevent a more draconian intervention from Moscow. Union leaders were sent to prison – but the nation's mood had changed. Solidarity's call had been heard in other Eastern European countries, too. The wind of change was blowing through the old Intervision empire.

1981

Date: 4 April
Venue: Simmonscourt Pavilion, Dublin, Ireland
Debut: Cyprus
Winner: Bucks Fizz, UK
Winning Song: 'Making Your Mind Up'

Johnny Logan's win in 1980 had been a triumph for Europe's periphery, and Ireland's staging of the next contest was another one. No expense was spared and the small island showed its growing potential to punch above its weight. The era of Ireland the Celtic Tiger was still a decade away, but the presentation of Eurovision 1981, especially the lighting, foreshadowed that era – as did the confident Celtic rock of the interval act, Planxty, which also looked forward to the Eurovision of the 1990s.

Of course, there was plenty of Euro-comedy, too. An Austrian lady singing in an American football helmet. Reggae (of a sort) from Finland. Luxembourg singing about how wonderful it is to be French. Robotic dancers from Portugal. A classic voting moment. 'Good evening, Yugoslavia.' Silence. 'Good evening, Yugoslavia.' More silence. Finally an answer, so Doireann Ni Bhriain asks for their vote. 'I don't have it,' comes the reply.

The contest belonged to Europe's big players. The UK's winning entry was bouncy and optimistic. Its title could be seen as a harbinger of the new decade, where consumers would make their own minds up about what they wanted to buy. The skirt-removing trick halfway through was playful rather than intensely erotic (intensity was so seventies . . .)

Germany came second again, courtesy once more of Siegel and Meinunger, whose 'Johnny Blue' told the story of a young blind man overcoming adversity to become a successful musician. The contest seemed to be taunting these clever songwriters – will you ever actually win?

France's entry took a less upbeat view of things. 'Humanahum', which came third, looked back at the world from 3000 AD. Didn't there used to be flowers, love (and so on) in the old days? Yes, but that was before The War. The comment, courtesy of Tahitian singer Jean Gabilou and the songwriting duo behind Marie Myriam's 1977 winner, José Graciano and Jean-Paul Cara,* was timely in a different way to 'Making Your Mind Up'. There was a new, hawkish president in the White House and nuclear weapons were building up on both sides of the Iron Curtain.

The Irish trio Sheeba came fifth, bemoaning how people rely on horoscopes. Work to create your own life outcomes, they said instead – sentiments in tune with the new decade, both in their stress on self-reliance and their rejection of pseudo-science. Back in 1963, with the white heat of technology intending to burn away the old Europe and its antiquated, unscientific ways, horoscopes had looked doomed. But the late sixties changed all that. Horoscopes remained a part of 1970s popular culture, which was unworldly and technophobic – as the writers of 'Ding Dinge Dong' had understood. But now it was the 1980s, and Europe seemed eager to get more real and to embrace technology again.

There was, at last, an exciting new technology to embrace. Large corporations had been using mainframe computers for a while to perform traditional clerical and complex computational functions. 1981 saw the US launch of the IBM PC, the first widely available 'computer on a desk'. Software for these machines would soon follow, which would help small businesses and private users with databases, accounts and word processing.

* Cara also wrote the lyrics to 'Un, Deux, Trois' (second in 1976). 'Humanahum' gave him his own Eurovision one, two, three .

Eurovision!

More exciting still, microprocessors – effectively, tiny computerized control systems – were beginning to create a whole new world of consumer gadgets. The classic Sony Walkman WM2 appeared in 1981, as did the world's first fully automatic network for portable phones, in Scandinavia. The phones were 'portable' only by early 1980s standards: the set was the size of a small suitcase – but mobile telephony had arrived.

The microwave oven was another product of the era. Some commentators argue that this made European men do more cooking, and thus played a role in the 'feminization' of Europe. It certainly saved time for European women, who, despite feminization, were still responsible for most domestic work. Its effect on the European diet was less beneficial.

Outside the kitchen, young Europeans could play Space Invaders on the new Atari 2600 console, though this was best not done on early-eighties polyester shag-pile carpets: static electricity caused the console to malfunction.

A new economic era was dawning; at its heart, the remorseless binary logic of the silicon chip.

Politically, in the new decade, there seemed to be a move to the right. But this trend was not Europe-wide. Greece's first Socialist government for nearly half a century, under the charismatic Andreas Papandreou, was elected in 1981. A month after Eurovision 1981, France voted François Mitterrand into presidential office. Mitterrand's campaign had been based on the Cartesian-sounding '110 Propositions for France'. These included newly unfashionable government spending to boost the economy, abolition of the death penalty, a wealth tax and a 35-hour working week, as well as odder notions such as control of the building of supermarkets. Europe did not feature greatly in the 110 Propositions, though no. 41 did call for the reform of the CAP, which was continuing to gobble the EEC's resources.

The new France would not be technophobic, however. Minitel, a unique proto-internet run by the French post office, made its national debut in 1981. The first TGV express ran on 27 September, halving the journey time from Paris to Lyon. Both were, of course, the creations of an earlier administration, but France's new rulers kept faith with them. In their first full year, *Trains à Grande Vitesse* carried six million passengers. A decade later the figure would be forty million.

But all was not joy in the once-again-technophile Europe. Two months after the TGV began barrelling its way down to Lyon, the German magazine *Der Spiegel* started running articles about *Waldsterben*. The disease of trees in the Black Forest had continued to spread. Half the forest was now in immediate danger, the articles claimed. The culprit was 'acid rain', sulphur dioxide spewed out by power plants, refineries and ironworks.

Waldsterben stayed in German headlines from then on. It cut deep into Germany's identity, which was (and still is) intricately bound up with the nation's great forests; their witchy mystery, their protection (the Germanic tribes had driven out the Romans with forest ambushes) and their opportunities for healthy hiking and fresh air.

Acid rain also ignored national boundaries. Germany could go as green as it liked, but this stuff would still come floating over from other countries. It made another powerful argument for the centralization of political power in Europe.

Of course, Katja Ebstein and Fred Jay had warned us, ten years before.

1982

Date: 24 April
Venue: Conference Centre, Harrogate, UK
Debuts: None (none till 1986)
Winner: Nicole, Germany
Winning Song: 'Ein Bisschen Frieden' (A Little Peace)

1982 was another year when Eurovision showed its ability to capture a moment in history via its winner. The gentle young woman asking for a little peace probably did not impress the feisty female activists then encamped around US missile bases at Britain's Greenham Common, but for many Western Europeans, Nicole's 'Ein Bisschen Frieden' hit the bullseye. I don't want these weapons or this warmongering. I want to live my life in peace. I'm scared. What the hell do I do?

By an elegant irony, last place – and not just any old last place, but the full *nul points* – also went to a song protesting the Cold War, Finland's Kojo with 'Nuku Pommiin' (Sleep Till The Bomb). The song featured a rock guitar solo, the first, I think, in the contest. Rock from Finland in Eurovision? No, it'll never work.

Russia and the United States were both filling their halves of Europe with missiles; Russia with newly built ones, the USA bringing in existing ones from elsewhere. A new weapon was in production, too: the neutron bomb, which would kill people with radiation but do less damage to infrastructure. The Western left portrayed this as a product of capitalism, but these monstrous things were being just as eagerly constructed by the followers of Marx and Lenin. Europe, as usual, was piggy in the middle.

A glimmer of hope came on 10 November, with the death of Russia's aged premier, Leonid Brezhnev. His younger replacement,

Yuri Andropov, made peaceful approaches to the West. These were rejected by the newly elected US president Ronald Reagan. Reagan's supporters argued that words were cheap. They argued that Russia was producing ever more nuclear warheads; the destructive capacity of its arsenal had risen from just over 5,000 to 7,000 megatons between 1980 and 1982 (America's level remained constant over this time, at around 4,000 megatons). Still, would a more Nicole-influenced response to the new leader have changed this?

Andropov (and Europe) didn't get one, anyway. In March 1983 Reagan would make his famous speech denouncing Russia's 'evil empire' and would announce his 'Star Wars' missile shield – over America: Europe would have to look after itself.

A war featuring a European nation was actually happening when Eurovision 1982 took place. On 19 March, a group of scrap metal merchants arrived on the remote island of South Georgia in the South Atlantic. Not startling news, perhaps – but the land belonged to Britain, and the new arrivals hoisted an Argentinian flag. A week later, Argentinian soldiers joined them. The Falkland Islands were invaded on 2 April, and the small British garrison had no option but to surrender. A fleet of 127 vessels was then dispatched from Britain. As Nicole sang for a little peace, this mighty armada was making its way into the South Atlantic.

The rest of Europe was not impressed by Britain's response, especially Latin Europe. Spain's Eurovision entry featured the Argentine national dance, a tango. The UK's 'One Step Further', by another made-for-Eurovision duo, Bardo, fared poorly, despite being a perfectly good song. Going to war does not win votes in Eurovision.

The conflict that followed was hard-fought but brief. Around 1,000 combatants died (unlike almost all other wars, there were few civilian casualties), including 323 people on the *General Belgrano*, an Argentine cruiser. The sinking of that vessel was controversial – but such, surely, is war: messy, vicious and tragic.

Eurovision!

Another 1982 contestant also went to war shortly after the contest. Israel invaded Lebanon on 6 June. This was a much bloodier business than the Falklands, with massacres (largely by Lebanese 'Christian' forces) at two refugee camps its nadir. Israel initially hoped that the war would drive terrorist organizations out of its northern neighbour and bring 'forty years of peace'. The effect was the opposite. The optimism of Eurovision 1979 at the Binyanei Ha-ouma Convention Centre was now a very distant memory.

Denmark's 1982 Eurovision entry was 'Video Video', which took us away from war and peace, and instead sung about a young man hooked on yet another new 1980s consumer goodie. Basic video cassette recorders (VCRs) could now be bought for the equivalent of about 100 euros. These machines subtly changed European life: gone would be the days when streets fell silent whenever popular programmes like Eurovision were aired, and with that would disappear the workplace ritual of discussing them next Monday morning. Instead, we could watch whenever we liked (provided the VCR hadn't chewed up the tape). It was a tiny decoupling from a shared social ritual towards more convenient but more private experiences.

One of the most unusual things about Eurovision 1982 was the absence of a previous stalwart, France. The new regime wanted to show its class, culturally as well as ideologically. 'This so-called pop music competition,' said Jack Lang, Mitterrand's minister for culture, 'is a monument to drivel.'

But it was Germany's contest, anyway. As well as being an excellent and timely song, 'Ein Bisschen Frieden' was beautifully presented. Alongside his gift for melody and counter-melody, Ralf Siegel was a master stager of performances, while (usually) avoiding extravagant dance routines or irrelevant props. Many other 1982 entries tried to reprise Bucks Fizz and featured gyrating couples in primary-coloured outfits made from fabrics that one shouldn't put too close to a radiator. Nicole wore a simple black and white dress, strummed a white twelve-string guitar, looked into the camera and sang with conviction. Half the juries – including Israel, the first time they had done this for a German entry – gave her *douze points*.

On 1 October, the winning nation had a new chancellor. Helmut Kohl was a portly, pragmatic Christian Democrat and a keen supporter of European integration. The big European national leaders of the decade, Thatcher, Mitterrand and Kohl, were now in place (Kohl would outlast the others, remaining in office until 1998). The fourth giant of 1980s European politics was currently Mitterrand's minister of finance – but more of Jacques Delors later.

1983

Date: 23 April
Venue: Rudi Sedlmayer Hall, Munich, Germany
Winner: Corinne Hermès, Luxembourg
Winning Song: 'Si La Vie Est Cadeau' (If Life Is A Gift . . .)

The 1983 contest was held in a hall named after the former president of the Bavarian Sports Association. There's something delightfully old-fashioned-German about that: this man was an Important Official. In 2017, the venue is sponsored and called the Audi Dome, which tells its own story, too.

The show was hosted by Marlene Charrell, who made every announcement in French, German and English. This made it a long evening, and showed the practical difficulty of a theoretically admirable policy of multilingualism. It was sixteen minutes into the broadcast before the first note of a competing song was heard.

The contest is not a classic, and so tends to be remembered for its worst aspects: the interminable announcements; the announcer joining in the interval entertainment – and two classic *nul points* entries.

The first of these was 'Opera' by Turkey's Çetin Alp and the Short Waves. It is often cited as the worst Eurovision entry ever – but maybe it was just twenty years ahead of its time. It was certainly bizarre: the piece segues from a tribute to Western European opera to a Dixieland jazz middle section (complete with jazzed-up Bizet), then back again to the tribute. The unfortunate Alp received a barrage of criticism on his return to Turkey. He had let the nation down in front of people it was eager to impress. He appears to have led a reclusive life afterwards.

If you want to be really clever about this, you can read 'Opera' as a comment about Kemal Ataturk (the nation's president from 1923 to 1938) and his forcing Turkey to modernize and become a European state. Part of this involved setting up a national opera, after which Ataturk commissioned three operas – about himself. Was Alp questioning the wisdom of this? Or was he celebrating it? Or did he just like opera and Dixieland?

1983's other great *nul pointer* came from Spain's Remedios Amaya. '¿Quién Maneja Mi Barca?' (Who's Sailing My Boat?) is most charitably seen as an attempt to merge flamenco, in which Amaya was a respected artist, with Eurovision. It didn't work, but unlike poor, disgraced Çetin Alp, she went back to her roots and continued to achieve success in her chosen genre.

'Hi' (Alive) from Israel celebrated Jewish traditions passed down across generations – in front of an audience in a country which thirty years before had tried to eradicate those traditions in the most vicious manner imaginable, and in a city where a decade ago terrorists fuelled by similar hatred had murdered eleven Israeli athletes.

The winning song was a ballad, probably not the best winner of its kind, but well sung. There is a line in it where the singer laments the child she was going to give her unfaithful lover, come the spring. I've always wondered if this was a reference to abortion; it would make the title particularly heartfelt.

It seems that numbers of abortions were rising in Western Europe during the latter decades of the twentieth century, though accurate figures are hard to come by. This can be used to point a moralizing finger at us, but rates were still lower in Europe than in the rest of the world. A study carried out in 1995 by the New York-based Guttmacher Institute and reprinted in Britain's ultra-respectable *Lancet* magazine showed that Western, Northern and (to a lesser extent) Southern Europe had lower levels of abortion than anywhere else. Eastern Europe, by contrast, had rates above the global average (and three times higher than those in the west of the continent).

After Monsieur Lang's comments about Eurovision, one might have expected a long absence on France's part, but 1983 saw the land of Marianne return to the drivel monument, with Guy Bonnet's rather old-fashioned 'Vivre' (To Live). The nation had to do similar *voltes-face* in political policy. President Mitterrand found his currency under attack from global speculators. In June 1982, the franc was downgraded 10 per cent against the deutschmark. In March 1983, after a defeat for his party in local elections, its value began to tumble again. Mitterrand was faced with a dilemma. He could leave the European Monetary System, the mechanism set up in 1979 to keep European currencies in step with one another, but this would mean admitting to being a second-rate European power. Or he could do a deal with the Germans, whereby they revalued the mark and France stayed in the EMS. Germany insisted on austerity measures as a precondition of the deal, and Mitterrand accepted. This was, arguably, the moment when European leadership began passing east across the Franco-German border. Turning sounds were heard from General de Gaulle's grave.

Not that there was much 'Europe' to lead at that time. In 1983, the EEC was still suffering from the sclerosis imposed by the Luxembourg Compromise back in 1966, with its insistence on unanimous votes on major decisions. CAP spending was spiralling out of control; Britain was clamouring for a rebate on its contribution; Spain and Portugal wanted to join the club but nobody could agree how or when. A meeting of the European Council in Athens in December 1983 found itself unable to agree even on the blandest communiqué to sum up its proceedings.

Meanwhile, the Cold War kept getting colder. On 31 August 1983, the Russians shot down a Korean airliner, KAL 007, that had strayed over the Kamchatka peninsula, killing all 269 passengers and crew. Three weeks later, World War Three nearly broke out.

On the evening of 25 September, Lt-Col Stanislav Petrov was manning the Soviet early warning system in its bunker south of Moscow, when a warning light went on. The US, apparently, had launched a missile. Then another. Then three more. The current Soviet plan at the time was to launch massive retaliation if attacked – but was this a real attack? Petrov had almost no time to decide, but had a gut feeling that the alarm was false: why would America launch just five missiles? He followed his intuition; the 'missiles' later disappeared from the screen. Europe woke up on the morning of 26 September with its population and cities intact, but it had been a close thing. The new K and K Calypso as *Totentanz*, the Dance of Death.

The incident was not revealed to the world till 1990, but Europe was angry about the missiles anyway. Across the continent, 22 October 1983 was a day of protest against their presence, with huge marches in Belgium, Britain, France, Italy, Spain and, especially, West Germany, where a million people are estimated to have taken to the streets.

As Eurovision said, *Ein bisschen Frieden, bitte.*

1984

Date: 5 May
Venue: Théâtre Municipal, Luxembourg
Winner: Herreys, Sweden
Winning Song: 'Diggi-loo, Diggi-ley'

Kooky presenter Désirée Nosbusch gave George Orwell a name-check in her intro to Eurovision 1984. The winning song would probably have brought a wry smile to the face of the great novelist, whose classic *1984* predicted, amongst other things, the existence of Prolesec, a department of the Ministry of Truth which churned out mindless entertainment for the masses, known as Prolefeed. Along with newspapers full of sport, crime and astrology, sexy films and sensational novels, Prolesec produced sentimental songs, with words composed on a machine called a versifier which combined random clichés. Both *diggi-loo* and *diggi-ley* would no doubt have qualified for feeding into this machine.

Orwell's dystopic vision also involved three massive power blocs, perpetually at war: Eurasia, Eastasia and Oceania. Orwell's Eurasia maps spookily onto the area participating in the 21st-century Eurovision Song Contest (Britain is the main exception, being part of Oceania along with the Americas and the old white Commonwealth). From Charlemagne's Holy Roman Empire to Big Brother's Eurasia?

Like 'Ding Dinge Dong', the earlier winner it is often compared to, 'Diggi-loo, Diggi-ley' opened the show. It set the tone: bright primary colours (red was a particular favourite for 1984), clean-cut performers, slick performance – the three Mormon brothers put on a great show. 'Diggi-loo, Diggi-ley' bubbled with mid-eighties optimism. The bad times are over; things are working well again; dream it and you can do it – as long as you have the right shoes.

The 1984 contest is best remembered for other things than the songs. The 'postcards' were quirky and imaginative. Désirée was a fun presenter, casually dressed in contrast to many of the performers, and genuinely European: she spoke four languages and solved the problem that had defeated Marlene Charrell by flowing effortlessly between them during the evening (ironically, she actually lived in the USA at the time, though she had been born and raised in Luxembourg). At the end of the show, she said 'see you next Saturday'. Many male viewers probably wished that were the case.

And then there was the booing . . . Eurovision audiences have sat politely through 'Boom Boom Boomerang' and 'Opera', but the Motown-influenced UK entry 'Love Games', composed by the UK's most prolific Eurovision writer, Paul Curtis, proved too much for a section of the crowd at the Théâtre Municipal. The main reason was the memory of the previous November, when English football hooligans had run riot in the Grand Duchy (not for the first time: back in 1977, England fans had damaged the Luxembourg national stadium). Maybe the booers were also protesting Margaret Thatcher's dogged insistence on her CAP rebate. Or perhaps they didn't like Motown. The boos certainly reveal a cultural clash: Luxembourg regularly wins polls for being the most European-minded nation in the EU, while Britain usually comes last.

The battle of Britain's EEC budget contribution was finally settled in 1984. François Mitterrand had taken over the six-monthly Presidency of the European Council at the beginning of the year, and decided to get political Europe moving again. Sorting out the rebate was part of that. The process of admitting Spain and Portugal to the club was put in motion. Some attempt was made to tackle the CAP and its mountains and lakes. CAP spending actually continued to grow in the late 1980s, but this was because of the new members. Less cash ended up in France, which made Mitterrand unpopular back home. He nevertheless stuck to his guns on these essential reforms.

Eurovision!

The Cold War remained intense during 1984 – but on 10 December, a senior Soviet politician called Mikhail Gorbachev gave a speech to a Communist Party conference on ideology, calling for *glasnost* (openness) and *perestroika* (economic reform). Shortly after that, he visited Britain, and in March 1985, he was elected General Secretary of the Party.

1985

Date: 4 May
Venue: Scandinavium, Gothenburg, Sweden
Winner: Bobbysocks, Norway
Winning Song: 'La Det Swinge' (Let It Swing)

The peripheral, Euro-cautious Nordics always go to town on Eurovision. The 1985 contest was the most spectacular to date. Eight thousand people attended: the capacity of the previous year's venue had been less than 1,000. Another contrast with 1984 was the announcements. 1966 contestant Lill Lindfors – dressed and made up to the nines* – introduced most of the songs in English (beneath a large sign reading 'Eurovision Song Contest'). The songs (by and large) had a modern, professional edge to them. Even the one that came last, 'Laat Me Nu Gaan' (Let Me Go Now) by Belgium's Linda Lepomme, was pleasant and well sung, just a bit dull. When the results were announced, there were no French-language entries in the top five (or, actually, the top nine). These differences all go to make 1985 feel like the first modern event.

This new-look Eurovision was a northern affair. Britain's Vikki came fourth, telling us what 'Love Is'. She is now better known as New Age artiste and composer Aeone – a journey many people were to make once the material-girl 1980s gave way to the 1990s. Above her came Sweden's Kikki Danielsson with 'Bra Vibrationer' (the title actually just means Good Vibrations) and Germany's Wind, with 'Für Alle' (For

---

* For most of the contest, anyway. After the songs, she came onto the stage and seemed to catch her dress on an impediment, ripping the bottom half clean away. After a moment of apparent embarrassment, she calmly rolled down what was left of her outfit to form an elegant new one, adding, 'I just wanted to wake you all up a bit.'

Everyone), one of those let's-all-be-nice-to-each-other Eurovision specials. Bouncing up to the winner's podium were Norway's female duo Bobbysocks, with Rolf Løvland's Abba-ish jive. The Land of the Midnight Sun and of Jahn Teigen's Braces had finally won!

By contrast, political Europe remained a project of the centre. It was in 1985 that Jacques Delors, a former banker, trades unionist, state planner and MEP, became president of the European Commission. Like his countryman's presidency of the European Council the previous year, this gave 'Europe' a new energy. Delors was to stay in the job for ten years, during which political Europe became the EU. He oversaw the implementation of the Single Market and of EU citizenship. He worked to introduce social legislation. He expanded Europe's two 'Structural Funds' (the European Social Fund, set up back in 1958, which largely funds training, and the European Regional Development Fund, founded in 1974, which helps finance job creation). Most significant of all, he drove the move to the creation of a common currency.

On 14 June, five of the seven original contestants from Lugano (Italy and Switzerland were the non-participants) signed an agreement at Schengen in Luxembourg to remove all shared borders. Like the EEC/EU, this zone would later be expanded. The agreement would become part of EU law in 1999.

All EEC nations were involved in drafting the Single European Act (SEA), the text of which was finalized at a European Council meeting in December 1985. This was essentially about creating a true Common Market in Europe, the 'Single Market', with free movement of goods, services, capital and labour. The Act was extremely thorough, specifying 282 measures needed to bring this about. The aim was to have the measures in place by 31 December 1992, and a special '1992 Programme' was launched to push them along the obstacle course of national and Europe-level legislative change they would face. The decision-making apparatus of EEC-level government was also speeded up, with more majority voting and less Gaullist insistence on unanimity.

Eurovision!

Britain, usually lacking in Euro-enthusiasm, was an eager participant in the creation of the Single Market. Margaret Thatcher was keen to increase trade, and the man who did most to both write and implement the SEA was Arthur Cockfield, a British commissioner. There is a fascinating puzzle here. Arguably (apart from the creation of the euro) nothing has done more to centralize EEC/EU power than this act. Its rules – essential for the functioning of an effective market – give huge power to the European Court of Justice, which in turn has the power to overrule national governments. The arch-intergovernmentalist Mrs Thatcher, love her or loathe her, was highly intelligent. Did she really not foresee this?

1985 also saw political Europe formally adopt its flag, the twelve gold stars on a blue background (the flag had been used by the Council of Europe since the 1950s), and its anthem, Beethoven's setting of Schiller's *Ode to Joy*. Many Eurovision fans still think Charpentier's *Te Deum* would be a better one.

The rest of the decade can be seen as a high point of European federalist idealism, on a par with those late forties/early fifties days of Jean Monnet and Robert Schuman. Delors worked tirelessly to turn the long-dreamt-of European currency into a reality. A committee would be set up in 1988 under his leadership, to work out how this should best come about. In 1989 it would report, suggesting three stages to monetary union. At the end, there would be a common currency issued by a European central bank, and rules on national government borrowing to ensure no one nation could devalue the currency by mismanaging its finances.

Part of the motivation behind the monetary union project was a desire to get away from the inconvenience of national exchange rates, which made both commercial and 'Eurocratic' planning difficult (and sometimes embarrassed good, loyal European nations whose economies weren't as robust as that of Germany). But the quiet driver of it all was the conviction that monetary union would lead to political union. Once nations share a currency, how much control can their governments have over interest rates, levels of borrowing or even tax regimes? Monetary union was never just about economics.

In November, the new K and K, Mikhail Gorbachev and Ronald Reagan, met for the first time. There was a high level of suspicion on both sides, but the two leaders began to develop a personal understanding. Both agreed that 'a nuclear war cannot be won and must never be fought'. The missiles, however, remained on Europe's soil.

1986

Date: 3 May
Venue: Grieghalle, Bergen, Norway
Debut: Iceland
Winner: Sandra Kim, Belgium
Winning Song: 'J'Aime La Vie' (I Love Life)

Like Sweden, Norway welcomed Eurovision with great enthusiasm. The host city of Bergen was *en fête* for the entire preceding week. The Norwegian royal family attended the contest, which took place in a mythological 'ice palace' that glowed with the various pastel shades shone into it. And presenter Åse Kleveland sang her famous 'Soon we will know who'll be the best . . .' version of the Eurovision theme to kick off the show.

1986 saw another move towards the modern competition, with the orchestra playing a much smaller part in the proceedings than before. Some acts dispensed with it altogether, replacing it with lead and bass guitars, keyboards (including a transparent grand piano), saxophones and white hexagonal syn-drums – 1986 was the year of the syn-drum.

It was also the year of the francophone fight-back, the three top songs being sung in French. Not France's however, for whom Cocktail Chic sang of being modern *Européennes*, moving between Paris and London and enjoying 'Musique USA'. *Non!* said the judges, and put them seventeenth.

The north made its presence felt visually, without greatly impressing the judges musically. Sweden's Lasse Holm and Monica Tornell sang in black, possibly out of respect for Olof Palme, who had been assassinated on 28 February.

The identity of Palme's killer remains a mystery. A loner convicted of the crime in 1988 was freed on appeal. Conspiracy theories abound. The South African government is in the frame, due to Palme's support for the African National Congress. Other suspects include Kurdish separatists, the Yugoslav Secret Service and Chilean fascists. The most bitterly ironic theory is the one that suggests his killing was a mistake and that the highly principled Palme was mistaken for a local drug dealer. As with JFK, we will probably never know the truth.

Norway's Ketil Stokkan sang about his failures as a 'Romeo' with two dancers behind him from the Great Garlic Girls, a drag act founded, initially as a joke, by three members of Norway's gay community in 1981. This was the first drag act in the contest (unless you count Charlie Rivel, the bizarre clown/pantomime-dame interval entertainment from 1973). Iceland made its debut, the first new nation since 1981, with a song about *Gledibankinn* or 'The Bank of Happiness'. Don't take out too much in one withdrawal, it recommended.

Such financial prudence was not on the menu in Britain, where October 1986 saw radical changes in the City of London, the most powerful financial centre in Europe. In what was called the 'Big Bang', fixed commissions were abolished, the old stock exchange floor was replaced by electronic trading, and regulations were relaxed. This set in motion a process whereby the world's major financial centres began to compete with one another to attract global capital by deregulating – which would have disastrous effects twenty-two years on. But in 1986, it just gave us the 'yuppie', the decade's model aggressive, acquisitive young professional. In many ways he or she was the polar opposite of the *soixante-huitard*, but both archetypes shared youth, arrogance and ideological certainty.

Yuppies weren't just to be found in London, but in Frankfurt, Paris, Milan . . . Their neo-liberal ideology was fast becoming domi-nant in Western Europe. Yuppies also believed in globalism, trading capital from around the world. The EEC, which looked a behemoth to old-fashioned nationalists, seemed too small to the globally minded City young.

This change is often represented as a move to the right, but it was to a new liberal, anarcho-capitalist, global-minded right, not the old authoritarian/nationalist one. Yuppies believed strongly in individual freedom of choice.

The old right had not gone away, however. In France's 1986 elections, Jean-Marie le Pen's right-wing Front National won thirty-five seats in the National Assembly. Austria was about to elect a man with a questionable Nazi past as its president. That country's Eurovision entrant, Timna Brauer, who was Jewish, was pressurized to pull out of the contest in protest, though she participated in the end – and came eighteenth out of twenty.

In contrast, Germany's 1986 Eurovision entry was – as its entries often are – about building bridges between peoples and nations. Especially, of course, in its own split country: 'Uber Die Brücke Gehen' (Go Over The Bridge) also recommends the listener to open his or her mind by looking behind a wall. The wall that Ingrid Peters had in mind showed little sign of weakening, though the two sides that eyeballed one another across it seemed ever less likely to obliterate each other. An explosion at the nuclear reactor at Chernobyl sapped the Soviet Union's already fading confidence even further. At a second summit, in the capital of Eurovision debutant Iceland, Messrs Reagan and Gorbachev found more personal chemistry. The idea that Germany might soon unite seemed a dream, however. Fine for a Eurovision song, but hardly realistic . . .

The contest was rounded off by 'Não Sejas Mau Para Mim' (Don't Be Mean To Me), a pleasant, contemporary song from Portugal's Dora, in a ra-ra skirt and Doc Martens boots. Her home nation was now a member of the EEC, having joined on 1 January. So had Spain, whose entry, 'Valentino', shared with 'Romeo' and Switzerland's 'Pas Pour Moi' (Not For Me) the topic of men's attempts to seduce women and their lack of success. Eighties women had become more tough-minded than the sad-eyed girls of the 1970s. The Swiss entry came second, beaten by Belgium's teenage Sandra Kim, who purported to be fifteen but later turned out to be thirteen. Switzerland tried to have Kim retrospectively thrown out, like an Olympic gold medallist found guilty of taking drugs, but this came to nothing. Probably for the best: Kim's song, poppy, high-tech and bubbling with 'Diggi-loo Diggi-ley' optimism, suited the era better. Switzerland and its song's composer, Atilla Şereftuğ, would have their moment later.

As she introduced the voting, Åse Kleveland said she wished we could all participate in it, but at the moment this was not technologically feasible. However, technology was now firmly in the driving seat of the new economic boom, filling people's homes with ever more gadgets and yuppies' wallets with ever more cash. Would it really enable us all to vote in Eurovision one day?

1987

Date: 9 May
Venue: Palais des Expositions, Brussels, Belgium
Debuts: None (no more till 1993)
Winner: Johnny Logan, Ireland
Winning Song: 'Hold Me Now'

The contest took another leap forward in 1987, thanks to the magnificent laser show. A giant globe shimmered behind the performers; beams of multicoloured light cut through smoky air, creating different patterns for each singer (the home representative, Liliane St Pierre, had a particularly spectacular backdrop). Look back to only a few years before, let's say 1983, and consider the huge change in the look of the show.

Despite this, 1987 is probably best remembered for Johnny Logan's victory, which made him the only person to win the contest twice – a record that still holds. He has also written two winners, including this one. 'Hold Me Now' remains popular with fans: in the 2005 poll of all-time contest favourites, it came third, behind 'Waterloo' and 'Volare'. It says something about the wonderful oddness of Eurovision that Logan's unparalleled achievement didn't really lead to success anywhere else. He continues to sing professionally, however, and has a couple of gold discs to put on his wall thanks to his wins. He is often referred to as 'Mr Eurovision'.

Elsewhere in the contest, Cyprus produced one of its better entries: 'Aspro Marvo' (Black And White), in which Alexia Vassiliou finds solace after a failed relationship by playing the piano. Belgian punk Plastic Bertrand reinvented himself as a Luxembourgeois Eurovision contestant, and got four points. *Nul points* went to Turkey, though with a much less bizarre offering than 'Opera'. This was not a good omen for that nation's application to join the EEC, which had finally been filed a week beforehand. Brussels then took two years to say '*Non*', or at least 'not yet'. By contrast, in July, former Eurovision contestant Morocco applied to join the Community but was quickly turned down on the grounds that it was not a European state.

The year saw a crisis in funding for the new, expanding political Europe – though you wouldn't have guessed this from the Eurovision interval act, which featured flautist Marc Grauwels riffing on the new European anthem, *Ode to Joy*, as gold stars (from the new European flag) whirled through the skies above delighted observers. The Brussels budget had doubled since 1980, and old ways of raising money – tariffs on imports, plus a proportion of each nation's VAT – were no longer up to the job. A new system would be introduced the following year whereby nations contributed sums commensurate with their GDP. The richest nation, Germany, was happy to sign up to this because of its enthusiasm for the European project. (Germany remains the biggest overall contributor to the EU, though if you look at contribution per member of the population, it is Europhile Luxembourgers and loyal Dutch who fork out most.)

Commercially, the eighties boom continued. On 19 October, a stock market crash around Europe (and the rest of the world) was spectacular at the time, but short-lived. A few traders tore out a few fistfuls of expensively coiffured hair on the day itself, but capital markets soon regained lost ground and continued their relentless rise.

Behind the dominant materialism of the era, there lurked a more caring eighties: no decade is totally one-sided. The cause of AIDS awareness was greatly boosted by Princess Diana, who in 1987 shook hands with victims at London's Middlesex Hospital. Previously many, maybe even most, people had thought that the disease could be transmitted by such contact. 1987 also saw Domenico Modugno, of 'Volare' fame, elected to the Italian parliament for the liberal/left

Eurovision!

Radical Party, where he became a fierce campaigner for disability rights, both physical and mental. He became particularly famous for his exposé of conditions in the psychiatric hospital at Agrigento in Sicily, and later, despite having suffered a stroke, performed a concert to raise money for former inmates.

1988

Date: 30 April
Venue: Simmonscourt Pavilion, Dublin, Ireland
Winner: Céline Dion, Switzerland
Winning Song: 'Ne Partez Pas Sans Moi' (Don't Leave Without Me)

The updating of Eurovision's look was effectively completed here, with the old-fashioned scoreboard getting a makeover: the new, computerized one flashed up onto a giant 'video wall' at the flick of a finger from co-presenter Pat Kenny. The set, designed by Paula Farrell and Michael Grogan, was as spectacular. Over the next few years, Irish broadcaster RTÉ would create a series of stunning sets, courtesy of Farrell (1988, 1994, 1997) and Alan Farquharson (1993, 1995). If Roland de Groot represented the second generation of Eurovision staging, Farrell and Farquharson are the stars of the third, the stage no longer so much a 'set' as a three-dimensional world of its own, a fantasy kingdom of light and colour.

This was the year of Céline Dion. She went on to sell 220 million records worldwide, but she only won Eurovision by one point, after losing an early lead in the voting to UK singer Scott Fitzgerald then staging a late comeback. Turkey also won in 1988: not its own rather lame 'Sufi', but via the composer of the winning song, Atilla Şereftuğ. A perfect counterexample to the argument that Turkey is incapable of being European, Şereftuğ was trained in western classical music. He later got into jazz, especially the piano of George Shearing, and then – back in the late 1960s – rock. He moved to Switzerland in 1975. After his 1988 win, he worked in both Europe and his original homeland.

It is sometimes said that Eurovision did little to boost Dion's career. But she had just turned twenty when she won the contest.

Her win enabled her manager to renegotiate the budget for her first anglophone album, *Unison*, quadrupling the record company's investment in her. That album went platinum in Canada and the USA, and she hasn't looked back since. *Merci, Eurovision.*

There were some other pleasant songs on offer (as well as a few clunkers: Eurovision wouldn't be Eurovision without these). Ralf Siegel and Bernd Meinunger's 'Lied Für Einen Freund' (Song For A Friend) was, perhaps, now sounding a little old-fashioned, but, as always with these writers, professional. Norway's Karoline Krüger sang 'For Vår Jord' (For Our Earth), about a wild female spirit protecting the world, a theme that looked forward to the 'New Age' that was on its way. Austria's Wilfried Schütz was unlucky to pick up *nul points* – in my view, anyway, though a poll carried out in 2003 asked which *nul points* song least deserved the fate, and put Schütz last, thus effectively voting 'Lisa, Mona Lisa' the worst Eurovision final entry ever.

For the history-lover, the most intriguing thing about Eurovision 1988 was the interval act. The Irish group Hothouse Flowers were sent on a trip around Europe, to show (as the previous year's had done) the unity of the continent. But the video actually showed the unity of *half* the continent: it did not occur to anyone to send them across the Iron Curtain. It would probably have been difficult to do this, though the contest was broadcast to the Soviet Union and its empire – but it's significant that in 1988 people said 'Europe' and thought of Western Europe. A whole Europe, united, with no barbed wire or watchtowers? Dream on . . .

One person who did dream on was Margaret Thatcher. In September 1988 she gave a speech to the College of Europe in Bruges, an elite postgraduate academy many of whose students go on to become senior Brussels officials. The speech is often cited as a piece of venomous Euroscepticism – by people who haven't read the text. Sadly, it was spun in this way to suit the prejudices of the

Eurovision!

UK media by her press secretary, Bernard Ingham, and some people in Brussels chose to pick up on the spin rather than the substance.

The speech is, of course, anti-federalist and anti-Socialist. It was at least partially given as a response to a speech by Jacques Delors, where he told British trades unionists that he envisaged Europe-wide social legislation as well as a Single Market. But it is not anti-European: it is intergovernmentalist, promoting a Gaullist *Europe des patries*. To say, as Mrs Thatcher does, that 'We shall always look on Warsaw, Prague and Budapest as great European cities' was radical and prescient at the time, and remains a statement more of European idealism than of nationalistic scepticism.

The Iron Lady later became much more critical of the European project. Like many leaders, she lingered in power too long and rather lost the plot at the end of her time (she was the first of the 1980s 'big three' to leave office, in November 1990). But it is odd that her speech is now so often misunderstood. Committed enthusiasts for a United States of Europe will not like it, of course. Maybe it blows the British trumpet louder than some might find tasteful. But it expresses a clear, positive vision of a view of Europe, both in what 'Europe' means and how its transnational institutions should work. Much of that vision subsequently became reality.

The dream of belonging to a truly continent-wide Europe was certainly not dismissed behind the Iron Curtain. Instead, it began to express itself in startling new ways. One of them was musical. Estonia – still a part of the Soviet Union – had a long history of song festivals, where thousands of people would gather to sing traditional tunes. There was even a purpose-built venue for these near the capital, Tallinn. Stalin had tried to change such events into Soviet propaganda-fests, but his censors oddly missed a song called 'Mu Ismaa On Minu Arm' (Land Of My Fathers, Land That I Love), which everyone sang with much more gusto than the *Internationale*. (It was finally banned in 1969 – but people sang it at that year's festival anyway, despite attempts by a Russian military band to drown it out.)

Singing became a unique expression of optimism and pride in this small, occupied nation. Two weeks after Eurovision 1988, a pop festival was held at its second city, Tartu, and the crowds began to sing patriotic songs by young composer Alo Mattiisen. The moment is regarded as the start of Estonia's 'singing revolution'. In June, people started gathering at the Tallinn venue during the long summer evenings to sing these and other, more traditional songs. Estonian flags were unfurled and flown. In September, a staggering 300,000 people, about a third of the population, attended a Festival of Estonian Song, where they sang again – and heard the head of the Estonian Heritage Preservation Society, Trivimi Velliste, call for national independence. Song as visionary politics: Marcel Bezençon (who had died in 1981) would have loved it.

On 7 December, Mikhail Gorbachev gave a speech to the UN General Assembly where he announced radical cutbacks in his armed forces. Did this mean a green light to Eastern Europe to break free? The stage was set for a remarkable year.

1989

Date: 6 May
Venue: Palais de Beaulieu, Lausanne, Switzerland
Winner: Riva, Yugoslavia
Winning Song: 'Rock Me'

Eurovision did its best to provide a barometer for its times in this game-changing year. The winning song was unmemorable, probably one of the weakest winners ever – but it came from the one Iron Curtain nation allowed to compete in the contest. Giving victory to Riva was a signal from Western Europe to the countries behind that once-impenetrable wall. Join us!

In another way, the contest was mute on the great events of the year, as those events took place in nations still unable to compete in it. Yet one can't tell the story of modern Europe without telling the 1989 stories of East Germany, Poland, Hungary, Bulgaria, Czechoslovakia and Romania – none of whom took part in Eurovision 1989 – so for this chapter, I'm going to leap across to the former territory of Intervision.

By 6 May 1989 the Iron Curtain already had a small crack in it. A few days before the contest, the Hungarian government had begun dismantling the fortifications along its border with Austria. This was partly an economic decision: the wall needed upgrading, and Hungary didn't have the money. But it wasn't just cash: an Interior Ministry spokesman commented, 'Not only do we need the world, but the world needs us. An era will be closed with the removal of this fence, and we hope that such systems will never be needed again.' At the same time, Hungary assured its eastern bloc critics that the border would still be policed.

Next month, (largely) free elections were held in Poland. Solidarity won 99 of the 100 seats in the nation's Senate, and all the 35 seats on offer in the second house, the *Sejm*, where a majority was still reserved for the Communist Party.

As summer drew on, many East Germans went to Hungary for their holidays. This was nothing new – scenic Lake Balaton had become a popular destination – but in 1989, when their tourist visas expired, thousands stayed on in a refugee tent city, convinced that a chance to escape west would soon present itself. It did. On 19 August, a 'pan-European picnic' was held at Sopron, a Hungarian city right next to the border, to which all Europeans were invited. (Central to organizing the picnic was the old Pan-European Union founded back in 1923.) For three hours, the nearby crossing-point was opened. Around six hundred East Germans attended the event, then walked or drove to freedom (many more had stayed in their tent city, believing the picnic was too good to be true and was actually a Stasi trap). The border was then closed again. The Hungarians were still nervous about what Moscow would do. Two days later, a young East German architect, Kurt-Werner Schulz, was shot trying to smuggle his family to the West. The Hungarian prime minister, Miklós Németh, decided this was intolerable: the border had to be opened. He consulted with Helmut Kohl (not Mitterrand or Thatcher), who in turn contacted Gorbachev, who hinted that no action would be taken. The gates opened on 10 September.

Protests were spreading to East Germany itself. Pastor Christian Führer had been conducting 'services for peace' at Leipzig's St Nicholas church since 1982. In September 1989, attendances began to skyrocket. The services would be followed by peaceful demonstrations. The Stasi tried to stop these with roadblocks and random arrests, but failed. Demonstrators began taking to the streets in other cities. Then on 2 October, East Germany sealed its borders. Next Monday, the 9th, the country's leader, Erich Honecker, ordered security forces to open fire on the demonstrators.

Eurovision!

This approach was not new. Back in June, China had come up with its own way of dealing with democracy protesters, killing around 2,000 people in Tiananmen Square. Was the German Democratic Republic about to have its own version?

Local Party leaders – unsung heroes of this story – refused to pass the orders on, and the demonstrations went ahead peacefully. Honecker was sacked and his place taken by Egon Krenz, a man a generation younger. Krenz tried to reform the existing system, but it was too late. A protest meeting on 4 November filled Berlin's vast Alexanderplatz with an estimated one million people. On the evening of the 9th, it was announced that visas would be issued to East Berliners wanting to visit the West. Crowds immediately gathered at the crossing-points. The press soon became so great that the guards let people through, to be welcomed by partying West Berliners. The wall had been breached.

The very next day saw the downfall of Bulgaria's leader of thirty-five years' standing, Todor Zhivkov. This was more due to internal Politburo politicking than 'people power', but a month later, that nation's Communist Party renounced its right to rule and announced elections for June 1990.

Czechoslovakia also had a hard-line leader, Miloš Jakeš. Would he resort to violence to preserve the old order? On 17 November, a peaceful protest meeting in Prague was broken up by baton-wielding police (reports that a young student had died turned out to be false). More and more people took to the streets. It is rumoured that Jakeš summoned special forces to Prague on 21 November to quell the unrest, but he did not order them into action.

Next day, a vast gathering of people filled Wenceslas Square, and within a week Jakeš had resigned, along with the rest of the politburo. By the end of the year, dissident playwright Vaclav Havel would be the nation's president.

Romania's dictator, Nicolae Ceaușescu, had no compunction about going down the Tiananmen route. Protests in the western city of Timişoara were met with a military crackdown. But even this old monster's days were numbered. On 21 December he addressed a rally in Bucharest. Cheering Party goons lined the front, but behind them people started booing and chanting 'Timişoara'. The army was ordered to shoot, but the minister of defence refused to pass on the order – and died in suspicious circumstances immediately afterwards. His death destroyed any loyalty the army might have had to Ceauşescu. Next day, the dictator tried to flee his huge white marble palace and was arrested and executed, along with his Lady Macbeth wife, Elena.

This leaves the winner of Eurovision 1989, Yugoslavia. Arguably it didn't need a revolution, peaceful or otherwise, to leave the Soviet bloc, as it had always been half-in, half-out. But it had protests, anyway, 'anti-bureaucratic' marches in Serb-dominated parts of the country. However, these were not spontaneous 'people power' but were orchestrated by Serb leader Slobodan Milošević, whose agenda was not liberation but Serbian nationalism. Their end result was not fewer pen-pushers but new leaders in three previously semi-autonomous provinces, Vojvodina, Macedonia and Kosovo, all of whom called for closer integration with Serbia.

Historians still argue about what caused the sudden collapse of Communism. I'd like to put forward a new thesis. It was the Eurovision Song Contest. Riva won, and six months later, down came the Wall.

Sadly, I'm not sure this would convince many people. Nevertheless it can be argued that Western popular music in general played a substantial part in the downfall. Many young Eastern Europeans – and young Russians – listened to it and wanted both the fun and, at a deeper level, the personal authenticity it talked of. Eurovision, especially in the 1970s when watching it was illegal in some Communist countries, did its bit in this subversive process. If it didn't bring the wall crashing down on its own, the contest certainly helped undermine it.

Eurovision!

The collapse of the Iron Curtain was a fitting end to a tumultuous decade for Europe. If the missiles were still on our shared soil, nobody now had any intention of using them. In the West, anyway, 1970s stagflation had turned to 1980s growth, fuelled by a new economic paradigm and based on a resource that seemed able to grow exponentially – throughout the decade computer chips just kept on getting smaller, cheaper and more powerful, following the 'law' formulated back in the 1960s by Gordon Moore, whereby affordable chips double in power every two years. To the east, nations were emerging from behind the Curtain, blinking in the light of democracy and freedom. The decade saw the end of 'Euro sclerosis' and the creation of real Europe-wide governmental institutions. It arguably saw the casting of the main roles in political Europe: Germany the leader, France the shrewd follower, Britain the bolshy outsider. (The next four biggest Eurovision economies are, in order, Italy, Spain, Turkey and the Netherlands. Italy is, perhaps, Europe's magician, perpetually appearing to be on the edge of chaos but actually doing rather well. In the 1980s Spain was still a 'dark horse', rediscovering itself after the Franco years. Turkey remained the outsider; the Netherlands the loyal European team player.)

The decade also saw business adopt a new, entrepreneurial attitude, replacing the old corporatism. It saw burgeoning opportunities for women. Right at its close, it saw legislative progress in gay rights – the first civil partnerships came into being in Denmark in 1989.

A darker side? Of course. Not everyone shared in the growth. Unemployment steadfastly refused to drop below 6 per cent. There was a prevailing tone of brashness, harshness and materialism. There was the spectre of AIDS and, among many people still, the prejudice that came with it.

In Eurovision, the eighties created a song contest that in most ways looks and sounds like it does today. The decade did the same for political and economic Europe, putting in place a template with which we are still living, working, and in some ways now struggling.

The
1990s

1990

Date: 5 May
Venue: Vartroslav Lisinski Hall, Zagreb, Yugoslavia
Winner: Toto Cutugno, Italy
Winning Song: 'Insieme: 1992' (Together: 1992)

Eurovision 1990 began with the now-mandatory travelogue, which stressed the cheerful diversity of the host nation. Later, co-presenter Helga Vlahović (already famous in Eurovision lore as the voice who had finally answered the phone to Doireann Ni Bhriain back in 1981) enthused about Yugoslavia being like an orchestra, where the strings, woodwind and percussion sections all sit next to each other and combine to create beautiful music.

Sadly, things weren't that harmonious in reality. The original, planned presenter had been Dubravka Marković, a Serb, but she had started to receive anonymous phone calls threatening to kill her if she hosted the show (the event was being broadcast from Zagreb, capital of Croatia). Vlahović replaced her. The Serb slated to direct the event was also suddenly replaced by a Croat. Yugoslavia's bubbly entrant for the contest, Tajci, was also from Croatia. If the show meant to represent the Yugoslav orchestra, it ended up showing just one section.

One might have expected the 1990 contest to celebrate the collapse of the Iron Curtain – but the Eurovision judges didn't feel that way. Norway's (perfectly good) 'Brandenburger Tor', about the once-blocked gateway in the centre of Berlin, which had been formally reopened on 22 December 1989, came equal last. Neither Germany nor Austria gave it any points at all. Austria's 'Keine Mauern Mehr' (No More Walls) ended up mid-table, with no votes from newly

Wall-free Germany. Germany's 'Frei Zu Leben' (Free To Live) suffered a similar mediocre fate.

Two songs, neither about the Wall, tied for second place. Guadeloupe-born Joëlle Ursull's 'White And Black Blues' marked a new direction for France, ditching the ballads and *chansons* and looking to its old empire and new immigrant populations for musical inspiration. The song sold well in its home market: French popular taste was opening up to new sounds like Ursull's Caribbean *zouk*, *raï* from North Africa and hip-hop (France's first rap star, MC Solaar, emerged at this time. His parents had come to France from Senegal when he was six months old).

Second equal was a much more forgettable Irish entry, 'Somewhere In Europe', one of those old-style Eurovision songs that just lists loads of internationally recognizable words, in this case, place-names. By contrast, Ireland itself was modernizing fast. In 1990 it elected its first female president, Mary Robinson, who had campaigned for the right of women to serve on Irish juries and been legal adviser to the Campaign for Homosexual Law Reform.

The year's winner, from Italy's Toto Cutugno, hymned the upcoming uniting of *Western* Europe via the Single Market in 1992 – an event that had been planned back in the mid-eighties and would have come about whether the Berlin Wall had been bulldozed flat or built twice as high with extra guns and watchtowers.

It's interesting to speculate why the judges felt as they did. Maybe it was just musical: the winning song was catchy, well sung and powerfully arranged. Its singer/composer was well-known around Europe. But maybe Europeans were also ambivalent about the end of the Wall. Germany seemed eager to reunite, but how overpowering would that new nation be?

I believe that 'Insieme', like Sandie Shaw back in 1967 or Nicole in 1982, won because it captured the mood of its era. The EU's Eurobarometer survey of European public opinion had showed increasingly positive attitudes toward Brussels over the 1980s. In 1990 that hit its peak, with 71 per cent of respondents saying that their country's membership of the EU was a good thing (and only 7 per cent saying it was bad).* The best Eurovision winners are 'postcards from a moment'. This is one of them.

Germany was uniting, whatever Eurovision judges said. Initially, there had been no rush for this to happen – a professor at the London School of Economics was confidently predicting reunification in fifty years' time. But the process developed a momentum of its own (helped by an extra push from the portly Herr Kohl). The old GDR economy, weak in the first place, went into freefall. Kohl concluded that action had to be taken fast, and visited Moscow to check that Gorbachev would accept reunification. He would, as would US president George H.W. Bush. Kohl then turned his attention to Europe, where misgivings were stronger. Margaret Thatcher, a child of the Second World War, and former resistance fighter François Mitterrand did not want unification. Italy's prime minister Giulio Andreotti said he loved Germany so much he preferred to see two of them. However, Mitterrand was bought off with a promise that Germany would support French plans for monetary union. Thatcher and Andreotti were ignored. Meanwhile, an election was held in the old GDR in 18 March 1990, and won by the 'Alliance for Germany', whose manifesto called for speedy reunification.

Two weeks after Eurovision 1990, East and West Germany signed a treaty on 'monetary, economic and social union', which came into effect on 1 July. East German citizens were allowed to exchange 4,000 old eastern marks for new western ones (a gift, essentially: the GDR marks were worth a fraction of that), and to swap further 'Ostmarks' at generous rates. Tons of old currency were carted away: the coins to be melted down, the notes stashed in a cave. (After an

---

* In 1980, the response had been 50 per cent good, 17 per cent bad.

attempt to steal some of the notes, the remaining ones were burnt. The last Ostmark note outside private collections went up in flames in July 2002.) On 3 October, less than a year after the opening of the Berlin Wall, East Germany ceased to exist. It was quicker to simply admit its five provinces (*Länder*) to the *Bundesrepublik* than create a new, united Germany.

The old West Germany had been, along, perhaps, with Belgium, Luxembourg and the Netherlands, the nation most true to Robert Schuman's 1949 'European spirit', happy to write out a large annual cheque in order to be one of the Europe club. But now, rather like a young man who suddenly falls in love and stops spending all his evenings with his mates, would Germany's enthusiasm for club membership wane? It had found its perfect partner, its 'other half', and had other things on its mind. Not old dreams of conquest, but, like many newlyweds, a shiny new home.

The dream home would not come cheap. Initial optimism that privatizing East German industry would pay for reunification soon vanished. Nobody wanted to buy old technology. Instead, money had to be poured into the East's inadequate telephone lines, crumbling autobahns and noxious power stations. Kohl insisted on honouring the pension obligations of the old GDR government, placing a huge (and lasting) burden on the more productive West. Unemployment soared in the uncompetitive East, necessitating yet more government assistance. According to some estimates, in the first three years after reunification, the exercise cost the new, expanded Germany 350 billion deutschmarks. Ill feeling between 'ossies' and 'wessies' resulted: the marriage turned out to be stormier than had been hoped. But it was still a marriage.

Iron Curtain technology also dogged Eurovision 1990. Croatian TV had a small budget (though the expenditure still horrified people in Zagreb, where wages were well below Western European levels). Spain's song had to be started twice due to a mix-up with the backing tape, and there were phone problems during the voting – worst of all, prophetically, with the line to Belgrade.

But elsewhere in Europe, technology marched on. The previous year, Tim Berners-Lee, a British scientist working at the European Organization for Nuclear Research (CERN: the acronym comes from the French) in Switzerland, had suggested creating a 'world wide web' of sites that other academics could access via their computers to make research easier. In December 1990, a prototype webpage went live on CERN's internal system.

1991

Date: 4 May
Venue: Cinecitta Studio 15, Rome, Italy
Winner: Carola, Sweden
Winning Song: 'Fångad Av En Stormwind' (Caught In A Storm)

It had originally been planned to hold Eurovision 1991 at San Remo, the home of an Italian song festival that had inspired Marcel Bezençon back in 1955, but security concerns meant that it was switched to film studios near Rome. Those concerns were caused by the outbreak of the first Gulf War. Iraqi dictator Saddam Hussein had invaded Kuwait; the United Nations told him to get out or face the consequences. He stayed put. A global coalition of troops, led by the US but featuring many European nations, liberated the small oil state. The main European participants were Britain and France, with back-up from Italy, the Netherlands, Sweden, Spain, Poland, Czechoslovakia, Greece, Denmark, Hungary and Norway.

Perhaps because of this late change of venue, Eurovision 1991 is now treasured as a vintage one for connoisseurs of Euro-cockups. Choose your favourite! The phone ringing offstage as the second song is announced. The awful sax solo in the Greek entry. The mysterious twang halfway through Luxembourg's song. The venue's PA conking out halfway through 'Fångad Av En Stormwind'. The lights going out before the (rather good) interval act. Or maybe it was just the presenters. Gigliola Cinquetti and Toto Cutugno chatted away in Italian between the songs (Eurovision announcements are supposed to be in English or French), testing to the limit the boundaries between charming informality and self-indulgent amateurism. The show went on way beyond its planned time – and then two songs tied for first place. Chaos threatened to engulf the whole proceedings, but luckily EBU scrutineer Frank Naef stayed calm and a winner was quickly announced.

It wasn't a vintage year for songs. Carola's victory was more a reward for her gutsy delivery than the quality of the material. Her French rival for the top spot, Tunisian-born Amina Annabi, continued that nation's new self-presentation as *la France mondiale* with the elegant eastern-influenced 'C'est Le Dernier Qui A Parlé Qui A Raison' (The Last One To Speak Is Right) – a dig, perhaps, at the ever more vociferous right in France. The result was the closest ever, apart from the 1969 farce: Carola won by virtue of having more second places than Annabi, both having got 146 points and maximum votes from five countries.

At the other end of the table, Austria's Thomas Forstner was unlucky to get *nul points*. One point clear of him was Yugoslavia's Bebi Doll with 'Brazil', a bland song covering up the fact that the singer's nation was about to implode. Looking behind the scenes at Zagreb 1990, we had seen the seeds of this. They were now sprouting.

During that year, whenever free elections were allowed in the different parts of the country, separatist politicians won. Serbs in the Krajina region of Croatia began to prepare for an uprising should Croatia declare independence. A month before Eurovision 1991, a shootout took place between Croatian police and Serb rebels. A month after the contest the Croatians made their declaration. Slovenia did the same.

Slovenia was at once invaded by the Yugoslav (now, essentially, Serb) army, but the half-hearted invasion was not a success: after ten days the army pulled out. Slovenia, the northernmost part of Yugoslavia and an area with little history of ethnic conflict, was essentially left alone to get on with making itself a modern nation. (A good sign of its success is the fact that since 1993 it has been a regular, if not hugely successful, participant in Eurovision, missing only two years.)

Beauty and the Box
France's Jacqueline Joubert, presenter of the 1959 and 1961 contests, with the machine that made it all possible.

Vol – aaaa – re!
(Wo – ho) Domenico
Mudugno (Italy, 1958)
about to take off in another
piece of game-changing
technology, the airliner.

Let it swing!
Shoeless and mini-skirted, the UK's
Sandie Shaw prepares to make
Eurovision fab and groovy in 1967.

Boom-Bang-a-Bad-Guys
The UK's Lulu in front of Salvador Dalí's bizarre 1969 tribute to
Franco and Mussolini.

European Conquerors
Sweden's mighty Abba plus their secret weapon, ready for Brighton, 1974.

A Little Peace
Germany's Nicole protests against the horrors of the nuclear arms race in 1982, with charm, vulnerability and grace.

Viva la Diva!
Dana International victorious in 1998, for Israel and for the LGBT community.

Eurovision heads East
What is 'Europe' and where does it end? Turkey's Sertab Erener winning Eurovision in 2003.

Orange Revolution
The 2004 winner, Ukrainian singer-songwriter Ruslana, later played a major role in the protests that toppled her country's anti-European president.

Silver Revolution

'Russia, Goodbye' is what we all heard in 2007, from Ukraine's off-the-wall Verka Sedushka.

Joyful and triumphant

Norway's 2009 winner Alexander Rybak reminding us that Eurovision is also about performing music and loving every moment of it.

A New Beauty?
'Transformed and reborn', went the lyric, but Austria's 2014 winner Conchita Wurst was just being true to herself – the core value of modern Europe.

Eurovision!

In Croatia, however, things got nastier and nastier. In July 1991, Serb forces invaded, this time with real resolve – and real brutality. On 1 August, Croat prisoners of war were murdered at the border village of Delj. Later that month, the siege of Vukovar began: the most vicious fighting on European soil since 1945. When the city fell, in November, hundreds of people were massacred. This was the old, riven Europe that Eurovision had been created to transcend, a place still haunted by Second World War hatreds, by memories of the atrocities of the pro-Nazi Croatian Ustaše and of reprisals by the Communist (and largely Serb) Partisans.

In January 1992, a peace treaty brokered by the USA received agreement – whereupon the tension moved to Bosnia. Both Serbs and Croats began to eye up chunks of the province, which was ethnically divided (about 45 per cent of the population were Muslim, 40 per cent Serb and 15 per cent Croat).

In 1991 the break-up also came of another state composed of cobbled-together nationalities: the Soviet Union. It seemed at the beginning of the year that Moscow was going to stamp on separatism within the Union. In January, two waves of Russian troops had stormed public buildings in Vilnius, Lithuania, killing eighteen people. But at that point Gorbachev realized where this was leading and backtracked, condemning the 'brutality' of the events. This was probably the moment he realized he couldn't both hold the Soviet Union together and retain his moral principles. After this, various republics started voting to leave: Estonia, Latvia, Georgia.

On the morning of 19 August 1991, however, Russian citizens awoke to the news that Gorbachev was 'unwell' and that martial law had been declared. A group of high-ranking conspirators had seized power. In the Baltic states, the Soviet army moved in on key targets, ready to use maximum force. Helmut Kohl's haste to reunify Germany suddenly seemed extremely prescient. But Moscow's citizens took to the streets, led by the president of the Russian

Federation, Boris Yeltsin. The conspirators did not do a Tiananmen/ Timişoara: they were reactionary old men, but not Stalin or Ceauşescu. By 21 August, the coup had failed.

On 8 December, the presidents of Russia, Ukraine and Belarus signed a treaty ending the Soviet Union and replacing it with a 'Commonwealth of Independent States'. The Supreme Soviet finally voted itself out of existence on Boxing Day.

One could regard the failure of the August coup as the final fall of Communism and thus the end of the Cold War. Amazingly, in the very same month Tim Berners-Lee's 'world wide web' became officially available to non-academic users – though there were few takers to start with. One era ends, another begins.

Two and a half years later, the nation that had spent forty years dominating Eastern Europe and threatening to obliterate the rest of the continent with nuclear missiles would be taking part in the Eurovision Song Contest.

1992

Date: 9 May
Venue: Malmö Ice Stadium, Sweden
Winner: Linda Martin, Ireland
Winning Song: 'Why Me?'

The 1992 contest was held on Europe Day, the anniversary of the announcement of the plans for Jean Monnet's European Coal and Steel Community back in 1950. This was appropriate: earlier in the year, the Maastricht Treaty had been signed, marking a huge step forward for European integration. At Maastricht, political Europe was given its new name, the European Union. Jacques Delors' timetable for the new currency became official: a new Europe-wide currency (it still had no name) was to be in place by January 1999 – in the financial world, at least, though not on the streets. Rules for joining the currency were formally put in place: 'convergence criteria' were supposed to ensure that no nation could participate if its economy wasn't in shape. Still-sceptical Britain and Denmark were allowed to opt out; everybody else was on board and heading in one direction.

As a sop to old-fashioned de Gaulle/Thatcher intergovernmentalists, a concept known as subsidiarity was written into the treaty. This held that European government was supposed to interfere in national government as little as possible. If a decision could be made at a regional or national level, it should be. Quite how this would be interpreted was up for debate – and still is.

But Maastricht was essentially a triumph for the federalists – its official name is the Treaty on European Union (TEU), not the Treaty on Subsidiarity. It showed just how far the European project had advanced from the confusion of the early 1980s. Historians see

Maastricht as the third major agreement in modern European history, alongside the 1957 Treaty of Rome and the Single European Act of 1986.

Oddly, in the year of such forward-looking Euro-triumph, there was a retro air to the 1992 contest. The set was elegant – designed around the prow of a Viking ship – but static, unlike the shape-shifting laser kingdoms of the 1980s. Alongside the electric guitars and Yamaha DX7 synths, we saw accordions feature in several numbers. Belgium's Morgane sung that her generation was, beneath its confident appearance, afraid, because it lacked emotion and connection to the past. Switzerland's Daisy Auvray wanted an old-style song with some tenderness from 'Mister Music Man'.

She got it in the winner, an unassuming ballad where the singer wonders, as many self-doubting people do when they finally find love, 'Why Me?' Back in the eighties, one feels, few people would have asked such a question, confident that their romantic success was due to their charisma, hard work, businesslike attitude and giant shoulder pads. The new decade was already assuming a gentler, more thoughtful tone. The composer of the winning song was Johnny Logan, a man it seemed impossible to keep off the winners' podium.

If Linda Martin's win was the start of Ireland's run as darlings of Eurovision, 1992 also saw an Irishman come to the fore in political Europe. That man was Ray MacSharry, who had once been MEP for Connacht-Ulster (the same role that would later be performed by 1970 Eurovision winner Dana) and was now European Commissioner for Agriculture.

In the 1980s, both François Mitterrand and Jacques Delors had tried to do something about the Common Agricultural Policy. They had briefly succeeded, but by 1991 the money was haemorrhaging out again. MacSharry was the man who finally grabbed the highly subsidized bull by its highly subsidized horns. The programme of price support was cut back and new measures introduced to encourage farmers to look after land rather than just overproduce, and to retire if their farms were no longer financially viable. Eurosceptics point out that *overall* EU expenditure continued to grow as fast after MacSharry as before, but it was no longer largely vanishing into wine lakes and butter mountains: the two Structural Funds and, after 1994, a new 'Cohesion Fund' created especially to improve transport links began to take up more budget, and what remained in the agricultural pot was more wisely invested.

The top three songs of 1992 were all in English. Britain, represented by stage star Michael Ball with 'One Step Out Of Time', came second: Linda Martin's gentleness seemed to suit the times better than Ball's grandiose power ballad. Malta, the only other competitor allowed to sing in English, came third.

Britain did not rule in political Europe, however. It was a grudging signatory to the Maastricht Treaty. Its prime minister, Conservative John Major, found himself under attack from ever more assertive Eurosceptics in his own party on his return home. In September 1992, the British pound crashed out of the European Monetary System (EMS) in a day of financial high drama, with UK interest rates flying through the roof and money pouring into the pockets of speculators (one of whom, George Soros, is reputed to have made $1 billion from 'shorting' sterling that day).

Other nations were cagey about European integration, too. In June, Danish voters refused to ratify the Maastricht Treaty (four specific opt-outs were later negotiated, and in a second referendum, next year, this new version was accepted). In September, France voted for ratification – but only just. During the summer, French polls had showed massive support for the treaty, but maverick Eurosceptic Philippe Séguin led an aggressive campaign, culminating in a three-hour eve-of-vote debate with an unwell President Mitterrand. On the day, 50.8 per cent of valid votes were in favour, the result not being certain until votes from France's overseas territories came in. The referendum became known as the *petit oui*.

In the same month the Swedish krona, which had been 'shadowing' the EMS currencies with the intention of joining them, was savaged by currency speculators: in 2017, it has yet to join the Euro.

Shadowing – when a government buys or sells on currency markets or pulls economic levers such as interest rates in order to keep its currency level with another one – is a risky business. Once speculators work out that you are doing it, they can milk you, and the interest rate changes make life difficult for domestic businesses and home buyers. Britain and Sweden learnt this the hard way.

Eurovision 1992 saw the last appearance of Yugoslavia – though technically this was no longer the old Yugoslavia but a new state that had come into being a month before the contest, consisting of Serbia and Montenegro. Snežana Berić, aka Extra Nena, sang her Alla-Pugacheva-ish 'Ljubim Te Pesmama' (Kissing You With Songs) with flair and grace. One line in the lyric talks of two broken glasses: the lovers in the song have had too much wine that evening. It's a neat flashback to those two cigarette ends from 1962. This was a much classier way to bow out than with Bebi Doll. *Nul points* for Berić's political awareness, however: at the pre-contest press conference, she insisted that her government and president (Milošević) were 'against all kinds of violence and armed conflict'.

Bosnia had declared independence a month before Eurovision 1992, and was soon invaded. The notorious siege of Sarajevo began on 2 May. Hills ring the Bosnian capital, and these were occupied by Serb forces who, after initial failed attempts to storm the city, blocked its main access routes, cut off its utilities and began shelling it. Snipers created lines of fire onto two of Sarajevo's main streets, and shot at random passers-by (an estimated 225 people would be killed this way, including 60 children).

So much for that happy orchestra.

1993

Date: 15 May
Venue: Green Glens Arena, Millstreet, Ireland
Debuts: Bosnia-Herzegovina, Croatia, Slovenia
Winner: Niamh Kavanagh, Ireland
Winning Song: 'In Your Eyes'

The evening that Linda Martin won Eurovision 1992, entrepreneur Noel Duggan wrote a letter to RTÉ, the Irish broadcaster, offering to host the 1993 event for free. The venue would be his equestrian centre in Millstreet, a small town – it had around 1,500 inhabitants – halfway between Cork and Killarney. Cue, one suspects, laughter at RTÉ headquarters. But Duggan meant what he said. He began lobbying influential people. A local committee was set up to co-ordinate the bid and convince visiting officials that Millstreet could really deliver. The officials agreed, and it got the gig.

There's a lot to be said for small Eurovision venues: they generate a special enthusiasm. Like Bergen in 1986, Millstreet went Eurovision crazy. Visitors can still see where one local resident decorated the wall of his house with the flags of the twenty-five contestants. Such venues generate good PR. The world's media descended and gave the contest a fresh injection of publicity. It did, of course, pose logistical challenges – the local railway station had to be enlarged for the event – but these were triumphantly met by RTÉ. Alan Farquharson's set was back to the standards of the late 1980s. Millstreet put on a great show: the mouse roared.

Such was the spirit of the times. Two weeks before the 1993 contest, CERN made the software for participating in the world wide web freely available for anyone to use. Soon the new 'internet' would be providing ever more opportunities for nimble entrepreneurs like Noel Duggan, with big ideas and can-do mindsets.

The 1993 contest was the start of a new Eurovision era, too, as entrants from Eastern European nations began to appear. The undoubted heroes of Millstreet were the six musicians from Bosnia, who had to run the gauntlet of snipers to leave besieged Sarajevo. The last part of their flight involved crossing the city's exposed airport in darkness, running across two runways to reach a ditch, from which one could crawl to a peninsula of Bosnian-held territory. The night that the musicians made their escape, six other people were killed trying to do the same. Muhamed Fazlagić, the vocalist, sang that 'Sva Bol Svijeta' (All The Pain Of The World) was in Bosnia at that time, and got a rousing reception from the crowd, as did the Bosnian representative when he finally got through to the rest of Europe on a whistling phone line to announce the results.

Croatia and Slovenia also made debuts that year. Croatia sang a lament for a young man killed in the war. Slovenia's entry, 'Tih Deževen Dan' (Rainy Day), is least remembered of the three debuts, but arguably the best musically. It's a dreamy song featuring acoustic guitar and a strange middle section where the singer seems to be recalling an unpleasant past – some kind of internment camp? Or was it just school? Sadly, none of these songs got much respect from the judges.

To be fair, they faced strong competition. This was a vintage year, with the periphery on particularly good form. Iceland, Portugal, Greece and Norway all came up with attractive entries. Spain's Eva Santamaria sang of the egotism of men – sentiments one would not have heard in Eurovision a few years back.

The centre, by contrast, was more out of touch. Several songs sounded dated. Denmark's Tommy Seebach sang a rather sweet lullaby, 'Under Stjernerne På Himlen' (Under The Stars Of The Sky), for his infant daughter. It came twenty-second. Freshly opted out from the euro, the Danes were much less happy about a probable exit from Eurovision.* Seebach was assailed by the Danish press on his return from Millstreet; he found solace in alcohol, and died in his early fifties. His son re-recorded the song in 2003, and it was a hit in the country that had been so vicious about it first time round.

Seebach's story highlights one of the less attractive features of the new decade: the rising power of the media, and with it, rising arrogance. Back in April 1992, Britain's populist *Sun* newspaper had claimed the credit for John Major's election victory ('It's the Sun wot won it', the paper crowed in its headline). Later that year, a cabinet minister who tried to curb media power, David Mellor, was exposed by the press for having an affair with an actress. He lost his job. Eurovision would see the media harpy in action again later in the decade.

Amongst other centre losers, Luxembourg came twentieth and left the competition, never to return. Their last two entries were wholly or partially in Luxembourgeois – and fared badly. Respect to the Grand Duchy for this: having prospered as France B for many years, they decided to return to their roots and to hell with the consequences. Belgium's Barbara Dex came undeservedly last, then suffered the added insult of having an annual award named after her for Eurovision's worst-dressed contestant (fortunately she seems to have taken this in good spirits).

The 1993 results were influenced by language again, with English-speaking entries taking the top two places. Again, too, an Irish song beautifully sung from the standpoint of an unconfident, reticent female beat a brassier UK entry by a big name (this time, Liverpool's chart-topping Sonia). Welcome to the 1990s. The song that came

---

* Because of the increasing demand for places in the contest, it was agreed that the worst-performing countries in 1993 would not get to participate next time round. Exactly where the line would be drawn was not made clear at the time, but twenty-second did not look good enough – and wasn't. Denmark sat out the 1994 contest, returning in 1995 with an impressive fifth place.

third was in the other official EBU language, French, and the fourth-placed entry a mixture of French and Corsican.

Croatia and Bosnia may have shared a stage at Millstreet, but the two nations were already at war. Croatia had initially sided with Bosnia when the latter was invaded by Serbs, but soon turned on its new ally, eager for territory. In April 1993, Croat forces killed over a hundred civilians in Ahmici, a largely Muslim village in Central Bosnia. The sinister term 'ethnic cleansing' was beginning to enter the vocabulary: the removal of ethnic groups from territory by violence (or at least by the threat of it). Croat forces also besieged the city of Mostar, 100 miles south-west of Sarajevo. In November its 500-year-old bridge, a masterpiece of Ottoman architecture, was blown up. It became a symbol of resistance for the oppressed Bosniaks. Their oppression did not go unnoticed in the wider Islamic world.

While this was going on, the newly powerful European Union did little. It was split. Germany had traditional links with Croatia. France and Britain feared the spread of German influence (they still hadn't really got used to reunification). Nobody wanted to drag Russia, keen supporters of fellow Slavs in Serbia, into a war. But critical voices were raised at the inactivity: this was a European tragedy, not some trouble in far-away Vietnam or Kuwait. One of the 'pillars' of the post-Maastricht EU (it had three) was supposed to be a 'Common Foreign and Security Policy'. In 1994, US president Bill Clinton came over and gave us a nudge. But the killing went on and Europe did little to stop it.

1994

Date: 15 May
Venue: The Point, Dublin, Ireland
Debuts: Estonia, Hungary, Lithuania, Poland, Romania, Russia, Slovakia
Winner: Paul Harrington and Charlie McGettigan, Ireland
Winning Song: Rock 'n' Roll Kids

This was the great year of Eastern accession to the contest. Four former Soviet satellites joined: Hungary, Poland, Romania and, recently split from the Czech Republic, Slovakia. Two Baltic states, Estonia and Lithuania. And, of course, Russia itself: the old enemy, now singing along with us on Paula Farrell's stage based on 'Dublin by night'.

Other European institutions were way behind Eurovision. Eastern bloc nations would not be admitted to the EU until 2004. Germany and Austria were worried about immigration, France about the watering down of its agricultural subsidy. Spain, Portugal and Greece feared they would get fewer handouts from the Structural and Cohesion funds as even poorer nations joined. Talks didn't even start till 1998. Sadly, the idea that the EU immediately welcomed these nations and thereby guaranteed freedom and democracy in them does not stand up to scrutiny. These nations chose freedom and democracy, then joined the EU when they were finally allowed to. NATO was only a little speedier, admitting the Czech Republic, Hungary and Poland in 1999, but nobody else till 2004. Eurovision alone opened its arms at once to these nations and said, 'You are European: welcome!'

The contest itself was a triumph for Ireland. It was superbly staged. Technology continued to improve: 1994 saw satellite links to each nation's announcement of their votes. The host's entry was a runaway winner. For 'Rock 'n' Roll Kids', the orchestra was not used. Two men sat on stage, played piano and guitar, and sang a wistful ballad. In the 1980s, it would probably not have featured in the top ten, but this was the 1990s, and quiet reflection was the order of the day.

Several other songs featured a quiet, confessional tone. Best of all was Hungarian singer Friderika Bayer's 'Kinek Mondjam El Vétkeimet?' (Who Can I Tell My Sins To?). Hungary has rarely bought into the 'Diggi-loo Diggi-ley' approach to Eurovision, usually preferring intelligent, sometimes troubling songs.

The answer to Bayer's question in 1990s Europe, especially in Northern Europe, was increasingly 'a therapist'. The decade was notable for a boom in counselling and therapy. Eurovision can't be accused of lacking emotion, but in many European countries – like my own – there still was a big difference between relating to a song and actually admitting to personal emotions, especially those which betray vulnerability. But this was beginning to change. Emotional honesty was becoming more valued than emotional restraint – all part of Europe's journey from an ethic of duty to one of authenticity, a journey which is a central theme of this book.

We heard twenty-five songs from all round an expanded Europe – but the best of Eurovision 1994 was yet to come. Interval acts in the contest have, let's say, varied in quality over the years. Britain in 1974 came up with the Wombles (a kids' programme not shown anywhere else in Europe). During Switzerland's 1989 William Tell act, the arrow was clearly seen missing the apple, though moments later a pre-pierced apple was held up for our admiration. But 1994 gave us *Riverdance*, a stunning display of traditional Irish dancing presented in a totally modern way by Jean Butler, Michael Flatley and a troupe of dancers, to the music of Limerick-born composer Bill Whelan. The six-minute piece began with a haunting vocal section from soloist Katie McMahon and the group Anúna. Next, Butler and

Eurovision!

Flatley took solo turns, then performed a *pas de deux*, before being joined by the ensemble for the finale. It brought the audience to its feet. *Riverdance* was turned into a stage show and ran for years. It's up there with Abba and Céline Dion.

It was also a perfect symbol for the Ireland that was arising at that time. Entry to the EEC had benefited that nation in several ways, widening the market for its products and allowing it to receive money from the Structural and Cohesion funds. In addition, the Irish government had provided a low-tax environment for both business and, true to its soul, artists.

The results would prove startling. In 1994, unemployment was 14.7 per cent; by 2001, the figure would have fallen to 3.8 per cent. GDP would grow by 8 per cent annually over the same period. People began talking about the Celtic Tiger, by analogy with the booming Asian Tiger economies of South Korea and Taiwan. Critics say this was false growth based on bribing foreign companies to invest in Ireland, but it takes energy and enterprise to attract and retain such investors, and Eurovision 1994 shows that Ireland had these aplenty.

Right now, the new arrivals to Eurovision could only look on and hope their economic turn would come. If Eurovision was anything to go by, Poland would be the next Tiger – Edyta Gorniak stormed to second place, showing off her remarkable vocal range in 'To Nie Ja' (That's Not Me). This barometer is not false: the newly liberated nation had restructured its economy after 1989, and by the mid-1990s was reaping the benefit. Growth for the five years after 1994 would average 6 per cent a year.

Less tigerish musically were the Baltic states, who came last and second last, with *nul* and *deux points*. They were still in recovery from escaping the Soviet Union – there had been 150,000 Russian troops in the three nations in 1991, and at the time of the contest, withdrawal was still incomplete – and had a lot to learn about Eurovision. Lithuania's *nul point*er Ovidijus Vyšniauskas was only belatedly asked to provide a song, and claimed to have written the tune of 'Lopšine Mylimai' (Sweethearts' Lullaby) in three minutes.

Economically, however, these nations were modernizing fast. Estonia, in particular, looked at Ireland's success and began courting overseas investment. It reformed its currency, cracked down on corruption, stopped subsidies to old Soviet-era enterprises and began looking at the potential of the fast-developing internet.

The arrival of such states gave a new shape to both the Eurovision and the political map of Europe. Arguably there was now a new, eastern periphery, out beyond the old periphery. As a result, the old periphery was starting to look like the old centre, at least more like a halfway house. Peripheral Britain was now directly linked to core France by a tunnel which opened a week before Eurovision 1994. Austria was preparing to join the EU. Scandinavia was signing up, too, with Finland and Sweden becoming members on 1 January 1995.

Looks, however, can deceive. Would these nations be as committed to the European project as its founders, the nations who had come to Switzerland to sing in 1956?

Norway, as usual, did differently and voted to stay out. An oil-rich nation, it had much less to gain from EU membership than other peripherals. At the same time, Norway had a love-hate relationship with Eurovision. Some years it didn't give a hoot (or the twang of a pair of braces). Others . . . Sitting in the audience during *Riverdance* was composer Rolf Løvland. He'd already won back in the bouncy eighties with Bobbysocks. A shrewd judge of the *zeitgeist*, Løvland heard the haunting vocal and the lone Celtic violin accompanying Jean Butler's solo dance, and knew the kind of piece he had to come up with.

1995

Date: 13 May
Venue: The Point, Dublin, Ireland
Debuts: None (none till 1998)
Winner: Secret Garden, Norway
Winning Song: 'Nocturne'

On 1995's dark, brooding, beautiful set, a dark, brooding, beautiful tune walked away with the competition. Not everybody approved, however. 'Nocturne' has only twenty-four words; Fionnuala Sherry on violin features a lot more than singer Gunnhild Tvinnereim. Sweden said the piece should not have been allowed to participate, and gave it no votes. The Norwegian press was furious at this – rivalry between the two nations runs deep (for most of the nineteenth century, Norway was the junior partner in a union with Sweden). A diplomatic row threatened, and the Swedish ambassador ended up apologizing. Fellow Nordics Denmark only gave 'Nocturne' one point, too: so much for the bloc vote. Almost everybody else loved it. If you're watching the YouTube video, the many-stringed instrument is called a Nyckelharp and the player is Åsa Jinder – who is Swedish: national grudges aren't held by everybody.

The New Age had arrived in Eurovision. Back in the 'white heat' of the early 1960s, it was assumed that religion would quietly wither away, as we Europeans all became scientific and rational. The *soixante-huitards* ditched the science and rationality, but wanted no truck with religion. That old stuff, all thoughtful people seemed to agree, was on its way out.

The stats support them. Between 1960 and 1990 the number of practising Catholics in Belgium fell by 31 per cent and in France by 23 per cent, while the Dutch Catholic and Reformed churches lost 24 per cent between them. The percentage of Scots taking communion halved between 1960 and 1995. If one assumes that most older people kept their faith, these figures show a very low take-up of established religion by the younger generation.* Some of these defectors became, as expected, technocratic atheists (a classic example being Richard Dawkins, appointed in 1995 as Professor for Public Understanding of Science at Oxford University).

Many more Europeans, however, took a third route, looking for new, more personal ways of pursuing the spiritual life. Some of these ways were, and still are, delightfully daft (or sinister, in the wrong hands), but for many, the New Age brought a sense of personal power and significance. One can imagine Judy's friend from Sweden, 1969, following this route.

Eurovision mirrors this change from orthodox religion to unorthodox spirituality. To listen to the 1995 winner is to feel the New Age's sense of yearning and mystery. A song with a more conventional religious message, Germany's 'Verliebt In Dich' (In Love With You) ('You' in this song is God), came last, only escaping *nul points* thanks to one vote (the award came near the end of the voting, and got a loud cheer from the sporting Irish crowd).

Of course, the nineties weren't one long hug. Eurovision 1995 also saw another musical genre debut in the contest: an angry import from America, rap. Critics of Eurovision say this is a rather late take-up, as people had been rapping since the mid-1970s. But that was in the South Bronx. The genre took a long time to go mainstream. If the cynics who say that 'go mainstream' means 'get taken up by white artists' are right, then Eurovision was ahead of its time, as the great white rapper, Eminem, had yet to make it big by 1995. Britain's 'Love City Groove' (by yet another made-for-Eurovision group, this time with

---

* This was much less true among Europe's non-Christian minorities. Muslims made up around 4 per cent of Europe's population in 1990, and Jews and Hindus about 0.5 per cent together.

the same name as the song) was a relatively gentle introduction to the genre; it came mid-table, but rap did not take root in the competition.

Russia participated for the second time, courtesy of the wild-haired Philipp Kirkorov,* who had recently married Alla Pugacheva. Kirkorov's song, sung sixth, was poor and came seventeenth – but in Russia, where the programme was not broadcast live, the running order was edited and 'Kolybelnaya Dlya Vulkana' (Lullaby For A Volcano) appeared to be sung last. The voting was then not shown, leaving viewers with the impression that Kirkorov had won. The Soviet Union might have vanished, but old habits die hard.

For Bosnia, Davor Popović sang about 'Dvadeset I Prvi Vijek' (The Twenty-First Century). The words were gloomy, but the tune quite upbeat. Tragically, words trump music here. In 1995 the Balkan war hit new depths.

The city of Srebrenica in the far east of Bosnia was one of three Muslim enclaves in that part of the country, which was otherwise now held by the Bosnian Serb army (VRS). The Serbs wanted them out.

The city had been under siege since 1993. UN troops had been struggling to keep it a 'safe area' since that date, but the force was under-resourced. By the time of Eurovision 1995, the situation was drastic, with ever fewer supply convoys getting through and ever more VRS troops in place around the city. The UN defence consisted of 370 lightly armed soldiers, mandated only to fight 'in self-defence'.

The final attack began on 6 July. It met little resistance; on 11 July, General Ratko Mladic was filmed walking through the deserted town centre. The town's Muslim residents had all fled to the UN head-quarters, an abandoned battery factory at nearby Potocari, and were camped around it. The next day, VRS forces came there and walked through the encampment, separating out men of military age. Some

---

* Eurovision 1995 was notable for wild hair, except for Malta's Mike Spitieri, who was totally bald.

tried to escape to Bosnian-held territory, but the columns of already hungry and weakened refugees made easy targets. In the end, over six thousand men and boys were rounded up. Over the next week, they would be systematically murdered by the VRS. Small groups were taken out to remote fields, shot, then buried in mass graves.

The UN troops supposed to be protecting these people were Dutch, and the massacre caused soul-searching in the Netherlands. Could more have been done? More deeply, was the likeable, easy-going nation tough enough for the emerging modern world? My sense is that the 370 'Dutchbat' soldiers were pawns in a much bigger game. There is certainly nothing to be proud of in their conduct, but the real blame lies elsewhere – primarily with the perpetrators of the massacre, of course, but also with allied politicians and senior commanders who did not give Dutchbat the mandate or the military support it needed.

What finally prompted decisive international action was the more visible siege of Sarajevo. On 28 August, a Serb mortar attack killed thirty-seven people in a crowded marketplace. Two days later, NATO began air strikes on the besiegers. These lasted three weeks, after which a joint Bosnian and Croat force was able to begin driving the VRS from their positions. Basic facilities were slowly restored to the city, but the siege was not officially declared over until February 1996.

In the meantime, an agreement had been thrashed out at a US airbase near Dayton, Ohio. Bosnia in theory retained its former boundaries, but was effectively divided into two similar-sized 'Entities': the Federation of Bosnia and Herzegovina (largely inhabited by Bosniaks and Bosnian Croats) and the Serb-dominated 'Republika Srpska'. Hostilities ceased. Had peace finally arrived in the land of Lola Novaković's sophisticated late-night lovers?

In April 1996, four army patrols were attacked in the southern Serbian province of Kosovo. A little-known group called the Kosovo Liberation Army (KLA) claimed responsibility.

1996

Date: 18 May
Venue: Oslo Spektrum, Norway
Winner: Eimear Quinn, Ireland
Winning Song: 'The Voice'

Thirty nations were eager to participate in the 1996 contest, so a pre-final was organized, whereby the juries listened to recordings of all the songs and put twenty-two through to the live event (to join the hosts, who qualified automatically). One of the nations not to make the cut was Germany, the country with the largest single TV audience and a major financial contributor to the show. All seven fallers at the pre-final fence had the disheartening experience of winning their national heats then being unable to compete in a live competition. This unsatisfactory system was not used again.*

Norway put on a stunning show, in front of 8,000 people. A range of material was on offer. Austria brought us gospel, courtesy of blind pianist/singer George Nussbaumer. Poland's Kasia Kowalska took us to a smoky intellectuals' bar with her dark, intense 'I Want To Know My Sin'. We went clubbing with Britain's Gina G and her saucy, techno 'Ooh Aah . . . Just A Little Bit', Eurovision's answer to a Donald McGill seaside postcard.

New Age was still the dominant genre, however: floaty and ethnic. France's entry was sung in Breton. France had once ruled the contest, thanks to its creative power and its dutiful satellites, Luxembourg

---

* A system based on recent past performance was introduced instead. In 2000, the four biggest financial contributors to the contest, the UK, France, Germany and Spain, were allowed to skip this. A semi-final, the only really fair system, would follow in 2004, though the 'Big Four' exemption remained, with Italy making it a 'Big Five' in 2011.

and Monaco. But now the satellites had crashed to earth and music had moved on. Since Joëlle Ursull back in 1990, the nation had been on a fascinating Eurovision journey of self-discovery, looking to its minorities and regions for inspiration. This policy had worked, with a string of Top Ten places in the early 1990s. From 1996 onwards, however, it would struggle in Eurovision, with long runs of poor results broken only by the occasional single-figure placing.

Politically, France was not faring so well. The reunification of Germany, a few months after Ursull took to the Eurovision stage, had been the *coup de grâce* for lingering Gaullist dreams of French supremacy in Europe.

France remained committed to the European project, however: being number two is, after all, not the worst fate in the world – some Eurovision second-placers are remembered as classics ('Su Canción', 'Theater', 'Never Ever Let You Go', 'Sanomi' and 'Lane Moje' are my personal favourites; you will no doubt have others). The project appeared to be coalescing even better than expected. Experts had forecast that only a few centre countries would initially meet the Maastricht criteria for membership of the new shared currency – named the euro at a meeting of the European Council in Madrid in December 1995. However as the nineties progressed, the 'Club Med' nations – Italy, Spain and Portugal – made unexpected progress in sorting out their public finances. The three nations that had joined the EU in 1995, Austria, Finland and Sweden, all seemed eligible, too (though Sweden was not keen to join).

Critics of the single currency argued that potential members were fudging their figures to fit the criteria – even centre ones: France, Italy, Germany and Belgium. But such criticisms were brushed aside. The euro was on its way, and nit-picking naysayers were missing the point. The currency now even had a physical form: in 1996 a competition was held to design the banknotes, and the winner was a young Austrian, Robert Kalina. The coins – the one, shared side of them – would follow next year, when Belgian Luc Luycx won another contest (look closely at euro coins and you can see his signature, interlocking Ls).

Critics also pointed at the huge differences between the economies of different regions of Europe. Could they really all be squeezed into one monetary system? To be fair to enthusiasts for the euro, there was little agreed knowledge on what makes a currency union work. Economists talked rather vaguely about 'Optimal Currency Areas' (OCAs), but there seemed to be limited agreement about what these exactly consisted of, and even less empirical evidence. The euro was in many ways a leap in the dark. Such leaps require, above all, faith.

There was not a complete absence of evidence, however. Europe had witnessed two attempts at creating shared currency areas, albeit in a previous century.

In 1872, Sweden and Denmark had merged their currencies. Norway joined them in 1875. Initially the Scandinavian Currency Union worked well, but in 1905 Norway sought political independence from Sweden, and Denmark decided to follow different economic policies to the other two nations. The Union, now under stress, lumbered on till the First World War, when the different experiences of the three countries (Norway was linked to Britain; Denmark shared a border with Germany and traded extensively with it) created such different economic conditions in the three nations that it finally collapsed.

By contrast, an earlier German attempt at monetary union had been a success. At the beginning of the nineteenth century Germany was a mass of independent states, mostly small but with two big players, Prussia and Austria. In 1818 Prussia began to set up a Customs Union, and over the next few decades more and more states joined it. Austria didn't want to participate, and in 1866 ended up at war with Prussia, where it was quickly defeated; afterwards it went its own way, forming a joint Balkan empire with Hungary. Prussia set up a North German Federation, which in 1870 went to war with France and won. South Germany (Bavaria and Baden-Württemberg) joined the Federation soon after, and the new nation became the *Reich* (Empire). A central German bank was only founded in 1876.

Looking at these examples, the prognosis for the euro did not look good. Monetary union had worked where, politically, one state ended up effectively taking over the others – and where this takeover was generally accepted: the German statelets became Prussian when they wanted to; Austria, unwilling to join the party, was excluded. It had worked where participants shared a language and a sense of national and cultural identity. It had, in other words, worked where there was already a high, agreed level of political union.

Ah, but maybe that was old stuff. Would this material from over a century ago have any relevance to our own post-modern, post-national continent? This was 1996, not 1876, after all.

Eurovision 1996 was won by Ireland, which gave the once-peripheral nation a record-busting sequence of four wins out of five (or four and a half wins, given that Secret Garden's Fionnuala Sherry had come from County Kildare). 'The Voice' was sung by former Anúna member Eimear (it's pronounced *Ee-ma*) Quinn and written by Brendan Graham, who thereby joined the elite double-winners songwriting group,* having also written 'Rock 'n' Roll Kids' in 1994. The lyrics talk of past pain, and the need to both remember that pain and transcend it if one truly wishes to find peace. The message was extraordinarily timely.

When this narrative last visited the UK province of Northern Ireland, it was to reveal an atmosphere of hatred and violence, psychotic in the 1970s, simmering in the 1980s. The nineties finally saw change. In 1993, a joint declaration had been issued by the British prime minister, John Major, and the Irish Taoiseach, Albert Reynolds,

---

* The others were Willy van Hemert (1957, 1959), Yves Dessca (1971, 1973), Johnny Logan (1987, 1992) and Rolf Løvland (1985, 1995).

renouncing both nations' theoretical claims on the province: its future was, instead, up to its inhabitants. In 1994 first Catholic then Protestant paramilitaries announced ceasefires. The much-discussed 'peace process' was becoming a reality. However, it then got bogged down in arguments about verifying the decommissioning of weapons. Some backsliding took place in 1996. The Provisional IRA detonated a bomb in London's Docklands, after which Sinn Fein, a party with links to the terrorists, was excluded from talks. 'The Voice' was a much-needed call to get the peace process moving again.

Meanwhile, European technology marched on. The results for Eurovision 1996 were beamed into a virtual studio. Presenter Ingvild Bryn was able to walk 'behind' a scoreboard that seemed to hover in space, while behind her was a virtual window into the 'Green Room', where we could see artists reacting to the latest allocation of points. Direct video links to the results announcers around Europe were shown on another part of the studio 'wall'.

More generally, the internet, whose public era had dawned back in 1991, was beginning to impact on ordinary citizens' lives. Nine million Europeans now had access to it. This figure was still overwhelmingly made up of business users, but 1996 saw AOL open up the net to private subscribers in Britain, Germany and France. And if you didn't have your own computer, you could go to a cybercafé: by June 1996, Paris had fifteen of these. We were becoming connected, in ways nobody could have dreamt of a few years before.

1997

Date: 3 May
Venue: The Point, Dublin
Winner: Katrina and the Waves, UK
Winning Song: 'Love Shine A Light'

Eurovision 1997 saw a runaway winner, Katrina and the Waves, from Britain (Katrina Leskanich, the lead singer, was the daughter of a US airman stationed in East Anglia). 'Love Shine A Light' is an anthem, the kind of song you stand and sway to while holding up a cigarette lighter.*

The song is often cited as the UK's best-ever Eurovision entry. It's certainly my personal favourite, by miles. And it was the performers' own, rather than chosen for them by the public or 'experts'. The powerful arrangement was by a friend of the band, Don Airey. Authenticity works in Eurovision.

Ireland's Marc Roberts came second with a rather tame ballad, prompting more mutterings about the unfairness of insisting on national languages in Eurovision: English was now the *lingua franca* of Europe – even the EU had dropped French as its main language – and entrants who could sing in it had an ever-increasing advantage. Having said that, 'Love Shine A Light' was the outstanding song of the contest. From the fourth sung bar on, Leskanich clearly loves performing the song, the way Agnetha and Anni-Frid did back in 1974.

---

* Assuming, of course, that you have a cigarette lighter. Over the last three decades, smoking has declined in Western Europe, especially Scandinavia – though not in Eastern Europe, where the habit has gained popularity. Lovers there can still turn the lights out and watch their cigarettes glow in the dark. In Britain, when Abba won Eurovision, 50 per cent of men and 40 per cent of women smoked. By 1997, the level for both sexes was 30 per cent. In 2017 it is around 20 per cent.

When asked to comment on her victory, Leskanich observed that it was the second landslide in a week. Two days before Eurovision, Tony Blair's 'New Labour' party had trounced John Major's Conservatives in the UK general election, gaining 41 per cent more votes than their rivals (Katrina and the Waves got 44 per cent more points than Marc Roberts).

The Blair victory marked a radical change in British life. New Labour was inclusive – there were twice as many women in the new parliament as the old one, and its approach to gay and other minority rights was much more liberal than its predecessor, which had passed a law in 1988 preventing local authorities from 'promoting homosexuality'. New Labour was pro-Europe, though still cautious about the euro. It was business-friendly but also seemed caring and compassionate. 'Love Shine A Light' resonates with this new mindset. It was originally written for the Samaritans, a charity that provides phone support for the suicidal.

Britain couldn't keep out of the headlines in 1997. On 31 August, Princess Diana was killed in a high-speed car crash in Paris. The outpouring of national grief, symbolized by the millions of flowers left at Buckingham and Kensington Palaces, caught the nation's stiff-upper-lip old guard totally by surprise.* Blair, by contrast, understood the new national mood instinctively, with a speech written that morning describing her as the 'People's Princess'.

Books paying tribute to Diana came out almost as quickly. If you went into a London bookstore to buy one, you might also have seen a newly published children's story called *Harry Potter and the Philosopher's Stone* – though you might also have missed it, as it was the first novel by an unknown author and the initial print run was 500 copies. Over the next decade, the book and its six follow-ups

---

* Two decades earlier, 'Swinging London' had temporarily wrong-footed the old guard, but not for long. In contrast, 1997 saw a more lasting revolution in the nation's sensibility.

would sweep Europe more fully than almost any other popular cultural phenomenon (The Beatles had been minority tastes in France and east of the Iron Curtain). Almost? No individual Potter book has come near the viewing figures for Eurovision. It is estimated that the seven books in the series have, in all, sold around 450 million copies, so that's about 64 million per book; audience estimates for each song contest now top 200 million.

Elsewhere in Eurovision 1997, Russia was represented by Alla Pugacheva, who was showing her years visually though not vocally: 'Prima Donna' was dated, but still a *tour de force* of showmanship.

Austria's Bettina Soriat came up with a line that probably wouldn't have got into the contest a decade earlier, complaining that her lover was too quick in bed.* Time was also the theme of the Netherlands' entry – nobody has enough nowadays – and of Germany's Bianca Shomberg, whose song was actually called 'Zeit' (Time).

It was appropriate. The pace of life seemed to be accelerating all round Europe, with economics growing and stock markets booming (a 'mini-crash' in October was soon reversed). Darlings of the market were new internet businesses. None of them was actually making a profit, but the argument ran that this was a race into uncharted but incredibly valuable territory; whoever rushed in most vigorously and staked out most ground (in terms of 'brand awareness') would later be able to reap huge rewards. Interest rates were low at the time, and borrowed money flowed into what became known as 'dotcom' start-ups.

Katrina and the Waves sang second to last in Eurovision 1997. Last to sing was Iceland's Paul Oscar. 'Min Hinsti Dans' (My Last Dance) was a dramatic farewell by a wealthy pleasure-seeker to that life, or maybe even to life itself. This was unusual enough for Eurovision, but the staging completely rewrote the contest's script.

---

* Lyrically, the 1990s saw Eurovision getting more daring. In 1994 France's Nina Morato had sung – or rather howled – *putain*, which can mean a range of things but in context clearly meant 'fuck'.

While a techno beat thumps away, Oscar, Eurovision's first openly gay contestant, is surrounded by four gorgeous but doped-looking women in PVC, boots and fishnet stockings, adopting a succession of poses with a suggestiveness that makes Gina G look homely. We are suddenly in a new world of sexual fantasy and fetishism, sex as power-play and transgression rather than just good old-fashioned 'naughty but nice' Euro-fun. Katrina and the Waves were the old post-Abba Eurovision at its best. A two-minute postcard later, here is a Eurovision that will emerge in the next decade.

Anyone familiar with the contest's fan base may be surprised that an openly gay artist had not appeared before. But even in 1997 most competing nations still reckoned that fielding such a competitor would damage their chances. In the host nation, Ireland, sex between consenting male adults had only been legal since 1993. In 1995, the highly respected annual BSA (British Social Attitudes) survey had shown that 44 per cent of the UK population still thought that sex between people of the same gender was 'always wrong', while only 22 per cent said 'not wrong at all'.

However, things were finally changing. 'Not wrong at all' would overtake 'always wrong' in the 2003 BSA survey, and by 2006 the figures would show 24 per cent condemnation and 38 per cent 'not wrong at all'.

Similar changes were taking place around Europe, though at different speeds. By 2005, when the European Social Survey asked for responses to the question 'Do you agree that gay men and lesbians should be free to live their own lives as they wish?', Holland and Scandinavia (excluding Finland) said a resounding 'yes' (over 85 per cent); most other Northern and Western European countries came in at around 75 per cent. Finland, the Czech Republic and Portugal were around 60 per cent; Slovenia, Greece and Hungary above 50 per cent; the rest of Eastern Europe around 45 per cent. Only about one-third agreed in Ukraine and Russia.

Eurovision!

After Paul Oscar had sung, it was time to vote. Televoting took place for the first time in Eurovision 1997. Five nations – the UK, Germany, Austria, Switzerland and Sweden – dispensed with juries and instead asked the public to phone in their chosen winners. Intriguingly, only one of these nations was an original 'Lugano 1956' EEC member, but four had belonged to the ill-fated EFTA. Make of this what you will: it can be argued that the centre countries tend to have a more top-down, experts-know-best culture – let the judges decide – while peripheral Britain and Scandinavia are more individualistic and democratic. What cannot be denied is the sheer technological achievement. In the UK, 250,000 votes were cast in the five minutes the lines were open. For viewers in these countries, another part of modern Eurovision was now in place.

The year ended with the signing of a new EU treaty in Amsterdam. This gave new powers to the European Parliament, putting it on an equal footing with the previously more powerful Council of Ministers. In theory this made 'Europe' more democratic, though this is only meaningful if people bother to vote in European elections and are given a genuinely broad range of political views to choose from. The treaty opened EU borders (with opt-outs for Britain and Ireland) and tried to simplify decision-making in EU institutions, with an eye to the future where new, Eastern nations – by now familiar faces in Eurovision – would at some time be joining.

1998

Date: 9 May
Venue: National Exhibition Centre, Birmingham, UK
Debut: Macedonia
Winner: Dana International, Israel
Winning Song: 'Diva'

The 1998 contest was much hyped in the media – or rather three contestants were, sharing different fates. Most memorable was Israel's Dana International, a transgender singer (she had undergone gender reassignment surgery in London in 1993). Her nomination as Israel's representative had been controversial back home, with members of the ultra-Orthodox Shas party calling her an 'abomination' and trying to prevent her being sent to Birmingham. She went, anyway, and on arrival received death threats. She defied these, sang her hi-NRG anthem 'Diva' and won.

Israelis of all sexual orientations celebrated. Her win was clearly a boost for gay culture, but Dana had stressed her national identity, too. The victory gave Israel much-needed PR, reminding the world that there was more to the country than its by now usual embattled, defensive image. However, the nation's political troubles remained. The Wye Deal, yet another attempted peace initiative between Israel and its Palestinian neighbours, was signed later in 1998 but quickly collapsed.

If Dana's win 'queered' the contest, using it to subvert conventional gender roles and narratives, Germany's Guildo Horn simply took the mickey out of it, tearing off various items of clothing, running into the audience, tousling Katie Boyle's hair and ending his set halfway up a gantry. His song 'Guildo Hat Euch Lieb' (Guildo Loves You) had *nul points* written all over it – but came seventh, beating a number of strong singers with reasonable songs.

Both Dana and Horn were shrewd users of the media – which mattered in Eurovision 1998, as televoting was now used by all participants except Cyprus and Hungary. A third contestant was not so shrewd. On winning her country's qualification heats, Switzerland's Gunvor Guggisberg had been feted by *Blick*, that nation's bestselling newspaper. But in the fortnight before the contest, *Blick* started running articles ripping her reputation to shreds. These increased in unpleasantness, and on the very morning of the contest, it ran a piece accusing her of having worked in a brothel. One has to admire her courage in going out to sing that evening, but it was in vain. 'Lass Ihn' (Let Him Go) was not a great song and Gunvor was no Céline Dion, but it and she didn't deserve the *nul points* they got. Such was the emerging power of the media, to take naïve, ostentatious people from obscurity, to build them up as 'celebrities', then to rip them down again in a vast, public and, inevitably, money-making (for the media) circus of humiliation.

There had, of course, always been 'celebrity' figures in European life – leaders, famous artists, movie stars – and media like *Paris Match*, *Bunte*, *Se og Hør* or *Oggi* to feature them. But the new era was generating a new type of celebrity, 'famous for being famous'. Such individuals are much easier to put through the build-'em-up, knock-'em-down mill than people of genuinely exceptional gifts, who always have their talent or achievements to fall back on.

New ways of generating willing fodder for this mill were emerging. Next year would see the start of Dutch company Endemol's *Big Brother* TV show, where 'ordinary' people are confined in a house and spied on by cameras, 24/7. The mill was ever busier, too. A survey of news media (in the US, but Europe followed this trend) showed that in 1985 coverage of news took 35 per cent of space and coverage of celebrities 4 per cent, but that by 2000 the figures were 29 per cent news and 8 per cent celebrity.

Eurovision!

Yet maybe that was what Europe wanted. The era also saw the consolidation of media ownership into fewer hands: hands that were ever less concerned about standards and ever more about profit. But profit means giving people what they want . . . So is democracy of taste a liberation from stuffy old elitism, or a new servitude to lowest-common-denominator mediocrity? In 1998 Eurovision was hurtling towards democracy, with the old, potentially elitist juries disappearing and continent-wide phone voting taking over. What would this experiment reveal?

The initial answer seemed to be 'not much'. Maybe the top-of-the-table songs were a bit more modern. There were two black artists in the top four. Did this show that the public were less prejudiced than the juries had been, or was this just a case of two good songs with good singers? The UK's Imaani Saleem was particularly impressive, producing that nation's third strong entry in a row: 'Where Are You?' came second.* Phone voting did little to change 'language bias', with English lyrics at positions two, three and nine, and the winning chorus of 'Diva' sung in fluent internationalese.

Amid the media noise, a new nation made its debut in 1998: Macedonia, with the brooding 'Ne Zori, Zoro' (Somebody Stop The Dawn). Macedonia was not allowed to call itself that, however, as Greece objected to the name, and Greece had got its foot into European institutions first. So Vlado Janevski sang for the 'Former Yugoslav Republic of Macedonia'. Parts of what used to be Macedonia lie in the modern country of Macedonia and parts of it

---

* The Brit-rot, however, would soon set in. Before 1998, the UK had only twice finished outside the top ten. After 1998, it would only twice finish *inside* the top ten, and would instead soon start racking up an embarrassing list of last or nearly-last places. Why? Critics of the contest say it was bloc voting once Europe's public was allowed to vote. British Eurosceptics add that this shows how unpopular Britain is in Europe. However a more likely explanation is the 1999 relaxation of the 'native language' rule, which took away the UK's advantage of singing in a language recognized around Europe. Ireland suffered a similar reversal of fortune at this time.

lie outside, largely in Greece. The Greeks object to the modern use of the name because they think it implies a territorial claim on their bit of former Macedonia. Modern Macedonian politicians deny this claim: they just want to use their country's name.

North of Macedonia, in Kosovo (still then a province of Serbia), the political situation was deteriorating. There had been tension in the region between ethnic Serbs and ethnic Albanians for centuries. In the 1990s the Serbs, despite constituting only around 10 per cent of the population, had the upper hand, controlling the media and education. In 1997, the collapse of order in neighbouring Albania led to an influx of weapons into the province. The stage was set for violent rebellion, and by 1998 this was escalating fast. By the time of the contest, the once-obscure KLA controlled around a third of the province: three weeks after it, the Serbs launched a counter-attack.

In September the bodies of an extended family of Albanian Kosovars were discovered near the village of Gornje Obrinje. A blood-spattered doll found with one of the murdered children became the defining image of the conflict. NATO threatened air strikes; a ceasefire was agreed, but that soon broke down; by the end of the year fighting had broken out again. In the new year, more talks took place at the beautiful Château de Rambouillet near Paris: more ceasefires, more subsequent breaches, more killing. In March 1999, NATO had had enough, and a bombing campaign against Serbia was begun.

In the same month, a 'Committee of Independent Experts' appointed by the European Parliament published its report on the European Commission, which since the retirement of Jacques Delors in 1995 had been led by Luxembourg's Jacques Santer. Tension between the Commission and the Parliament had been rising for a while: the Commission refused to share information with the Parliament, while the Parliament accused the Commission of arrogance and corruption. In 1998 a Commission official, Paul van Buitenen, blew the whistle on financial irregularities – and suffered the usual fate of such brave, conscientious individuals: dismissal and personal defamation. But he had been heard. The report was damning, saying of the Commission at one point: 'It is becoming difficult to find anyone who has even the slightest sense of responsibility.' The members of the Commission resigned shortly afterwards.

Europeans seemed relatively unfazed by these events. According to Eurobarometer, the European project had been losing popularity since the days of 'Insieme: 1992'. This trend actually came to a halt shortly before the time of the Santer fiasco (with levels around 50 per cent in favour of the EU and 15 per cent against: pretty much how things had been in 1980), and the figures would remain constant from then on. However, turnouts at European elections continued to fall. In the first European election, in 1979, turnout had been over 60 per cent across the (then) EEC. In 1994, that had slipped to 57 per cent. In 1999 it would fall to 49.5 per cent.

The concept of 'Europe' was changing, too. Eurovision led the way, with its Eastern accessions of 1993 and 1994. Now, political Europe would clearly soon be following it. On 19 April 1999, the German *Bundestag* (federal parliament) met for the first time in Berlin, making official the move of the new nation's capital from sleepy little Bonn. Europe's centre of gravity made a huge move to the East.

1999

Date: 29 May
Venue: Binyanei Ha-ouma Convention Centre, Jerusalem, Israel
Debut: None
Winner: Charlotte Nilsson, Sweden
Winning Song: 'Take Me To Your Heaven'

The 1999 contest saw two major changes in the rules. Singers were now allowed to use any language they wished, and they could also perform with no orchestra, just a pre-prepared backing track (Johnny Logan commented that this second change had reduced the contest to karaoke). Dispensing with the language rule opened the door to non-periphery winners, but removed some of the quirkiness and authenticity of the contest – a baton which would soon be taken up by the Liet Festival, of which more later.

A pre-contest poll was also taken on the now-booming internet to identify favourites – though it did not prove very accurate. It selected two songs, one of which came second last with two votes. But the net was here to stay. There were now over sixty million users in Europe, with Germany leading the way, followed by Britain, Italy and France. This represents an astonishing take-up since 1996: essentially, Europe had caught up with the USA. By 2014, some smaller European countries would have over 90 per cent 'internet penetration' (that means the percentage of people with access to the net, not what some of those people end up watching on it).

The 1999 contest was not a classic. Several singers had trouble with the sound system, meaning that they wandered off key. The English lyrics of many of the non-native English songs were banal (as were those of the native-speaking English ones, but there was nothing new in that). But the new language rule did allow new nations to appear at the top of the table. Sweden was back in business, and Iceland's techno 'All Out Of Luck' earned the far-northern island, and the lovely Selma Björnsdóttir, second place. Germany and Bosnia experimented with mixing languages – something judges and televoters both liked, putting these entries third and seventh.

The German entry had lyrical fun with their term for the game of 'musical chairs', 'Reise Nach Jerusalem' (Journey To Jerusalem), and broke that country's mould by featuring Turkish performers. This reflected a new national mood. In 1998, a Social Democrat/Green coalition, led by Gerhard Schröder, had replaced the last of the eighties/early nineties titans, Helmut Kohl. Marieluise Beck from the Green Party was made Commissioner for Migration, Refugees and Integration, and took a more positive, welcoming line with that nation's immigrant population, many of whom were second- or third-generation residents, but still found it hard to get formal German nationality.

France's entrant, Nayah, was a member of the *Mouvement Raëlien*, a cult whose members believe that humans were created by extraterrestrials who now come back and visit us in UFOs: a true citizen of the New Age. French officialdom has always had an uneasy relationship with alternative religions, and calls were made for her to be replaced as the national representative. She was – rightly, surely – allowed to sing on, though 'Je Veux Donner Ma Voix' (I Want To Give You My Voice) did not do well.

Songs in Eurovision 1999 were largely presented in a conventional way, with singers singing at us, sometimes with backing support discreetly tucked away behind microphones (Iceland winged out a bit and gave us two manic dancers in macs). It was left to Dana International to put on a truly extravagant show as the interval act.

On the twenty-fifth anniversary of Abba's victory, the eventual winner was, perhaps, fitting. The backing track to 'Take Me To Your

Eurovision!

Heaven' could have been borrowed from 'Waterloo'. Less fittingly for the anniversary of a runaway winner that became a Europe-wide hit, bloc voting was a feature of 1999. Academic treatises have been published on the subject – for example biologist Dr Derek Gatherer's, which coined the phrase 'eurovisiopsephology' (the study of Eurovision voting), in which, surely, Terry Wogan should have been given an honorary doctorate. Gatherer pointed out – and demonstrated mathematically – the formation of voting blocs in the late 1990s (televoting no doubt increased this phenomenon, though it has been in the contest arguably since the very first one). The most notable blocs were the 'Viking Empire' (Scandinavia and the Baltic states), the 'Balkan bloc', and those old favourites Greece and Cyprus. The start of the next decade would see the arrival of the 'Warsaw pact' group, initially featuring Latvia, Lithuania, Poland, Russia, Estonia and Romania, and later expanding to include other parts of the former Soviet Union. Eurovision shows that national and regional identity matters to people, as do surveys that we will look at later.

The final act of the contest – once Charlotte Nilsson had received her prize and Dana International had tried to steal the show by falling over when presenting it to her – was for all the contestants to join in singing 1979 winner 'Hallelujah', as a tribute to all the victims of the Balkan war.

That war was still going on as the contestants sang. Serbia was still refusing to quit Kosovo, and NATO was still carrying out air strikes to persuade it to change its mind. It would be another month before Slobodan Milošević accepted a peace plan to end the fighting.

Once he had done so, a joint NATO/Russian peacekeeping force entered Kosovo. There was little harmony between the new allies. Russia wanted autonomy and its own sector to occupy; NATO wanted overall command of a province-wide operation. This led to a race to control the airport at Pristina, the province's capital, which was won by the Russians. American NATO general Wesley Clark then ordered British forces to block the runway. The officer leading these forces queried the order, and was supported by his commander, General Mike Jackson. This officer was James Blount, who later became singer James Blunt, and is thus the only person both to avert a Third World War and have a platinum-selling album.

The decade ended with relative peace in the Balkans. It ended with shares in dotcom companies booming on Europe's stock markets. A 'millennium bug' that was supposed to wreak havoc on the continent's computers at midnight on 31 December had no effect at all, though the fuss about it did highlight how dependent on information technology our lives had become. The euro was now a reality, though not on the streets. It had been traded on global financial markets since 1 January 1999, as mandated by the Maastricht treaty. The currencies of eleven nations were locked to its value: the old centre countries of Lugano 1956 (less Switzerland) were joined by Austria, Spain, Finland, Ireland and Portugal. The Vatican and San Marino also participated.

Despite the East/West confrontation at Pristina airport, academics, especially in America, began to talk about 'the End of History'. Neoliberal economics and democratic government were now going to spread out across the world, Taking us to their Heaven slowly but benignly and inexorably.

The
2000s

2000

Date: 13 May
Venue: Globe Arena, Stockholm, Sweden
Debut: Latvia
Winner: The Olsen Brothers, Denmark
Winning Song: 'Fly On The Wings Of Love'

Eurovision opened the new millennium with ambition: the stadium was the biggest venue yet used for the contest, with an audience of 16,000. It was also the first Eurovision to be broadcast on the internet, though this was not a success: Europe's IT infrastructure was not yet up to the job. The bubble in internet-related stocks had popped a few months earlier, but figures for internet use around Europe kept rising: the net was here to stay.

Eurovision 2000 began in a youthful, albeit out of tune, manner, with a hi-NRG entry from Israel's Ping Pong, telling us to 'Be Happy'. The singers unfurled Israeli and Syrian flags at the end of their song. Most of the other contestants were young, too. Ines from Estonia sang of the adventure of being seventeen; Russia's Alsou, eager to go 'Solo', was a year younger. By contrast, Denmark's Olsen Brothers, Jørgen (aged fifty) and Niels (forty-seven), had been performing together since before most of the contestants were born. Their first band, The Kids, had supported The Kinks when the UK sixties supergroup played Copenhagen. In 2000 the likeable Danes had won their national heats with a song, written by themselves, called 'Smuk Som Et Stjerneskud' (As Beautiful As A Shooting Star), in praise of a woman who 'gets more beautiful year after year'. This beauty-in-middle-age theme was toned down for the new, English lyrics used in the final. A shame, in a contest that is often obsessed with youth.

Fourteen of the twenty-four songs were in English. Sadly, this meant overtime for George Orwell's *1984* 'versifier'. The clichés flowed thick and fast, and the subject matter of far too many songs was 'I fancy you', with no reflection, irony or poetry. All part of life, of course, but after the sixth repetition it gets a bit samey. Add to this odd phrasings and pronunciations from singers for whom English is not a native language, and you have a recipe for mediocrity.

Between the songs, postcards neatly stressed the interconnection of modern nations. After recording a scene of Swedish life, the camera would zoom in on some item in that scene that actually came from the country about to sing: an Amos Oz novel from Israel, lighting from Denmark, clocks from Switzerland (and so on).

When voting began, the Olsen Brothers stormed into the lead, and they kept it, pulling ever further ahead of the opposition. Jørgen became the first competitor aged over fifty to win.

Beneath them was a scoreboard that would have looked bizarre five years before. The north and east of Europe ruled (the top five entrants all had coastline on the Baltic Sea, as did the nation that came seventh). The old centre was slipping down the chart – the two entries in French were last and second-last. The most impressive singer in the contest was probably Switzerland's Jane Bogaert – who came twentieth. Germany alone defied the trend, with Stefan Raab taking the Guildo Horn route of poking fun at the contest (he had co-written Horn's 1998 entry) and coming fifth with 'Wadde Hadde Dudde Da' – the title comes from a comment overheard by Raab by an old lady to her dog which had just messed on the pavement. Dutch viewers did not see this turnabout, as that evening, an explosion killed twenty-three people at a fireworks distributor in the eastern city of Enschede, and NOS, the nation's broadcaster, pulled the show, feeling it was too light for such a solemn moment.

Two representatives of the old Yugoslavia sang in the contest, balladeer Goran Karan from Croatia and the bouncy but not very tuneful XXL from Macedonia. The terrible drama of that region was coming to its end. Elections in what was effectively Serbia (though it still called itself Yugoslavia) had been announced for 24 September. The main opposition parties teamed up to challenge the incumbent President Milošević. On 25 August, one of the main opposition figures, Ivan Stambolić, a former Milošević ally turned reformist, disappeared – it later turned out he had been murdered, almost undoubtedly on the president's orders.* The opposition went on to win the election but with less than half the votes, which would mean a rematch. Complaints were made, of vote-rigging . . .

Serbia had had enough. People took to the streets, chanting '*Gotov je!*' (He's finished!). A construction worker drove a heavy vehicle into the State TV building: the events of October 2000 became known as the Bulldozer Revolution. Milošević resigned two days later and Serbia began its journey towards modern nationhood – one that would soon include participation in Eurovision. In April next year, the ousted president would be arrested for war crimes.

One nation absent from Eurovision 2000 was Greece. That nation had other things on its mind. On 1 January 2001, it became the twelfth member of the euro club. Critics of this move pointed out that both Greece's inflation and its public sector debt were way beyond the official 'convergence criteria' that had been designed to keep unstable economies out of the new currency. But optimism was the order of the day. Greece met *some* of the Maastricht criteria, and, more important, it was eager to join.

In the same upbeat mood, 2000 saw the European Council produce its Lisbon Agenda. 'The Union has today set itself a new strategic goal for the next decade: to become the most competitive and dynamic knowledge-based economy in the world, capable of

---

* On 18 July 2005, a court in Belgrade found one of Milošević's paramilitary commanders and his former secret police chief guilty of the murder. It intended to then try the former president, but he died before this could happen.

sustainable economic growth with more and better jobs and greater social cohesion.'

While producing a number of sensible policy ideas – better education, more expenditure on research, less 'red tape' for business (especially smaller business) – the agenda didn't really explain how these would make Europe overtake the USA, Japan or China, who were also busting a gut to be biggest and best. More worrying still, it didn't explain what Europe had to do if faced with a choice between social cohesion and competitiveness. The agenda simply assumed that such a trade-off shouldn't be necessary.

A serious lack of realism seemed to be creeping into the European project. But maybe mood is what really matters. Let Ping Pong set the tone. Be happy!

2001

Date: 12 May
Venue: Parken Stadium, Copenhagen, Denmark
Winner: Tanel Padar and Dave Benton, Estonia
Winning Song: 'Everybody'

Literal-minded people had spent much of 1999 and 2000 pointing out to the rest of us that the millennium really began on 1 January 2001. For them, *this* was the first Eurovision of the new era.

Eurovision 2001 certainly had more of a 'start-of-an-era' feel to it than 2000. It was the biggest yet (and is still the biggest ever): Denmark stuck a roof over their national football stadium and made a venue for 38,000 fans. The first song of the contest, 'Out On My Own', by the Netherlands' Michelle, was about walking away from the past in a new spirit of freedom, though the song's restrained tone carried a measure of sadness. Freedom, we infer, comes at a cost.

Michelle later put her words into practice by marrying her girl-friend in 2006. The month before Eurovision 2001, the Netherlands had become the first nation in the world to allow same-sex couples formally to marry (the contest's host nation, Denmark, had instituted something similar, a 'registered partnership', back in 1989). Belgium would be next in 2003. The rest of Europe is still slowly catching up.

Twenty-two songs followed, many with soaring vocals over punchy, techno beats: Slovenia, Malta and Greece stand out. Russia's Mumiy Troll, from distant Vladivostok, went down a different route, indie rock (or 'rockapops' as the band, still big in Russia and the Far East, called their style). Lead singer Ilya Lagutenko brimmed with adolescent attitude. France also eschewed techno, and returned to its traditions with 'Je N'ai Que Mon Ame' (I Have Only My Soul).

Natasha St-Pier did the song proud, putting herself up there with the contest's classic francophone power balladeers: Vicky Leandros, Anne-Marie David, Marie Myriam, Corinne Hermès, Céline Dion (St-Pier is also from French Canada). Unlike them, she sang the last verse of her song in English. *Mon dieu!* Popular with the crowd was the final act of the night, Denmark's own Rollo and King, with their catchy 'Never Ever Let You Go'.

Denmark, France and Estonia featured well in the early voting, and Estonia eventually came out the winner. Tanel Padar and Dave Benton had also avoided techno, preferring to go back to late 1970s funk. The song was not that special, but it was performed with gusto, especially by Benton. His spontaneity was a contrast to the heavily choreographed stage shows of some other entrants, and voters seemed to warm to this. He took Jørgen Olsen's short-lived record for the oldest victor, and also became the first black contestant to win.

About time, too, given the contribution of black artists to European popular music. Can we read from this that there is still more racial prejudice in Europe than liberal optimists like to think? I trust Eurovision as a barometer, so must sadly admit that we probably have to.

In Eurovision's defence, there is now a growing list of non-whites who have done well in the contest. 2016 would see a Muslim winner and a second-place artist born in Korea. But pessimists on this topic argue that much racism is particularly directed at black people, so Jamala and Dami Im don't count.

Research carried out in 2013 by the World Values Survey, an institution based in Vienna, seems relevant here. People all round the world were asked if they would mind someone of a different race moving next door. Europeans came out pretty well from the survey, especially Northern Europe. Eastern Europe was less tolerant, especially the south-east. France doesn't look good. But Europe is still better than much of the rest of the world.* Thoughtful Europeans can take some comfort from this, while accepting that there is still much to do to make our continent a kinder, more civilized place.

But back to 2001 . . . The win was a triumph for the small Baltic state (it has a population of 1.3 million: on the list of European countries ranked by population, it comes forty-first). Ten years earlier Estonia had been an occupied 'republic' of the Soviet Union; in 2001 not only was it competing in Eurovision as a free, European nation, but it was winning. Centre, and even old-peripheral, nations can easily take their European identity for granted. Estonians do not. People partied all night in Tallinn after the win. Padar and Benton were welcomed by the country's prime minister, Mart Laar, when they returned from Copenhagen, with his promise: 'We will sing our way into Europe!'

The 2001 contest is one of my favourites, with exciting, energetic songs. This is despite the presenters, who spoke in arch rhyming couplets (Terry Wogan treated them with particular derision / but he'd long since stopped enjoying Eurovision). Technologically, another attempt was made to stream the contest live, but Europe's IT infrastructure was still not yet up to it. There were also facilities for viewers to go online and chat with the contestants: there is something both modern and ironic about the apparent intimacy of such chats and the actual impersonal vastness of the stadium where the contest was held.

Later in the year, three events took place that would mould Europe's new era. Maybe the pedants were right about 2001 being the start of the millennium.

Enough has been written of the 9/11 attacks in New York; I don't need to add anything here, except, perhaps, to point out that nationals of twenty Eurovision contestant nations died in

---

* The survey does not cover every country, in Europe or the world. But enough, I feel, to show patterns. See the reference at the back of this book for a link.

them, almost half (sixty-seven) from the UK. A great feeling of solidarity with America swept over Europe – '*Nous sommes tous Américains*' (We are all Americans) commented Paris newspaper *Le Monde* the next day. (More revolving sounds from a grave at Colombey-les-deux-Églises?)

Three months later, China joined the World Trade Organization. That nation's exports to the West had been quietly growing since it liberalized its economy back in 1978. They stalled a bit at the end of the 1990s, but the new decade would see them skyrocket. With seemingly boundless supplies of poorly paid labour and a currency kept cheap by its government, China began to drive European manufacturers out of business. That Lisbon Agenda aim of being both the world's most ruthlessly competitive economy and its cuddliest society was already beginning to look unachievable.

Finally, at the stroke of midnight on 31 December, the euro became the everyday currency in twelve European nations. In Germany, it became the only currency, though you could take your old deutschmarks to banks and change them (you still can). Elsewhere there was a two-month period when you could use both, though ATMs only dispensed euros and traders of all kinds were expected to give all change in the new currency. Despite complaints about prices being rounded up, the Euro's birth was essentially trouble-free.

The euro was justified on various economic grounds, such as ease of transactions and simplifying cross-border price comparison. But it had always meant more. On the day the new money hit the streets, Wim Duisenberg, the Governor of the European Central Bank, observed that the change was 'not only the completion of economic and monetary union . . . but one of the major, if not the major, steps forward in the history of European integration'.

2002

Date: 25 May
Venue: Saku Suurhall Arena, Tallinn, Estonia
Winner: Marie N, Latvia
Winning Song: 'I Wanna'

When the post-victory partying in Tallinn had died down, Estonian TV was left with a headache: could they afford to stage the 2002 contest? After some national soul-searching the answer was yes, Estonia could and must put on the show. It was all part of their new European status and their pride in that status. The decision was justified from the moment two presenters walked out onto the stage of Estonia's brand-new and largest venue and shouted 'Hello Europe!'

The contest's 'theme', an innovation in 2002, was 'A Modern Fairytale'. Fairytales are supposed to have happy endings, and Eurovision 2002 was a celebration of such a story, Estonia's freedom.

The contest produced some interesting controversies. A campaign had been launched to get Israel, represented in 2002 by a big star, Sarit Hadad, banned. It failed, but on the night, TV commentators in Sweden and Belgium actually asked people not to vote for 'Light A Candle'. 'She may be wearing white, but don't be fooled into thinking that Israel wants peace,' said the Belgian.

Tension between Israel and Palestine had been mounting since late 2000, when the peace process between the two nations had broken down. The tragic but oft-repeated cycle of atrocity and counter-atrocity had been ratcheting up since then, with youngsters killed by both sides, then suicide bombings, then Israeli military action. In May 2002, both the second Palestinian *intifada* and Israel's reaction to it were in full swing.

Slovenia was less used to controversy. But its 2002 entrant – selected by local juries – was Sestre, a drag act. When this was announced, anti-gay protesters took to the streets of Ljubljana. Slovenian TV changed its decision, and it was the turn of gay activists to hit the streets, flying a huge rainbow flag outside the TV station. The issue was raised in both the Slovenian and European parliaments. Dutch MEP Lousewies van der Laan commented that homophobia could not 'be deemed acceptable in a candidate to join the European Union'. The broadcaster reversed its decision, and Sestre went to Tallinn, where they came thirteenth.

As a sign of the times, both Britain and Spain featured artistes discovered via televised talent contests: *Pop Idol* in the UK and, from Spain, a special series designed to find the year's Eurovision contestant, *Operación Triunfo*. Both selections appeared to pay off. Britain's Jessica Garlick came third; no British entry has done as well since. Rosa López' performance was watched by more Spanish TV viewers than any other event, until that nation played in (and won) the 2008 European Cup Final. Plucked from obscurity by the contest, she went on to have a successful singing career. Talent contests, once regarded as cheesy, would loom big in European media from then on.

The contest was won by Marija Naumova, a Latvian jazz singer. 'I Wanna' often appears in polls of worst-ever Eurovision winners. Like the previous year's top song, its victory was more about the performance than the material: Naumova produced an immaculately choreographed show whereby she came on in a tuxedo and ended up in a long, flame-red dress. During the song she flirted with both female and male backing singers. The lyrics, especially the last line of the chorus, show the danger of singing in non-native languages. She wants to be the last *what* in my eyes? No, it's 'love spark', apparently.*

---

* Most Eurovision fans have their favourite easy-to-mishear lyrics. My personal fave comes from the previous year, when Malta's Fabrizio Faniello spent the second verse of

Eurovision!

France stood up for older traditions with a power ballad about peace, 'Il Faut Du Temps' (It Takes Time), and did well, coming fifth. But English did seem to be engulfing the competition. As a welcome contrast, a new contest for songs in European regional and minority languages was held around the same time as Eurovision. The first Liet International Festival took place in Leeuwarden in Friesland, near the northern coast of the Netherlands. Competitors sang in Catalan, Frisian, Breton, Sami, Basque, Gaelic, Kashubian (a Polish dialect), North Frisian, Occitan (from southern France/northern Spain and Italy) and Welsh. The winners were a duo from Catalonia. The contest was a success, and has been held annually from then on, apart from a break in 2013.

The Netherlands were not competing in Eurovision 2002, having finished too low in the previous year's contest. That was perhaps painful enough to this long-standing, eager competitor, but May saw the nation suffer another blow to its identity, when a Dutch politician was assassinated. In Holland you say what you think, to the point of tactlessness if necessary; you take similar criticism if it comes your way; you never doubt the other person's right to speak, however wrong they seem. Pim Fortuyn's anti-immigrant views were unattractive to many, but his silencing by the gun horrified Europe's most liberal nation. It was another blow, like Srebrenica. Conspiracy theories bubbled up briefly, but the assassin, as often happens, turned out to be a loner.

Violence was an underlying theme of the year. Events in Iraq were drifting towards war. American president George W. Bush was determined to remove Iraqi dictator Saddam Hussein, incorrectly believing he was in some way implicated in the 9/11 atrocity. Would Europe get embroiled in this conflict? America was stepping up the

---

'Another Summer Night' summoning up a picture of a scorching hot summer beach, then appeared to end it with 'And a snowman passing by'.

pressure. There was doubt that the United Nations would sanction an invasion, the way it had done in 1991. Instead, Bush sought to build a 'coalition of the willing'. However, in Europe, only Britain seemed seriously willing. The rest of the continent was split between half-hearted support and no support at all. Transatlantic relationships, warm after 9/11, were fast deteriorating.

This was not a good time for Europe-level government. There was no common position on Iraq. Fresh accusations of corruption began leaking out of Brussels. Earlier in the year, the Commission had appointed Marta Andreasen as its chief accountant. Andreasen soon found out that the accounts were a mess. Attempts to sort the matter internally failed, and she finally went public with her criticisms, which led to her dismissal for 'failure to show sufficient loyalty and respect'. Her tale, of corruption, smugness, sexism and bullying, did not reflect well on an institution that was supposed to lead, and thus exemplify the best values of, Europe.

Eurovision was coming in for criticism, too. The last two winners had been weak and had failed to sell on the streets. Was it, like the European Commission, losing touch?

2003

Date: 24 May
Venue: Skonto Olympic Hall, Riga, Latvia
Debut: Ukraine
Winner: Sertab Erener, Turkey
Winning Song: 'Everyway That I Can'

The 2003 contest took place in the shadow of a war. Militarily, the second Iraq war had been won by the time Marie N and Renars Kaupers welcomed Europe to Riga. But the real battle, to win the 'hearts and minds' of Iraqis, had only just begun.

The early months of 2003 had seen America pressing ever harder for European nations to join its coalition, but to little avail. George W. Bush is reputed to have phoned French president Jacques Chirac and told him that events were the fulfilment of a prophecy from Chapter 38 of the book of Ezekiel. Even despite this, Chirac did not alter his refusal either to participate in the coalition or vote for war in the United Nations.

On 15 February, huge anti-war demonstrations were held in major European cities. As many as three million people are rumoured to have taken to the streets of Rome; Madrid and London both probably saw a million protesters. The marches were notable for the wide range of people participating; not just political radicals but individuals from all walks of life felt an overriding need to speak up.

The mood was seized upon by philosophers Jürgen Habermas and Jacques Derrida, who wrote a paper that was published in the *Frankfurter Allgemeine Zeitung* entitled 'What binds Europeans together: a Plea for a common foreign Policy, beginning in the Core of Europe'. That last part is perhaps the most interesting. In their eyes, the Iraq war split Europe back into 'Lugano 1956', who are the true torchbearers of European civilization, and the rest, who aren't.

The piece is also notable for its uncompromisingly academic tone. Although it was published in the mainstream media and both authors were men of the left, neither seems to have been interested in addressing the ordinary, working man or woman in language they could understand. Their 'Europe' was an elite project. One can argue that most big projects are elite ones: they are usually driven by a small group of highly motivated, very able people. But in the end, they will fail if they cannot go on to involve the rest of us. Nations, for good or ill, are very good at that. Is political Europe?

Third, the piece is interesting because it shows a new mood of reflectiveness about questions of European identity. The war was making us look at ourselves again and ask, who are we and what do we believe?

I doubt that either Habermas or Derrida watched Eurovision 2003. If they had, they would have seen an interesting show. After two years of rather samey (though fun) techno, contestants were looking to be different. Belgium's Urban Trad sang their haunting, Celtic-influenced 'Sanomi' in a made-up language – and were rewarded for their imaginativeness with second place. Austria, as it often does, went left-field and produced joker Alf Poier making fun both of the contest and of humanity's attitudes to animals. Others turned off the synthesizers and just sang pleasant songs – I liked Malta's easy-listening 'To Dream Again', though not many other people did, as it came second last.

Media focus before the contest was on Russia's entrants, t.A.T.u.: two young women who arrived with a reputation for being shocking – a reputation that had sold a lot of records (their single, 'All The Things She Said', had reached number one around Europe in 2002). Part of their 'shock' was that they claimed to be lesbians, though by 2003 this was hardly radical in Eurovision – and they turned out to be heterosexual, anyway. In Riga, they behaved like spoilt teenagers, turning up late to rehearsals then complaining about the facilities. They threatened to sing their song naked, but actually performed in old jeans and T-shirts, thereby earning themselves the 2003 Barbara Dex award. The most shocking thing about t.A.T.u. turned out to be the quality of their performance. The crowd booed, partially no doubt because of Stalin but mostly because the duo had behaved like brats and put on a bad show. Their third place was a reward for pre-existing notoriety rather than for anything they brought to Latvia.

But perhaps they didn't want to bring anything to Latvia. There's a sense that t.A.T.u. was a giant V-sign from Russia to the West: 'You think you're so liberal – well, put up with this then!' Fifteen years ago, that nation had been a superpower. Now it was struggling to find its identity (and even its geographical boundaries – in 2003 it was at war with separatists in Chechnya). Fifteen years ago, it had claimed political and moral superiority to the West. Now its old ideology had been discredited and it was recovering from a financial crash (its government bonds had been rated as junk from 2000 to 2002). To add to its pain, Russia's old arch-enemy was now trampling round the Middle East, unchecked. And in Eurovision, the last two winners had come from countries which had once been part of its innermost empire and which now made no secret of their unmitigated delight that this was no longer the case. Ouch!

It is often said that the voting (which could, for the first time, be done by SMS) in 2003 was a European comment on the Iraq war. The UK, America's sidekick in the conflict, came last, getting *nul points* for the only time in its competition history. Turkey, which had resisted attempts to drag it into the coalition and had not allowed US forces an invasion route into northern Iraq, won.

It wasn't purely political. Britain's entry, 'Cry Baby', was dire, with the singers, Jemini, a boy/girl duo plucked from obscurity, hideously out of tune (to be fair, they had problems with the on-stage sound system, but one feels that a more experienced act would have overcome this). Victorious Turkey, on the other hand, set out to win. An established star, Sertab Erener, was chosen to represent them. She insisted on singing in English – an unpopular move back home, until her song won, after which all was forgiven. A lush pre-contest promo video set 'Everyway That I Can' in a harem, and an imaginative choreographic routine was built around her for the live performance. After the contest, the song sold well round Europe, reaching number one in Greece and Sweden as well as back home. It still does well in 'greatest ever Eurovision songs' polls, long after Turkey's stance on the Iraq war has been forgotten.

And yet . . . the 2003 contest does seem to come from a different, golden age, rather like that of 1956. In May 2003, most of Europe was distancing itself from America's adventure in Iraq. It was reaching out to an Islamic country, awarding first prize to a song steeped in that country's culture: 'Everyway' might have been in English, but its music and dance were thoroughly Turkish. An exciting new future beckoned,* with a friendly, confident, liberal Europe reaching out to the world.

But poison was seeping out of Iraq. The victorious coalition was not greeted by cheering crowds and spontaneous order but by looters and bombers. Liberation began to turn into occupation. As 2003 progressed, reports of US treatment of prisoners in Abu Ghraib prison began to emerge. The coalition's attempt to control the conquered country became a recruiting drive for militant Islamist organizations, as young men watched videos of the war over the internet. The ugliness

---

* 2003 also saw new beginnings for Eurovision, with the first Junior Song Contest, for singers aged between eight (later ten) and fifteen, held in Copenhagen in November of that year. It was won by Croatia's Dino Jelusić, who went on to have a successful international career as a rock singer. Since then, Junior Eurovision has remained a fertile hunting ground for peripheral nations. Georgia has won three times (including the 2016 contest). Malta and Belarus have both won twice. Britain's Cory Spedding came second in 2004, the UK's best result in any Eurovision contest this century.

of these organizations would become ever more apparent. In early 2004, a few terrorists – it only takes a few – let off a horrendous set of bombs on Spanish commuter trains. Later that year, a school in Beslan, in the south of Russia, would be attacked and nearly two hundred children killed.

The world, which had seemed to be coming closer together in liberal, democratic harmony, was suddenly becoming messy and scary again.

2004

Date of the final: 15 May
Venue: Abdi Ipecki Arena, Istanbul, Turkey
Debuts: Albania, Andorra, Belarus, Serbia/Montenegro
Winner: Ruslana, Ukraine
Winning Song: 'Wild Dances'

On 1 May, ten new states joined the EU: Cyprus, the Czech Republic, Estonia, Hungary, Latvia, Lithuania, Malta, Poland, Slovakia and Slovenia. The eight Eastern European countries became known as the 'A8'. If Frankfurt's philosophers wanted to concentrate on Lugano 1956 Europe, political reality was pushing in the opposite direction.

Eurovision was expanding, too. 2004 saw a record number of entries: thirty-six nations, all eager to join in and thus be European. A semi-final was held on the Wednesday before the Big Night. This featured nations who were neither one of the previous year's ten highest-placed finalists, nor the host, nor the 'Big Four' (Germany, France, Britain and Spain). The top ten songs from the semi would join the above in the final. Several Eurovision stalwarts failed to jump this hurdle: Israel, Denmark, Portugal, as well as new stars Estonia and Latvia.

The contest stayed peripheral, too – this time, it was hosted by long-term EU aspirant Turkey. The contest's slogan was 'Under the Same Sky', a hint to negotiators in Brussels (and a quote from 1990's hymn to political Europe, 'Insieme: 1992'). The nation's prime minister, Recep Tayyip Erdogan, was among the enthusiastic, 12,500-strong audience. Eurovision mattered.

A better slogan for the contest would probably have been the name of the eventual winning song, as 2004 was the year that choreography took over from singing. Much of that choreography was sexually explicit, with pawing and pelvic thrusting and plenty of thighs, cleavages, rippling pecs and six-packs on show. Several contestants seemed to have got their outfits from Ann Summers.

This might lead one to assume a certain dimwittedness about the event, but, as usual, there is more to Eurovision than meets the eye or ear. The winner, Ruslana, who bounded onstage clad in (not a lot of) leather, was a classically trained musician who later went on to become a serious politician and social activist. She co-wrote 'Wild Dances' and plays the drums on the backing track; while she clearly had one eye on modern Eurovision trends, the piece reflects a long-standing interest in her country's traditional folk culture, especially that of the Carpathian mountains where she grew up.

Ukraine's Eurovision win coincided with its arrival on the European political stage. After breaking from the Soviet Union, it had suffered a major economic collapse in the mid-1990s, but by the end of the decade, things had picked up. Voices then began to be raised about its leadership. An investigative journalist was murdered in 2000. A tape of President Leonid Kuchma revealed him to be doing deals with Iraqi dictator Saddam Hussein. In the 2004 presidential election, Kuchma was not eligible, so his prime minister Viktor Yanukovytch stood.

Yanukovytch's opponent was Viktor Yushchenko, a former finance minister who favoured closer links with Europe. During the campaign, Yushchenko developed a mysterious and debilitating illness – most likely a result of dioxin poisoning, which, if true, means that a deliberate attempt was made to kill him. The election appeared to be won by Yanukovytch, but few people apart from his core supporters believed the results to be fair. Ukraine took to the streets despite the midwinter weather. Huge rallies were addressed by opposition politicians – including Ruslana, who soon became a key figure in the opposition movement. The Orange Revolution was under way.

Eurovision!

On 26 December, Ukraine's Supreme Court declared the election void and ordered a fresh one, which was held in January 2005. It was won by Yushchenko and his Our Ukraine Party. Ruslana became a member of the Ukrainian parliament for that party.

The Orange Revolution was at least partially about removing a corrupt administration. But it was also about belonging. A look at political voting patterns reveals trouble in store for Eurovision's 2004 winner. It shows a country facing two ways, its east towards Russia, its west towards Europe.

Another country placed on the European map by the 2004 contest was Serbia. We left this country having finally ousted Slobodan Milošević. In 2003, now known as Serbia and Montenegro, it had begun its application to join the EU. In the same year, its prime minister had been murdered, part of a conspiracy by old-guard loyalists and organized crime. However, the assassination made Europe-friendly liberals more determined than ever to move on from the past. The country's debut in Eurovision 2004 was a sign of this – and was rewarded with second place. Željko Joksimović's 'Lane Moje' (My Sweetheart) was a powerful contrast to the winner, melancholy and gentle (though it shares with 'Wild Dances' musical influences from its country's folk traditions).

Greece came third, courtesy of heartthrob Sakis Rouvas' 'Shake It'. Later in 2004, that nation would host an impressive Olympic Games, another apparent triumph for Eastern Europe.

The other results from Eurovision 2004 reflected this new, eastern bullishness, too. Of the top nine countries, only Germany and Sweden were not located in or around the Balkans. Of the top fourteen, ten were Balkan/eastern Mediterranean. 'Old Eurovision' – France (despite featuring a bizarre lady on stilts), the UK, the Netherlands, Austria, Belgium, Ireland, Norway – languished at the bottom.

Old Europe was further embarrassed by the publication in November of a report by Dutch politician Wim Kok on the EU's progress – or rather lack of progress – towards the goals outlined in the 2000 Lisbon Agenda. Europe was not becoming the world's most dynamic economy. Instead, other economies were surging past it: China, India, even the EU founding fathers' old foe, the USA. More depressing still, the report didn't question the agenda or the realism of its goals, it simply berated European governments for not fulfilling it properly.

Around the same time, Greece admitted to having fudged the figures that allowed it to join the euro. It could hardly be thrown out, so nothing was done. Nothing was done, either, when France announced that it had broken the Maastricht rules. Europe's economy was doing OK. Perhaps the rules weren't needed anyway . . .

Arguably a more pressing concern for political Europe was the continuing lack of public identification with it. While people generally accepted the EU, they felt little passion for it. Back in 1992, Eurobarometer had asked people around Europe how they saw themselves. Were they European, national, or a mixture of both? The replies had been:

- purely European and not national at all – 4 per cent
- European first and national second – 7 per cent
- national first and European second – 48 per cent
- purely national and not European at all – 38 per cent

By 2004, these figures . . .

. . . were almost exactly the same. More than a decade of European flags, anthems, a Treaty on European Union, the introduction of the euro, the Lisbon Agenda, etc., had had no effect at all on Europeans' perception of who at heart they were.

The 2004 findings were reported by Eurobarometer as good news. Look how many people see themselves as (in some way or other) European: 62 per cent! But by the same criteria, 96 per cent saw themselves as in some way national.

It is also interesting to see the breakdown *by nation* of these figures (this data comes from Neil Fligstein's excellent book, *Euroclash*).

Eurovision!

The most Europhile EU member in (pre-accession) 2004 was Luxembourg. Its citizens saw themselves as:
- purely European and not national at all – 19 per cent
- European first and national second – 12 per cent
- national first and European second – 41 per cent
- purely national and not European at all – 28 per cent

So even Luxembourgers were more national- than European-minded.

No other EU member had double-figure percentages in either of the first two categories. The core, 'Lugano 1956' countries were less purely national-minded than the periphery (scores in the 'purely national' column were Italy 29 per cent, France 30 per cent, Germany 35 per cent, Belgium 40 per cent). At the other end of the scale, most Scandinavians still saw themselves as purely national (Sweden 58 per cent, Finland 60 per cent). And guess which nation was most Eurosceptic of all ...
- purely European and not national at all – 4 per cent
- European first and national second – 4 per cent
- national first and European second – 27 per cent
- purely national and not European at all – 65 per cent

That was, of course, the UK.

Fligstein went on to analyse support for 'Europe' among the various social classes, and found that it dwindled as you went down the social ladder. This seemed to be true across the continent, not just in the more sceptical nations. (There was one piece of good news for Europhiles: younger people were more positive about the EU than their elders. Maybe the European project will take generations, rather than decades, to take root.)

Eurovision is sometimes derided as being 'nationalistic'. But so, it seems from the above data, are we – at the moment, anyway. That's partly why so many of us watch the contest.

Is this a bad thing? I think it depends how you 'do' nationalism. Nationalism à la Eurovision is gentle. It is a nationalism of enjoyment and participation, that does not seek to demean or disrespect others but welcomes different cultures and celebrates with them. We're there waving our flags, but so is everyone else, and we're really all there for a big party. Two things would destroy that party. One would be if some (or all) participants became aggressively, unpleasantly nationalistic. But another would be if national pride disappeared, if we all became cut-out model 'Europeans', ashamed of our different histories, traditions and identities.

2005

Date of the final: 21 May
Venue: Palace of Sports, Kyiv, Ukraine
Debuts: Bulgaria, Moldova
Winner: Helena Paparizou, Greece
Winning Song: 'My Number One'

Ukraine's hosting of Eurovision 2005 was another example of the contest blazing a trail for European modernity beyond the continent's traditional boundaries. A lasting legacy of this was the nation's visa policy. In order to make it easy for people to attend the event, Ukraine temporarily dropped its visa requirements for visitors from Europe and, while they were about it, North America. The plan was to reintroduce them once the circus had left town, but the removal proved so popular with local business leaders that it was made permanent.

The slogan for the contest was 'Awakening'. It was certainly very loud. Rock and punk found their way into the repertoire ('Rock is the new *schlager*,' proclaimed Norway's glam-rock entrants Wig Wam). Most of all 2005 was the year of onstage percussion. This took an intriguing range of forms, from Romanian oil drums to a smiling elderly lady tapping a traditional *doba* during Moldova's anarchic entry. Over many of the beats, folk instruments twirled, taking Eurovision audiences to new Balkan and Middle Eastern musical worlds. By contrast, a few balladeers stuck to their guns, standing and singing and being well rewarded: Chiara from Malta came second and Israel's Shiri Maimon fourth. Choreography triumphed in the end, however, with Helena Paparizou's stage show (literally, at one point) lifting her to become Europe's number one.

Lyrically, much of what was on offer was bland – but there were some exceptions, mostly towards the end of the evening. Walters and Kazha, two young Latvians, sang 'The War Is Not Over'. The lyric contained a dig at the 'fairytale' theme of Estonia's 2002 Eurovision. The Cold War might be history, but life remained tough. France's Ortal Malka knew why: in the modern world, 'Chacun Pense À Soi' (Everyone Thinks Of Themselves). Russia agreed: the dream offered by 'sweet America' had disappeared, according to Natalia Podolskaya – who then went on to reference the victim of a serial child killer.

More obvious politics came from the hosts, for whom GreenJolly half-sang, half-rapped a street anthem from the Orange Revolution, 'Razom Nas Bahato' (Together We Are Many). This entry itself was controversial – aren't Eurovision songs supposed to be non-political? Another Ukrainian singer, Ani Lorak, who happened to be a supporter of the old regime, had been pushed aside at the last minute to allow GreenJolly to participate. 'Razom' was, sadly, not very melodious, and finished way down the table – a disappointment, no doubt, for President Yushchenko, who at the end of the contest presented the winner with a special award (though he probably enjoyed kissing Helena Paparizou more than he would have Roman Kalyn, GreenJolly's stocky, crop-haired lead vocalist).

Perhaps the most intriguing thing about the lyrics of 2005 was their tendency to concentrate on the obsessional aspects of love: love as fantasy, love as a drug. Together with the pouting and posing of many of the acts, the spirit of Paul Oscar's 1997 'Final Dance' seemed to have won the day.

It was a timely metaphor. Europe was beginning to dope itself up with credit. Within the Eurozone, countries that had traditionally had to pay high rates of interest on loans, because they had been considered weak economically, suddenly found themselves able to borrow in the new currency at low rates. So that's what they did. Governments such as Portugal and Greece borrowed, borrowed, borrowed to keep sleepy public sectors chugging along. Banks in Ireland and Spanish regional banks lent, lent, lent to property speculators.

Outside the Eurozone, British banks were perhaps the daftest of the lot, both lending irresponsibly and, intoxicated with 'sweet America's dream', trading new financial products that they did not understand in the bizarre belief that these 'derivatives' would somehow automatically find realistic prices.

One exception to this folly was Germany, a nation traditionally obsessed with keeping its economic house in order. Perhaps as a punishment for not joining the credit-addicts club (or perhaps because their song wasn't very good), that nation was awarded the wooden spoon in Eurovision 2005 – to which the singer, Gracia, philosophically observed, 'Well, somebody has to come last.'

The German economy seemed to be in the doldrums, too, with slow growth and uncharacteristically low levels of investment. People were smugly talking about the continent's former economic powerhouse as 'the sick man of Europe' – though in fact all it was doing was staying off the steroids. It would not be long before that tune changed. In September 2005, the person to bring the change about came to power: Angela Merkel, a former chemistry student from the *Land* of Brandenburg in the old GDR. She would soon outshine even Helmut Kohl (and Helena Paparizou) in being Europe's number one.

European leaders had been working on a European constitution since 2001. By the end of 2004 they had agreed on its contents and signed a treaty bringing it into being, once it had been ratified by member nations. Ratification can take several forms. Usually a vote in that nation's parliament is enough, but seven European countries decided this was so important that a national public vote was required. Shortly after Eurovision 2005, the people of France went to the polls, and rejected the constitution by 55 per cent to 45 per cent (a relative of Ortal Malka's reportedly voted *non* because her song did so badly in

Eurovision – it came second last). The Netherlands followed, even less enthusiastic: no, by 61 per cent to 39 per cent. Only one more vote was taken, in Luxembourg, where it, predictably perhaps, won, but by that time the European constitution was dead. Federalists were shocked. If they had studied the figures cited in the last section they would have been less so.

Voting of a less political kind took place on 22 October, when a special programme, *Congratulations*, was broadcast from Copenhagen to celebrate fifty Eurovision Song Contests (Euro-sulky Britain and snobby France didn't bother to broadcast it). Viewers were polled for their favourite Eurovision song of all time. To create a bit of suspense – well, a tiny bit, anyway – I've put the results in an appendix.

2006

Date of the final: 20 May
Venue: OAKA Olympic Arena, Athens, Greece
Debuts: Armenia
Winner: Lordi, Finland
Winning Song: 'Hard Rock Hallelujah'

In Eurovision 2006, thirty-seven nations competed, from tiny Andorra, who gave us four backing singers in stockings and suspenders, to vast Russia, with three ballerinas, one of whom seemed to have got stuck in a piano. In contrast with the previous two years, a wide range of musical styles was on offer. There was comedy from Iceland (even though it backfired: lots of people didn't get the joke and thought that Silvia Night, a caricature materialistic narcissistic young woman created by actress Ágústa Eva Erlendsdóttir, was genuine). There was a cappella from Latvia, a football chant from Lithuania's LT United, country and western (plus Stetsons and onstage cacti) from Germany, a poppy girl band from Spain, rap from the UK's Daz Sampson, techno from Romania, beautiful *sevdah* from Bosnia, and, of course, Gothic metal from Finland.

Other nations went back to their Eurovision roots – a singer plus violins for Norway, ballads from Ireland and France, an Abba-like entry from Sweden. Greece put on a superb show, to match the extravaganzas of the late 1990s. It was all great fun. Critics of Eurovision say it is 'formulaic', but looking through the varied entrants from 2006 shows that this isn't true. This contest was about Europe's diversity.

It showed old traditions. The first record of a *sevdah* song goes back to 1475. The Bosnian genre, one of melancholy love songs, has influences from Turkey and both Jewish and Islamic Spain.* It showed new traditions. Metal has become a part of Nordic life, not to everyone's taste but a passion for some. It showed cross-cultural borrowing. Romania's Mihai Traistariu sang his catchy chorus in Italian: 'Tornerò' (I Will Return) came fourth in the contest and became popular around Europe.

Russia stopped stirring, took Eurovision at face value, and nearly won. It sent an established star, Dima Bilan, singing an attractive ballad, 'Never Let You Go'. This reflected a new mood in the land of past European cultural giants, of Tchaikovsky, Tolstoy and Stravinsky. It seemed at last to want a place in modern political Europe.

Geographers have traditionally split Russia in two, calling the 38 per cent of the country west of the crest of the Ural Mountains 'European' – a minority of its space, but home to 77 per cent of its people. The Russians themselves have been more ambivalent about being European, in both imperial and Soviet times often using the term 'European Russia' for subject states like Ukraine and Belarus. But in 2006, there seemed little ambivalence: the Bear wanted in, and a Eurovision win would help.

It didn't get one, however. An old adversary, Finland, pushed it firmly into second place. The victory of 'Hard Rock Hallelujah' was seen as a national triumph. 'Years of humiliation, frustration, and "zero points" were wiped away,' said one Helsinki newspaper (forty-three years to be precise, the longest time any nation has gone in the contest before winning). The Finnish prime minister suddenly announced he was a fan of heavy rock. An estimated 100,000 Finns attended a rally to welcome the winners to the capital (the city's population is half a million). A square was named after them in Rovaniemi, home town

---

* The word *sevdah* also means a particular feeling: that mixture of sadness and joy that comes from looking back at past happiness, especially in a relationship that has ended. It is untranslatable into English, though the poet Tennyson understood it when he wrote "Tis better to have loved and lost, than never to have loved at all'.

of lead singer Mr Lordi. Pepsi started marketing Lordi Cola. It was announced that the band would feature on a commemorative stamp (the odd, cloud-shaped stamps appeared in 2007, to celebrate the holding of that year's contest in Helsinki).

Who says Eurovision is just a TV show?

It wasn't just a win, either, but a very Finnish win. The band's monster outfits and Mr Lordi's autobiography (he is the son of a troll and a demon, and rides a sleigh pulled by vampire reindeer) resonate with the violent, mystical world of the great Scandinavian myths. Finland had tried paying tribute to this tradition before in the contest, back in 1977, but 'Lapponia' had pulled too many punches. Lordi did it the Eurovision way: go for broke!

At the same time, 2006 showed Eurovision's odd ability to spot-light countries where interesting things are happening. In 1997, 18 per cent of the population of the developed world owned a mobile phone. Ten years later there was a mobile for *every* citizen: no doubt some were owned by businesses, but the increase is still astonishing. Even more remarkable, in 2006 almost half these phones were made in Finland – by one company, Nokia. The 2000s was the decade that the western world 'went mobile', and it was Finland that drove the change, not the US or Japan. The year after Lordi's win, Nokia's turn-over would peak at 51 billion euros – about one-fifth of the entire nation's GDP.

It didn't last. Sales began to plummet in 2009, due to competition from the new iPhone. In that year Finland came last in Eurovision, with a song called 'Lose Control'.

'Hard Rock Hallelujah' followed 'Everyway That I Can' and 'Wild Dances' in presenting Europe with splendidly dramatized visions of its periphery. Yet for one of those nations, the new sense of belonging was already beginning to decay. Negotiations about Turkey's accession to the EU stalled in 2006. The main reason was the continuing stalemate over Cyprus, but behind that was a lingering lack of political will in

Europe. In 2007 French presidential candidate Nicolas Sarkozy would claim, 'Turkey has no place in the European Union.' In Turkey itself, the old aims of Europeanization inherited from Kemal Ataturk – and celebrated (or was it parodied?) by Çetin Alp – were beginning to be questioned. Would Turkey, such an eager Eurovision host in 2004, be better off pursuing a 'neo-Ottoman' agenda, forgetting Europe and concentrating on its relations with members of its former empire?

Back in core Europe, a (relatively) old institution was notching up a success. The European Space Agency had been founded in 1975. Its founder members were the same nations who had been part of the third Eurovision Song Contest in 1958 (minus Austria) – Hilversum Europe, not Lugano. In 2006 its VEX spacecraft arrived at its destination and went into orbit, examining a planet's atmosphere – it is still there, sending back information. That planet, appropriate given the subject matter of most Eurovision songs, is Venus.

2007

Date of the final: 12 May
Venue: Hartwall Areena, Helsinki, Finland
Debuts: Czech Republic, Georgia, Montenegro, Serbia (as solo nation)
Winner: Maria Šerifović, Serbia
Winning Song: 'Molitva' (Prayer)

This contest, more than any other, represented the Triumph of the East. The results table divides very simply. The top fifteen songs are all from the eastern half of the continent. The next three are classic Baltic bloc members. The bottom six are old Europe. This, many people argued, was the end of Eurovision as a song contest; with expansion and televoting, they said, the event had degenerated into an exercise in regional back-scratching. A group of British MPs tabled a motion in parliament, saying that the contest had 'become a joke' as countries voted on 'narrow nationalistic grounds', and calling for the BBC to either renegotiate the rules or pull out (sound familiar?).

The trouble with this line is that if you listen to the songs, the Eastern ones are, by and large, much better. Old Europe offers cliché and/or rather soggy camp; it's the songs from the East that are (with a few grim exceptions) impassioned and imaginative. If you look at the performers, it is the ones from the East who have studied classical music and/or already have big followings. It's the West that wheels out the cruise-ship entertainers and thinks a little pre-contest PR will make Europe, old and new, love them.

'Water', a piece of tribal trance from Bulgaria's Elitsa Todorova and Stoyan Yankoulov, might not be to everyone's taste (I love it), but it takes risks and is performed with passion by two serious musicians (Yankoulov is a superb jazz drummer). Compare that with the UK's feeble and pointless 'Flying The Flag For You', from the nation that had once gifted Europe (and the world) The Beatles, Cream and The Kinks.

From elsewhere in the East, Hungary's Magdi Rusza gave us Janis Joplin-esque blues (and for the first time the word 'evanescent' appeared in a Eurovision lyric). Slovenia produced opera: Alenka Gotar was an experienced classical soloist – she had played Pamina in Mozart's *Magic Flute*, his most Eurovision-like opera. There was mighty Gothic rock from Moldova. The song that won, from Serbia, newly split from Montenegro and appearing for the first time as itself, was a beautiful ballad sung with great intensity.

Just like Lordi, winner Maria Šerifović received a tumultuous welcome on her return to her home country. 'This is a new chapter for a new Serbia,' she told a crowd of fifty thousand people. The old Serbia had not exactly been kind to Šerifović, with the popular press criticizing both her Roma roots and her assumed sexual orientation (not exactly hidden by her stage show, although she did not come out until 2014), but she rose above this.

The old Serbia had also been rattling its sabre politically, with the speaker of the nation's parliament calling for an end to rapprochement with the West. Šerifović's win changed the mood at once. The speaker resigned and the anti-Western rhetoric abated. Europe welcomed the win, EU Enlargement Commissioner Olli Rehn commenting that it was 'a European vote for a European Serbia'. On 13 June, the EU reopened its accession talks with the Eurovision winner, which had stalled over the issue of Serbia's apparent reluctance to arrest accused war criminals. Šerifović was made an EU 'ambassador for intercultural dialogue' – possibly not the wisest appointment, as tact is not one of her virtues.*

---

* Šerifović didn't exactly delight the Finns with her post-victory description of them as 'yellowish, see-through people' – though she later claimed this was a joke, as she was fed up with being asked how she liked Finland. The three-fingered salute she was seen giving in the Green Room as her votes ramped up was tactless, too: a relic of Milošević-era Serb nationalism.

Eurovision!

However the new, European Serbia was soon in for a test: next February, the Assembly of Kosovo would declare independence. How would the province's old master react?

Second to Šerifović's *cri de coeur* was a splendidly different piece, 'Dancing Lasha Tumbai' from Ukraine's Verka Sedushka, a comically vulgar lady railway sleeping car attendant created by actor Andriy Danylko. The lyrics are essentially nonsense, though 'Lasha Tumbai' sounds a lot like 'Russia Goodbye' – the way Sedushka sings it, anyway. When questioned about this, Danylko kept a straight face and said the words are actually Mongolian for whipped cream. (Don't try asking for *lasha tumbai* in your coffee next time you're in Ulan Bataar, however. The actual phrase is *tashuurduulj tos*.)

Ukraine itself remained a divided nation. In a snap presidential election in September 2007, the eastern half of the country voted for the party of Russophile Viktor Yanukovytch, while the west voted *Lasha Tumbai* and supported Europhile Yulia Tymoshenko (who won by a narrow margin).

Whatever Viktor Yanukovytch wanted, political Europe was edging closer to Ukraine, with Bulgaria and Romania members of the EU since the start of 2007. In Eurovision, Romania celebrated its new status by fielding a weak entry and came near the bottom of the 'eastern fifteen'. Bulgaria, however, came fifth. 'We love you, Europe,' called out Stoyan Yankoulov at the end of his piece.

While these countries were keen to join Europe, a mood of disenchantment about the EU was beginning to build among its older members. In May 2007, Toto Cutugno was booed by an audience in Valletta when he announced he was going to sing 'Insieme: 1992'. Later that year, on 8 September, Italian comedian and activist Beppe Grillo held *Vaffanculo* Day. *Vaffanculo* means 'fuck off' (well, literally 'go and do it up the arse'). One of the institutions being told to do so was the EU. Grillo addressed an estimated 100,000 people at a rally in Bologna that day. The Five Star Movement, which grew out of this, was a serious political organization which got over eight million votes in Italy's 2013 election, making it the country's third biggest party.

Grillo had other targets, especially the elite of his own country, which he believed to be irredeemably corrupt. But the EU was seen as part of that corruption. The Five Star Movement wanted, and still wants, out.

In response to these signals, Brussels did little. Instead, it decided to put (or 'sneak' if you are a Eurosceptic) chunks of the recently rejected constitution into a treaty. This was finally signed by leaders of most EU states – Britain's Gordon Brown missed the signing – in Lisbon in December.

The Lisbon Treaty extended majority voting to more areas of EU business. It formally incorporated a Charter of Fundamental Rights into EU law. It allowed opt-outs from certain of these changes for more Eurosceptic countries like Poland and Britain. It created two new key roles. One was a 'High Representative of the Union for Foreign Affairs and Security Policy': an EU foreign minister. The other was a European president – or rather another one, as the EU already had a clutch of presidents, the most important being those of the Commission and of the Parliament. This new president was of the European Council.

The Council had had presidents before, but only on a 'rotating' six-month basis. This job was more permanent, and went beyond running the Council. The incumbent would be a kind of EU head of state, the public face of the EU.

Finally, the treaty created a formal mechanism whereby a nation could leave the EU. No such mechanism had existed before. The only countries to have left were those who had gained independence from existing members of the old EEC: Algeria back in 1962 and Greenland in 1985. But would any actual member use the new 'Article 50'? Surely not . . .

Eurovision!

Unsurprisingly, the new treaty was criticized by Eurosceptics. In 2008, Irish voters refused to ratify it.

But it wasn't all Euro-gloom. In December, the Czech Republic, Estonia, Hungary, Latvia, Lithuania, Malta, Poland, Slovakia and Slovenia all joined the Schengen border-free zone. Eastern Europe was becoming an integral part of Europe, and bringing gifts to the table. The 2007 Eurovision Song Contest was a celebration of this fact.

2008

Date of the final: 24 May
Venue: Belgrade Arena, Belgrade, Serbia
Debuts: Azerbaijan, San Marino
Winner: Dima Bilan, Russia
Winning Song: 'Believe'

The 2008 final nearly had to be relocated, as in February of that year, rioting broke out on the streets of Belgrade in protest at Kosovo's declaration of independence. On 21 February, a group from a mass 'Kosovo is Serbia' rally in the city broke off and attacked the embassies of some countries thought to support Kosovan independence, including near neighbours Slovenia. It was felt that the Belgrade authorities had not done enough to prevent the attacks, and the EU stopped its accession talks with Serbia. However this was 2008, not 1999. The violence was brought under control. While discontent simmered in the north of Kosovo, where most of the province's Serbs live, the Serbian capital became peaceful again. Eurovision went ahead.

Instead of going to war, Serbia smuggled a reference to Kosovo into its rather beautiful 'Oro' (*Oro* is a Balkan circle dance, similar to the Israeli *Hora* celebrated in that nation's 1982 Eurovision entry). 'Wake me up on St Vitus' day,' sings Jelena Tomašević. As every Serb, but no EBU official, knows, St Vitus' day, 28 June, is the anniversary of the Battle of Kosovo in 1389, when a Serb army took on the invading Ottoman Turks. Serbia effectively lost – both armies were almost wiped out, but the encounter exhausted Serbia, while the much larger Ottoman Empire was able to call on new forces and, after a pause, push west again. Despite this, the battle is seen as the event that created the modern Serbian nation. The location of the battlefield, a few kilometres north-west of Pristina, is a major cause of Serbia's determination to hold onto the province.

Politics also found its way into Georgia's entry, 'Peace Will Come'. Diana Gurtskaya sang that her land was 'torn in half'. The two halves were Georgia itself and two breakaway regions, Abkhazia and South Ossetia, who wanted independence and close links with Russia. There had been a vicious war in 1992–3, especially in Abkhazia, where ethnic Georgian inhabitants had been massacred. Peace of a kind had then been brokered by international institutions, but it had remained fragile. In 2008, Russia began ramping up the rhetoric, insisting the two areas should have their independence.

By the time of the 2008 contest, Georgian drones had been shot down over the disputed areas and the issue was being discussed at the UN. Over the summer both Russia and Georgia massed troops on the borders of the disputed areas. War would eventually break out in early August, with Russian forces entering South Ossetia and Georgian forces attacking the area's capital, Tskhinvali. Needless to say, both sides claim that the other moved first; the truth is hard to establish. Russia launched air strikes and the Georgians were quickly driven back. Soon after, Russian troops were in Gori and Poti, two cities in undisputed Georgian territory. They did not press on, however: they had got what they wanted.

The EU still regards Abkhazia and South Ossetia as Georgian, but the issue is complex. If the majority of the areas' inhabitants wish to be independent, why should they not be? To which one can answer, 'if that majority has indulged in ethnic cleansing in order to become the majority'. But what does one do now to undo this past wrong? The two statelets remain in what political scientists call 'frozen conflict', unresolved issues left over from the collapse of the old Soviet empire, as does Transnistria, the russophile eastern region of Eurovision contestant Moldova. Eastern Ukraine has now effectively joined this list.

Croatia produced the contest's oldest competitor to date, in the form of Laci, a 75-year-old singer who turned into '75 Cents' for the competition. In 'Romanca' (Romance) he bemoaned the modern world, especially the internet, which he didn't understand, and ended up 'scratching' an old 78 rpm record on a horn gramophone.

The ageing of Europe's population is a matter of considerable concern among some commentators. We are living longer and having fewer children. Many EU countries are expected to lose population in the next generation. By 2030 nearly a quarter of the EU population will be over sixty-five, and by 2050, nearly a fifth could be over eighty. There is an 80 per cent chance that by that time, the 'old age dependency ratio' (the ratio of people aged over sixty-five to those aged between fifteen and sixty-four) will have fallen from the current one in four to one in two. Looking at the bouncy, youth-obsessed Eurovision stage, these figures seem unreal, but they are not.

Optimists argue that these figures don't matter. We are getting healthier and can do productive work long after we reach sixty-five. Machines can do ever more of the heavy manual 'support' work once done by the fit, strong young. If we are having fewer offspring it is because we are choosing to have smaller families, where children can be given more time and attention. At a deeper level, the optimists continue, reading too much into trends is dangerous, as the future is inherently unpredictable, despite what 'experts' tell us. Who, watching the first few Eurovision Song Contests, would have foreseen Sertab Erener, Lordi or Bulgarian tribal trance? Europe (and humanity in general) is nothing if not creative. Even if deep demographic trends are set in stone, our responses to them are not.

Pessimists point to the teeming, overpopulated world that demographers predict will surround our European island of ageing *rentier* contentment. What will be the consequences of this imbalance?

Eurovision 2008 was won by Russia's Dima Bilan with 'Believe', a song based on Rhoda Byrne's bestselling, and quintessentially New

Age, book *The Secret*, which argues that you can achieve anything you want through belief and positive visualization (a force called the Law of Attraction will bring this about). Critics of the book point out that visualizing a nice outcome doesn't always make it come true. Europe's 2000 Lisbon Agenda leaps to mind as an example.

Bilan, who comes from just north of disputed Abkhazia, had not been happy at coming second in 2006, and did more than just visualize success for 2008. He appealed to Western European taste by getting an American songwriter, Jim Beanz, who has worked with Britney Spears, Rihanna and Whitney Houston, to co-author 'Believe', then toured Eastern Europe in the run-up to the contest.* An elegant stage show featured Evgeni Plushenko, an Olympic champion skater, floating round the singer. And he took his shirt off at the end. Intriguingly, Bilan also changed the last word of the song, which was supposed to say things would work out if he fully believed in himself ('me') – the concept expounded by *The Secret* – to the more romantic, less New-Agey belief in an imagined listener: 'you'.

Ukraine's Ani Lorak made 2008 a Slavic double. Having been elbowed out of the way in 2005 to let GreenJolly celebrate the Orange Revolution, she participated in this contest and came second with the steamy 'Shady Lady'.

Meanwhile at the other end of the table, old Europe struggled. Germany's No Angels outdid Britain's 2003 Jemini in singing out of tune, and came equal last. Fed up with a string of poor results – largely due to the 1999 change in the native language rule – Ireland cocked a snook at the contest via Dustin the Turkey, a satirical character from Irish TV. 'Irelande Douze Points' accused Eastern Europe of bloc voting, got booed at the semi-final and didn't make it to Saturday. Belgium, the Netherlands and Switzerland (the last of

---

* Modern Eurovision is seeing ever more build-up tours, and a 'circuit' is developing, including the London Eurovision Party, the first of which took place in 2008.

these with the pleasant 'Era Stupendo') didn't make it, either. France's Sébastien Tellier,* an automatic qualifier, came nineteenth. Britain's Andy Abraham shared last place with the tuneless No Angels. Only Norway bucked the trend, with Maria Haukass Storeng's 'Hold On, Be Strong' coming fifth – but then Norway always does different.

Old Europe had had enough. Britain's Terry Wogan quit the commentary box. Even the peace-loving Nicole wrote a shirty article in *Bild Zeitung*.

A new system of judging the final was announced for 2009, based on the one that had been used in Sweden's *Melodifestivalen* selection process since 1999. Every nation's vote would be split 50/50 between televotes and 'experts', a panel of five national music-industry professionals. The latter would assess each piece on 'the originality of the composition, act, quality of the vocal performance and overall picture'.

The year did not give the world a vintage Eurovision, but it will surely turn out to be a pivotal one in global geopolitics. On 8 August, the Beijing Olympics opened with the most magnificent opening ceremony ever seen; a fortnight later, China was top of the medals table. A fortnight after that, Lehman Brothers bank collapsed in New York. Two days later, British bank HBOS collapsed, and had to be rescued by a rival. Another British bank, RBS, followed. Oh well, thought mainland Europe, that's Britain, enslaved to US-style neo-liberalism . . .

Shortly after the collapse of Lehman Brothers, Spain's prime minister, José Luis Rodríguez Zapatero, told Wall Street bankers that Spain 'has perhaps the most solid financial system in the world. It has a standard of regulation and supervision recognized internationally for its quality and rigour.'

---

* Tellier caused a national scandal by threatening to sing 'Divine' in English. A French MP raised the matter in parliament, asking the culture minister why France was 'giving up the defence of its language in front of hundreds of millions of television viewers'. In response, Tellier added some lines in French.

On 29 September the Belgian bank Fortis had to be rescued by the three Benelux governments. On the same day, the Irish government agreed to underwrite the debts of its nation's banks. Iceland's banks crashed a week later, and could not be saved by the government of the tiny northern nation. The crisis had spread.

2009

Date of the final: 16 May
Venue: Olympic Indoor Arena, Moscow, Russia
Winner: Alexander Rybak, Norway
Winning Song: 'Fairytale'

In terms of the relationship between Europe and Russia, 16 May 2009 seems an age away, as distant as those black-and-white images of Alice Babs and Margot Hielscher. On that date, Russia put on a magnificent Eurovision finale, one that cried out to the world that the mighty Eastern nation was European and proud of it. An estimated 30 million euros were spent on the event, which involved creating a stage surrounded by LED screens – 30 per cent of the screens in existence at the time were used in the former Olympic Arena on that night. Twenty thousand people filled the auditorium to hear twenty-five songs from around the continent, from Lithuania to Spain.

There were rumblings in the background, however. Lithuania, Latvia and Estonia nearly backed out in protest at the host's continuing support for the two breakaway republics in Georgia. In the end, they came to Moscow, Estonia doing so as the result of a public vote: few countries have embraced democracy as passionately as the most northern of the Baltic states.

Georgia did not come. It had initially wanted nothing to do with the contest, given its recent mauling by the host nation. But after it had won junior Eurovision (thanks partly to the award of twelve points from Russia), it relented. The song that topped its domestic heats, however, was a Trammps-influenced disco number called 'We Don't Wanna Put In' ('put in' being pronounced like the Russian leader, just in case anyone missed the joke). The EBU said this was too political: could the lyrics be rewritten, please. Georgia said 'no' and so didn't go to Moscow.

And then there was the Gay Pride march. The authorities attempted to ban it (Moscow mayor Yuri Luzhkov had described an earlier attempted Pride march as 'satanic'). But they were foiled by the protesters, who changed their venue at the last minute, arriving at the garden in front of Moscow State University in limousines (the garden is a popular place for wedding parties). They then unfurled banners, chanted slogans and were arrested by riot police with what most observers agreed was unnecessary force: eighty or so people waving banners hardly represents a serious threat to public order.

2009 was the first Eurovision final to be judged under the new half-and-half split between experts and televoters. The main beneficiaries from the new system were the UK, France, Denmark, Malta and Israel; the biggest losers were Azerbaijan, Turkey, Greece and Russia. This seemed fair. The UK, France and Denmark had all put special effort into their 2009 entries. The UK's 'It's My Time', sung by Jade Ewen, was composed by Andrew Lloyd Webber, who also played the piano for the evening, and American lyricist Diane Warren. France featured well-known *chanteuse* Patricia Kaas. Denmark's 'Believe Again' was co-written by Boyzone star Ronan Keating.

Armenia threatened to cause a big stir, but didn't. There was a rumour that the small Caucasus nation planned to field rock stars System of a Down, four Armenian Americans whose song 'Holy Mountains' had protested the Turkish genocide of Armenians in 1915. Turkey, which continues to deny the genocide, was not amused. In the end, folk duo Inga and Anush Arshakyan got the gig. Armenia created a smaller stir instead, by featuring a statue on its semi-final 'postcard' that stands in the disputed territory of Nagorno-Karabakh. This did not go down well in Azerbaijan. The two nations had fought a war over the enclave in the 1990s, and control is still disputed (more post-Soviet 'frozen conflict'). After the contest, police in Azerbaijan contacted a number of their citizens who had voted for Armenia's entry by SMS. The Azerbaijani authorities later gave the Orwellian explanation that the people contacted had simply been 'invited to explain' why they had voted that way.

The contest produced a popular runaway winner, Norway's violin-playing Alexander Rybak with 'Fairytale'. Rybak (pronounced Ree-bak) was born in Belarus but brought up in Oslo. 'Fairytale' was very catchy (rather clunky English lyrics let it down a bit) and well arranged: it had probably won the moment the accompaniment came in on the fifth bar. Rybak performed with immense gusto: like many winners – Abba and Katrina Leskanich leap to mind – he exuded a sense of simply loving being up there, and viewers couldn't help being caught up in it. Iceland's Yohanna pipped Azerbaijan for second place (Europe's televoters preferred the Azeris).

Outside the confident, new-look Eurovision, the world's financial system tottered along. Despite difficulties with some banks, mainland Europe seemed to have suffered less than Britain or the USA. The 2008 crash was surely the swansong for the pure form of Anglo-Saxon neo-liberalism, the idea that if financial markets were left to their own devices, resources would be efficiently allocated and we'd all be better off. The demise of the theory did not, of course, necessitate a return to 1970s-style socialism, but it did restate the old European wisdom that good government is a balancing act between market freedom and other social desirables – a balance understood by Konrad Adenauer and Ludwig Erhard back when Lys Assia and Corry Brokken were winning Eurovision.

Europe's new currency seemed to have weathered the storm. Germany's finance minister even admitted to being 'close to euphoria' about the success of the euro (I doubt if his words influenced Loreen, three years later, but you never know).

In October, however, a new government came to power in Greece. A fortnight afterwards, the country's new leader, George Papandreou, admitted that the official figures for the nation's finances were completely wrong. The ratio of a Eurozone member's annual government borrowing to its annual GDP is meant to be 3 per cent. Officially Greece had been a bit naughty, running the ratio up to 3.7 per cent. Papandreou announced that the ratio for 2009 was actually going to be 6 per cent. The rate on Greek government bonds went through the roof – leaving the nation that had to borrow most having to pay more for that borrowing than anyone else. The new government reluctantly admitted that it would have to cut back public expenditure – upon which Greek public sector workers went on strike.

A grim cycle of events kicked in. More bad news would come out of Athens (usually a new set of figures showing the country to be in even more of a financial mess than had been previously admitted). Interest rates on Greek bonds would then rise, making borrowing even harder for the government, which would announce further austerity measures. Eurozone leaders would make funds available to bail Greece out, but by this time there would be public disorder on the streets of Athens as people protested the austerity. This would push bond yields up even higher and swallow up all the bailout funds . . .

Just before Eurovision 2010, a rescue package of 110 billion euros was announced by the Eurozone nations and the IMF, the global fund that had saved struggling mid-seventies Britain.* (If you had 110 billion euro coins and could pile them one on top of the other indefinitely, you would have a column that reached two-thirds of the way to the International Space Station.) Relative calm seemed to settle. Rather than breathe a sigh of relief, though, financial markets started looking around to see who else's bonds were risky. Two veteran Eurovision contestants came into their sights: Ireland and Portugal.

---

* The IMF, the European Commission and the European Central Bank, which all started buying Greek government bonds at this time, make up the 'Troika' that now controls European finance.

Eurovision!

Russia, who had been through financial turmoil in the past and whose oil-producing economy now suddenly looked rather stronger than that of the West, could watch the goings-on with some sense of superiority. But the triumph was muted.

Eurovision 2009 did not win the former superpower the friends it should have. The arrest of the Pride marchers did not play well with the rest of Europe. There was the business of those Georgian republics (though Russia could argue that Europe was being hypocritical and anti-Slavic, insisting that Kosovo should follow its majority and become independent but that Abkhazia and South Ossetia should not). One gets a sense that the nation was like a teenager who throws a big party but still ends up sitting alone in the kitchen at the end of the evening.

The 2009 contest and Europe's lukewarm response can be seen as a turning point in Russian foreign policy. It began to look elsewhere for friends. On 14 October, Vladimir Putin proposed revamping the old Intervision Song Contest. This time it would involve members of the Shanghai Cooperation Organization, a body founded in 2001 and consisting of Russia, China, Kazakhstan, Tajikistan, Uzbekistan and Kyrgyzstan.

For the rest of Europe, the 'noughties' also ended on a downbeat note, with the once-mighty euro project suddenly looking flaky amid disagreement about how best to rescue it. The indebted countries, led by France, wanted money thrown at the problem. Germany and other financially sound nations such as Finland, Austria and the Netherlands insisted the old rules be kept to.

Eurovision itself ended the decade on a high, with a popular winner. A gentle tinkering with the rules seemed to have brought about a subtle rebalancing of the outcomes. The queue of nations wanting to participate was as long as ever. Roll on the new decade; roll on Oslo!

The
2010s

2010

Date of the final: 29 May
Venue: Telenor Arena, Oslo, Norway
Winner: Lena, Germany
Winning Song: 'Satellite'

2010 was the first Eurovision of the new financial era. Europe's econo-mies had stopped growing halfway through 2008, and governments all over the continent were trying to cut back on expenditure. Traditionally, the way to counter recession had been that suggested by John Maynard Keynes in the 1930s: governments should borrow money and spend it in order to get cash flowing round the economy again. But (to quote Alexander Rybak) that was then. Now, European nations were already up to their armpits in debt. This time it was agreed that the only way forward was austerity.

The new mood was reflected in national selection procedures for Eurovision. Many countries stopped having special shows with public votes and just let 'experts' decide. Hungary was, apparently, warned off from participating at all by the IMF, from whom it was trying to secure a loan after its banks got into trouble.[*] The host broadcaster had to sell its rights to cover the 2010 FIFA World Cup in order to pay for staging the final – which was still an expensive business, costing them 211 million NKr (around 24 million euros at current rates).

Eurovision was still a matter of national pride for the hosts – in their own usual intriguing way. A set of stamps was issued to

---

[*] Participants have to pay a fee to join Eurovision. Exactly how much a nation pays seems to depend on the size of its home audience for the contest. My guess is that Hungary saved about 60,000 euros. The IMF presumably didn't consider the amount of TV that Hungary would then have to produce to fill the gap . . .

celebrate the contest. Three of them featured past Norwegian winners (Bobbysocks, Secret Garden and Alexander Rybak) and the public was asked to decide who should appear on the fourth one. The winner, by a huge majority, was Jahn Teigen, of *nul points* and braces fame. Norway remains very happy to be outside the EU: a poll taken around the time of this contest showed 58 per cent in favour of the status quo. As part of the European Economic Area, the country participates in a number of Europe-wide initiatives. Yet it values its independence hugely. Teigen is a symbol of this. We do things our way, thanks, Europe.

The semi-finals removed long-time regulars Sweden, the Netherlands and Switzerland, as well as Lithuania's InCulto with 'Eastern European Funk', a song complaining about how Eastern Europeans were doing a lot of the hard work in Europe but not getting the respect they deserved. After 2004, when the 'A8' joined the EU, there had been a flow of immigrants to more prosperous Western Europe. It's hard to get full, accurate figures for the whole of Europe, but for Britain, by 2010 there were 472,000 Eastern Europeans working in the country (about 1.6 per cent of the workforce). At least as many had already come to Britain, worked for a while, then returned home. Breaking these figures down by nationality, around seven out of ten were from Poland; Lithuania and Slovakia provided around 10 per cent each.

Britain seemed to be dealing with the influx well. Some right-wingers complained that immigrants were putting a 'burden' on the nation's health service, but the newcomers were young, healthy people who did not use these services much. They complained of crime, even when a survey showed falling crime in areas which had experienced high levels of A8 immigration. They complained of jobs being taken, but got their taps fixed quicker. The pressure was most strongly felt in eastern rural towns, previously quiet places which had kept themselves to themselves and weren't used to outsiders.

Eurovision!

Overall the nation appeared to be coping. Britons are a tolerant lot, underneath it all. Aren't we?

The broadcast of the 2010 final began with a neat recreation of watching Eurovision back in 1956. A woman dutifully brings dinner for the family watching on a brown Bakelite TV which then conks out. Her husband, who has chilled out for the evening by removing his jacket but not his tie, has to get up and give it a thump to get it to work. On comes the *Te Deum* – then we're back in 2010.

Several early songs – Azerbaijan, Spain, Moldova, Cyprus – set a timely tone of bemoaning how things had gone wrong, as did Ukraine's much darker, ironic 'Sweet People'. (Like Hungary, Ukraine can do dark in Eurovision when it feels like it.) Belgium's entry was resonant of the new cure. Tom Dice did away with backing singers, fancy outfits or pyrotechnics; it was just 'Me And My Guitar'. Eurovision has rarely seen anything so simple – and rewarded it with sixth place.* Greece replied by singing about 'burning the past'. Ireland tried to recreate the past by fielding a previous winner with an old-style ballad, but did not prosper.

Ireland's economy was faring the same. The former Celtic Tiger was now deep in trouble thanks to its government's promise to back its banks, and in November it became the second EU member to receive a bailout. The glory days of the 1990s seemed a long way in the past, both economically and in Eurovision.

Iceland created a model volcano in the Green Room, jokily reminding viewers of the eruption of Eyjafjallajökull the previous month. This had both given media commentators lockjaw and closed European airspace for five days. Many Europeans had been stuck overseas for that time (some Nordic holidaymakers in Spain had been taken home by bus, a journey of two and a half days, non-stop).

---

* The judges ranked the song second. Televoters like a bit of razzmatazz and only placed it fourteenth.

The continent's skies were spookily empty. While the eruption caused some environmental damage, the flight cancellations are estimated to have prevented two billion kilograms of CO_2 being pumped into the atmosphere.

A few days before the eruption, air transport had been in the European news for a darker reason, the crash of a Polish military jet carrying many of the nation's leading figures to a ceremony to mark the Katyn massacre of 1940. This should have been a moment of reconciliation between Russia and Poland, but instead both sides blamed each other for the tragedy. As often with accidents, more than one factor seems to have been involved – including linguistic difficulties with air traffic control: a reminder of the international nature of modern European life. English is the *de facto* language of Eurovision because it connects people.

Russia was represented in Eurovision 2010 by Peter Nalitch, a new kind of contestant. Forget talent contests; they're so 2000s. Nalitch had become famous on the internet. He had posted a home-made video of his song 'Gitar' on YouTube. 'Gitar' doesn't take itself too seriously, as he invites female listeners into his 'Yaguar', which is actually a beaten-up old Lada. The video became a hit, with over two million views, and Nalitch, an architecture student, assembled a band of friends and started gigging. The gigs proved popular. Russia, not forced into austerity, staged a full-on national selection TV show for Eurovision 2010, which the band entered and won by a large margin.

Social media were now a part of Eurovision life. A Facebook petition to get the orchestra reinstated was initiated in 2010 (given austerity, it had no chance). Britain even had a Facebook campaign to get the nation's Eurovision entry into its national charts – which showed the limitations of the new medium's power: Josh Dubovie's 'That Sounds Good To Me' only got to number 179.

There was unanimity about the 2010 winner. Lena, from the HQ of austerity, Germany, had discreet backing singers, a simple black dress, no props and minimal instrumentation: no pounding techno beat or soaring strings. She simply sang her kooky 'Satellite' in her idiosyncratic voice. This was Germany going back to traditions, both broadly cultural (Lena sounds like a modern version of those half-sung, half-spoken 1920s/30s songs from Bertolt Brecht and Kurt Weill) and specifically Eurovision (Germany's other winner, Nicole, had kept it simple, too). On returning home, she was greeted with the same enthusiasm that a peripheral nation would have given a winner in the previous decade. Germany was no longer the accommodating embodiment of that 1949 'European spirit' and was instead forcefully insisting on European austerity – but it clearly still wanted to be liked.

2011

Date of the final: 14 May
Venue: Esprit Arena, Düsseldorf, Germany
Winner: Ell and Nikki, Azerbaijan
Winning Song: 'Running Scared'

Germany had to put on a great show – and it did. The set, designed by Florian Wieder and lit by Jerry Appelt, featured a 1,250 square metre LED screen backdrop which weighed thirty tons. Ninety truckloads of lighting created towers, wigwams, pyramids and cones of light, turning the vast hall of the former football stadium (36,000 people attended) into a magical, perpetually changing world. One of the great Eurovision stagings, the next generation on from the great RTÉ shows of the 1990s, it showcases the mastery of practical technology on which the host nation's economic success is built. The *Bundesrepublik* makes things excellently, and people round the world want to buy them.

The semi-finals proved their worth by seeing off 'Haba Haba', 'Boom Boom' and 'Ding Dong'. It also got rid of the entry from Belarus, subtly titled 'I Love Belarus', about how great it is to be young and free in that country. Politically, the most interesting non-survivor was Portugal's 'Luta é Alegria' (The Struggle Is Joy) from the colourful, fist-clenching, banner-waving Homens da Luta (Men of the Struggle – though two of the band are women).

In the run-up to the contest, Portugal had become the third country to have its bonds savaged by international capital markets, and, after repeated denials that it needed help, a bailout had been organized, conditional on the usual austerity measures. Portugal, as is its tradition, found a way of putting political comment into Eurovision. A 'tight belt' is no use, complained Homens da Luta.

Instead, let's bring bread, cheese and wine and have a half-protest, half-party! Germany did not enter a song called 'Who's going to pay for it, then?'

The final gave us a Moldovan lady on a unicycle plus musicians in crazy conical hats – the small nation (population 3.5 million) east of Romania has developed a reputation for off-the-wall entertainment in Eurovision. It gave us sign language from Lithuania. It gave us Jedward: after 2010, Ireland modernized its act and featured John and Edward Grimes, identical twins from Dublin who had come to fame on Britain's *X Factor* talent show thanks to their exuberance, cockerel quiffs and ability to annoy lead judge Simon Cowell. Their song 'Lipstick' won the Marcel Bezençon award (awarded by the event's commentators) for best song, which perhaps says something about the other entries. 2011 was not a vintage year. Maybe the music was overwhelmed by the setting.

Iceland produced a touching entry. After the selected artist, Sjonni Brink, had suddenly died aged thirty-six, his friends got together and performed 'Coming Home' as a tribute.

Italy gave us some jazz, via 'Madness Of Love'. Jazz is normally a recipe for failure in the contest, but singer/pianist Raphael Gualazzi surprised everybody, including himself, by coming second. The judges made him a runaway winner, giving him 251 points and the next song 182, the biggest majority ever. Televoters were less convinced, rating 'Madness Of Love' eleventh, with 99 points. Among the thudding synthesizers and chant-like backing vocal lines of 2011 it was good to see some real musicianship on display, both from Gualazzi and his trumpeter Fabrizio Bosso.

Italy was back in Eurovision after a thirteen-year break, now as a fifth automatic qualifier thanks to its financial contribution. It was no doubt happy so to be after its near-triumph. Other kinds of attention proved less welcome. As 2011 progressed, it was the southern nation's turn to come into the markets' sights. This was particularly worrying for Europe, as Italy's economy was much larger – around 12 per cent of the whole of Europe's – than those of Ireland, Portugal or Greece, which are all around a tenth of Italy's size.* Italy's government debt was estimated at 1,800 billion euros.

In November, rates on Italian bonds began heading towards 7 per cent, a figure generally agreed to be unsupportable, as borrowing at that rate is crippling. Its alternately comical and sinister prime minister, Silvio Berlusconi, had to step down, and former EU commissioner Mario Monti took over: a 'safe pair of hands', but not democratically elected. Soon after, his new labour minister Elsa Fornero was in tears as she announced the inevitable austerity measures.

Meanwhile, Spain – for whom Eurovision 2011 meant the bouncy Lucia Perez telling viewers 'Que Me Quiten Lo Bailao' (They Can't Take The Fun From Me) – was also in trouble. As with Ireland, the problem was indirect, not government incurred debt but private-sector debt. In Spain, the villains were regional banks (*cajas*), which the government ended up having to guarantee to stop the nation's financial system collapsing. A month later Madrid announced massive cuts in government spending. Unemployment, already high, headed past 20 per cent. In reply, the *indignado* protest movement took to the streets. A new anti-austerity political party, *Podemos* ('We can'), would follow. The Eurozone now had five deeply troubled economies, which became known by the unflattering acronym PIIGS (Portugal, Italy, Ireland, Greece and Spain).

One place where austerity was not an issue was oil-rich Azerbaijan. Like Israel, Azerbaijan is not regarded as a 'European' country, but its geography makes it eligible to join the EBU, which it had done in 2008. Since then, it had enjoyed great success in the contest. In 2011

---

* In the EU's GDP stakes, Germany leads, comprising around 20 per cent of the Union's economy, followed by France (16 per cent) and Britain (15 per cent). Italy is fourth. Behind it come Spain (8 per cent), the Netherlands (5 per cent) and Sweden, Poland and Belgium (all around 3 per cent).

it took that to the ultimate by winning. 'Running Scared', sung by
Ell and Nikki (Eldar Gasimov and Nigar Jamal), was in many ways
a Western European product. It was written by Swedes Stefan Örn
and Sandra Bjurman and Briton Iain Farquharson. Singer Nikki has
lived in north London since 2005. The four backing singers were
Swedish. Such is modern Europe: free movement of labour is a key
foundation of the single market.

2012

Date of the final: 26 May
Venue: Crystal Hall, Baku, Azerbaijan
Winner: Loreen, Sweden
Winning Song: 'Euphoria'

When Ell and Nikki tearfully collected the trophy for Eurovision 2011, the site of the Crystal Hall, Baku, was a piece of waste ground near Azerbaijan's 162 metre National Flagpole. A year later, an astounding venue hosted Eurovision. It was covered in 9,500 LED lights, which magically lit up to show the flag of each participant as they sang. It seated 25,000 people. It cost 105 million Azerbaijani manats (about 120 million euros) – though the Baku government spent much more than that on infrastructure (including upgrading the national football stadium in case the Crystal Hall wasn't ready on time).

A spokesman for the country's ruling party observed: 'It is very important for Azerbaijan to make itself recognized in the world . . . There is no better opportunity than Eurovision to show the world that we are secular, not a radical Islamic country. We should demonstrate . . . that we have a developed economy, we have good infrastructure.' He couldn't resist adding: 'The world should see that we are a peaceful nation, not aggressive as Armenia describes us.'

The builders of the Crystal Hall were German, as were Eurovision 2012's lighting designers (the same team responsible for 2011). As with its 2011 winning song, the 2012 hosts knew how to get the best from Europe.

The hosts were criticized for their politics. In 2011, *The Economist* magazine scored Azerbaijan 140th out of 167 in its Democracy Index. There was some debate about the ethics of setting the contest there at all, but the EBU's determination to be apolitical prevailed. Swedish entrant Loreen met opposition activists before the event. Later in the year, she would do the same when performing in Belarus.

To be fair to Azerbaijan, it was also criticized for being too liberal. Iran withdrew its ambassador, disgusted that its fellow Shi'ite nation was hosting an event which might involve a 'gay parade'. There were fears that terrorists from Dagestan, Azerbaijan's northern neighbour, would target the contest. There are nastier people out there than the Baku government.

The semi-finals deprived us of Montenegro's Rambo Amadeus, a colourful performance artist whose other work includes hosting an erotic quiz show, writing a cadenza for a Mozart piano concerto and doing gigs backed by concrete mixers and vacuum cleaners. During his 'Euro Neuro', banners were unveiled demanding a rescheduling of debt. A loss to the final.

The semis also weeded out San Marino's 'The Social Network Song', despite its having music by Ralf Siegel, now aged sixty-six. From 2008, the use of 'Web 2.0' online social networking tools had blossomed in Europe, especially in the north. Around 50 per cent of people now used Facebook, YouTube or Twitter in the Netherlands, UK, Scandinavia and the Baltics. Southern Europe (and, strangely, Germany) lagged behind, averaging around 30 per cent.

Even without Rambo Amadeus or Ralf Siegel, the final was a classic. We had more fun from Moldova: you've not seen anything till you've seen my trumpet, sang Pasha Parfeny, to an infectious, jazzy *lăutărească* beat.* Azerbaijan, Bosnia, Estonia, Germany, Serbia and Spain – my personal favourite: Pastora Soler's 'Quédate Conmigo' (Stay With Me) – produced excellent ballads. Of these, Serbia's 'Nije Ljubav Stvar' (Love Is Not A Thing) did best, coming third. Singer/

---

* Another Eastern European musical tradition Eurovision has introduced us to. A mixture of Russian, Turkish and gypsy music – with a healthy dose of improvisation – it has been played at Romanian weddings since the sixteenth century.

composer Željko Joksimović already had an outstanding track record in Eurovision, having written songs that had come second, third (the lovely 'Lejla' from 2006) and sixth.

Albania's Rona Nishliu pushed the boundaries furthest. An artist who works in areas from dance to experimental jazz, she produced something different, both musically and lyrically, for Eurovision with 'Suus' (the title is Latin for 'his or her own': it's usually translated as 'Personal') and was rewarded with fifth place. Like a number of other recent Eurovision entrants, especially from the East, she is also a social activist: after the contest, she campaigned against domestic violence.

Albania and Kosovo – where Nishliu had lived since the age of thirteen – were suffering from historical legacies in 2012. The unemployment rate in Kosovo was nearly 50 per cent, and Albania was still recovering from both the psychotic Stalinist regime of Enver Hoxha, who had died in 1985, and a bizarre series of financial scandals that happened after the country had abandoned Communism. Albania had been the last former eastern bloc nation to make this change. Multi-party elections were held in 1991 and won by the Communists. Their government collapsed the next year, and was replaced by the Democratic Party. In 1996–7 a billion euros of the nation's savings had vanished in Ponzi schemes (at the time, Albania's GDP had been around 10 billion euros). It is estimated that two-thirds of the population lost money in one or other of these schemes, one of which was started by a former adviser to the prime minister.

Legacies of financial folly were stalking much of the rest of Europe, too, especially among young people (who had done nothing to bring these consequences about). Spain had joined Greece in having official youth unemployment figures of over 50 per cent. Croatia would soon make it three nations. The figure for the three other PIIGS hovered between 30 and 40 per cent. Britain, France and Sweden were at just over 20 per cent and Belgium just under that. In many parts of Europe, people began talking about a 'lost generation'.

The ultimate cause of this – in the Eurozone, anyway – was the euro, in two ways. One was the irresponsible borrowing that euro membership had allowed. The second was the removal of the traditional safety valve for underperforming economies. Outside a shared currency, the currencies of the PIIGS countries would have been devalued. This would have made their exports competitive again, and their economies could have picked up. Without this safety valve, weak economies suffered 'internal devaluation', with economic activity stalling and jobs leaching away.

Eurovision 2012 had a clear winner, according to both juries and televoters. Loreen's soaring 'Euphoria', co-written by the prolific Eurovision composer Thomas G:son, went on to be the most successful Eurovision song for decades, selling two million singles and topping charts all round Europe (except in France and Italy, where it got to numbers twenty-six and twenty-seven respectively).

Second place went to Buranovskiye Babushki, six grandmothers from a village 1,000 kilometres east of Moscow (but still in European Russia), singing partially in Udmurt, a language spoken by about 500,000 people. Any proceeds from their participation were to go to the rebuilding of a church destroyed in the Second World War. The oldest of the *babushki* was Natalya Pugacheva. Aged seventy-seven, she had been born when Stalin's show trials were at their height and had grown up during the war.

Other minority languages were getting song contest exposure via the Liet International Festival, which in 2012 took place in Gijon in northern Spain. Songs were sung in Asturian (the eventual winner), Gallic, Catalan, Corsican, Basque, Sami, Friulian (from north-east Italy), Breton, Low Saxon, Udmurt and Frisian.

As if inspired by an outstanding Eurovision, political Europe finally began to sort out its financial mess. Estimates of how much it would cost to refinance the economies of the PIIGS countries had been rising, and were now well past the 1 trillion euro mark. The financial markets

Eurovision!

doubted Europe's ability to find the money, but on 26 July Mario Draghi, the president of the European Central Bank, made his definitive statement that the ECB would do 'whatever it takes' to save the euro. The markets finally believed him. The turmoil that had begun in October 2009 began to subside. But how long would it take to repair the damage? Was the damage even reparable with the single currency apparently doing more harm than good in so many countries? And, beneath it all, was the banking system really safe? Had it really purged itself of all its bad loans and incomprehensible, worthless derivatives?

Still, Draghi's announcement brought calm, and calm was what Europe, and the world, needed.

Even better things were to come for European political institutions in 2012. In October, the EU was awarded the Nobel Peace Prize. On 10 December (the anniversary of Alfred Nobel's death in 1896), European Council president Herman Van Rompuy, European Commission president José Manuel Barroso and European Parliament president Martin Schulz travelled to Norway to accept the prize. The ghosts of Marcel Bezençon and Jean Monnet would have watched the event with huge pleasure.

Eurosceptics argue that peace in Europe has been brought about by other factors, such as a distaste for aggressive nationalism since 1945, the need for greater co-operation in the face of the Soviet threat until 1991, the growth of multinational business and media, and simple technology: we can all telephone, travel and now email all round the continent. To this, Europhiles simply point to the peace that has reigned within EEC/EU borders since 1958, and highlight the achievement of bringing the old Soviet empire into a bloc of liberal democracies with relatively little pain.

My own view? Well, there's one European institution that has been peaceful for even longer, since 1956, and which invited the East on board a whole decade before the EU did. But I suppose giving a Nobel Prize to the Eurovision Song Contest might be a step too far . . .

2013

Date of the final: 18 May
Venue: Malmö Arena, Malmö, Sweden
Winner: Emmelie de Forest, Denmark
Winning Song: 'Only Teardrops'

After the extravagance of Azerbaijan, it was time for Eurovision to calm down a bit. Eurovision 2013, in Malmö, cost a mere 12 million euros to stage, and seating was only provided for 11,000 people.

The contest still managed spectacle, however. There was an Olympic-style opening, where contestants processed into the arena behind national flags, to a new 'Eurovision anthem', 'We Write The Story', composed by Bjorn and Benny from Abba and Avicii, a young Stockholm-born DJ. And once the show began, we had a man in a cage mimicking the moves of Azerbaijan's Farid Mammadov, and Aliona Moon from Moldova in a strange expanding skirt that lifted her five metres off the ground.

Apart from the opening ceremony, nationalism appeared to take a back seat. The postcards, which had of late become tourist-board adverts for the home country, reverted to scenes from the relevant participating nations. The interval act was an affectionate self-parody of Sweden and Swedishness – reserve, tolerance, industriousness, Abba . . . 1991 winner Carola even took a deliberate 'pratfall' after a bar or two of 'Fångad Av En Stormvind'.

Yet it is a mistake to say Sweden's show was not nationalistic. In its own way, it waved the flag fiercely for its country, as an intelligent, competent, liberal state. In recent years, Sweden has used the contest very effectively as a vehicle for 'soft power', for showing the world what a good place it is. Well-crafted, genuinely felt, brilliantly staged songs, year after year, build up a cumulative impression in (now) 200 million viewers that it is a country that knows what it is about, and that its values are decent, humane and solid.

The UK, by comparison, which should have soft power coming out of its ears, given the success of British popular music since the early 1960s (not to mention Shakespeare, Newton, Dickens and other assorted cultural superstars), continued to blunder around the contest. In 2012, it had entered Engelbert Humperdinck, who was not exactly at the height of his career (his greatest hit, 'Release Me', came from the era when Eurovision was still being broadcast in black-and-white). His 'Love Will Set You Free' came second last.

The most controversial aspect of the 2013 contest was probably the brief kiss between Finland's Krista Siegfrids and her female backing singer. Controversial in some parts of the world, anyway: most of Europe took little notice, but Turkey quit the contest when it found out that was going to be part of the act. Chinese TV, which has broadcast the event since 2011 but does not do so live, edited it out.

Turkey's departure probably had other causes, too. The nation had been hammering on Europe's political door for decades, and was no doubt tiring of being told it could come in 'soon', especially since a horde of ex-Communist countries had been allowed in ahead of it. Europe, maybe, became tired of the hammering, too – though one can't help feeling its tiredness is that of a flirt who has suddenly found that the object of their attentions takes them seriously. In 2013, Turkey did its European ambitions few favours with a crackdown on demonstrators in Istanbul's Taksim Square. The old sticking points – human rights, Cyprus, Armenian genocide denial – didn't go away. Perhaps the split was best for both parties.

Turkey signalled its new mood not only by quitting Eurovision, but by setting up an alternative televised international song contest, Türkvizyon. This featured countries or regions that either spoke Turkic languages or contained people of Turkish descent (or both).

Eurovision!

The net spread wide. Amongst the twenty-four participants in the 2013 contest were Iraq, Kazakhstan, Bosnia, Northern Cyprus and parts of Siberia.

The show was clearly modelled on Eurovision – a similar logo, his 'n' hers presenters, shots of flag-waving spectators, postcards between acts and staging that tried to be as high-tech as possible (Türkvizyon did not have Eurovision's huge budget). The main difference was the intro: two long speeches from the Turkish minister for education and the governor of Eskisehir, the city where the contest was held. The tone was more restrained, too. Some of the smaller participants simply fielded solo singers in regional dress; the bigger acts featured backing dancers but ones that showed much more decorousness (except for the couple in the background in Gagauzia's entry) than we are used to in Eurovision. Eurovision experience clearly told in Türkvizyon 2013, however, with Azerbaijan winning, Belarus coming second and Ukraine third. But the point was made to Europe: we can do this, too.

Russia, Europe's other peripheral giant, was also creating clear space between itself and Europe, even though its 2013 Eurovision entry, Dina Garipova's 'What If', was on the popular contest theme of let's all be nice to each other. On 20 September, President Putin gave a speech to the Valdai Club, a leading national think tank, where he argued that Russia was steering a middle course between its old totalitarianism and 'extreme, western-style liberalism'. In doing so, he was taking a time-honoured Russian position of the guardian of moral values in the face of backsliding Europe, a position previously taken by Communism and before that by the Orthodox Church.

Russia was also expanding its territory. Across its border in Ukraine, russophile Viktor Yanukovytch had become president in 2010. In November 2013, he refused to sign a planned Association Agreement with the EU, which would have provided financial and technological assistance and granted Ukraine privileged access to EU markets, with the ultimate goal of Ukraine joining the club. A month later, he signed a deal with Moscow instead, securing aid and cheap gas.

These events brought crowds out onto the winter streets, especially the large central square in Kyiv. Some flew EU flags, and the place became known as the *Euromaidan*: Europe Square. Eurovision 2004 winner Ruslana threw herself into the protests, camping out with the protestors and making speeches (and receiving death threats from opponents). In early 2014 she started touring Europe to raise awareness of the protesters' desire for a liberal, democratic, European state, meeting José Manuel Barroso in January. (Later that year she was honoured with an International Woman of Courage award, presented by Michelle Obama.)

Matters came to a head on 20 February 2014, when a stand-off between protesters and police erupted into violence leaving more than fifty demonstrators and three police dead. Two days later, Yanukovytch stepped down and fled to Russia. Four days later, his new hosts invaded Crimea. *Lasha hello.*

Crimea was, arguably, debatable land: traditionally part of Russia, it had been ceded to Ukraine by Khrushchev back in 1954.* But the incursion did not stop there. After Crimea was secured, Moscow began to foment unrest in russophone eastern Ukraine. Two Eurovision contestants were effectively at war.

The EU, despite now having a foreign minister, found itself unable to do anything. Eurosceptics mocked the minister for this – but NATO, an organization much more popular with Eurosceptics, did nothing either.

Elsewhere in Europe, the economies of Portugal, Italy, Ireland and Spain had stabilized, albeit still with unacceptable levels of youth

---

* Nobody really knows why he did this. Some say it was sentiment: his wife, Nina, was Ukrainian, and the Soviet leader felt a genuine shame at Stalin's unspeakable mistreatment of the country. Or was it just politics, an attempt to win allies at a time when his grip on power in the Kremlin was still not totally secure?

unemployment. But that of Greece had not; unemployment kept rising and GDP kept falling. In contrast, Greece's 2013 Eurovision entry was one of its best for years. 'Alcohol Is Free' featured *rebetiko* singer Agathonas Iakovidis and the group Koza Mostra. The group's leader, Elias Kozas, said that the song was simply about taking a positive attitude to troubles, but one can't help seeing defiance towards the powers forcing austerity onto the South European country. 'We're going to party and you can't stop us.'

Safe from this turmoil thanks to monetary independence, the Nordic countries produced strong entries. Iceland's ballad 'Ég Á Líf' (I Have Life) should surely have fared better than seventeenth. Norway's Margaret Berger came a powerful fourth. The contest winner, Denmark's Emmelie de Forest with 'Only Teardrops', added to that small nation's list of well-made, well-performed Eurovision high achievers.

2014

Date of the final: 10 May
Venue: B and W Hallerne, Eurovision Island, Copenhagen, Denmark
Winner: Conchita Wurst, Austria
Winning Song: 'Rise Like A Phoenix'

In 2009, Russia had hosted one of the most extravagant Eurovisions ever, showcasing how European it was. In 2014, its entrants, the Tolmachevy Sisters, were booed by the crowd. In return, one Moscow politician commented that the contest's eventual winning song marked 'the end of Europe'. Russia seemed ever more intent on turning away from the West. It was busy stirring and arming discontent in the east of Ukraine. By August 2014, there would be virtual civil war in that region, and in September an airliner with 283 crew and passengers, 193 of them Dutch nationals, would be shot out of the sky near Donetsk, killing everybody on board. There is substantial evidence that Russian-backed separatists were responsible.

What a difference five years makes.

The 2014 contest took place on 'Eurovision Island', Refshaleøen. The district is a neat symbol of the changes in the continent's economic life over the last sixty years. Back when Lys Assia won Eurovision in 1956, Refshaleøen was home to docks and a large shipbuilding company, noted for the left-wing militancy of its workers. Forty years later the company went bankrupt; the area was derelict for a while, but by 2014 was being rejuvenated as a location for small businesses and fashionable restaurants. After Eurovision, it became a symbol of the most recent chapter of Europe's economic life, financial ineptitude, when it was revealed that the staging of the contest, including refurbishment of parts of the island, had gone way over budget.

The winner of the contest was Conchita Wurst, a female stage personality created by actor/singer Tom Neuwirth. When she appeared with her dress and beard to sing 'Rise Like A Phoenix', many viewers probably thought she would be another in the long line of Austrian novelty acts stretching back to Ferry Graf's 'K Und K Calypso Aus Wien', but she proceeded to show she was a fine singer with a strong song. Juries and televoters both gave her first place.

The results revealed a cultural split. Most of the traditionally liberal Western European countries voted enthusiastically for her: *douze points* from Greece, the Netherlands, the UK, Sweden, Israel, Portugal, Ireland, Spain, Belgium, Italy, Switzerland and Slovenia. By contrast, Belarus gave her *nul points*, as did Armenia and Poland. (The split wasn't completely East/West. She got *nul points* from San Marino and *cinq points* from Russia – thanks to its public, who ranked the song third. Russia's judges voted it down: an interesting sign that maybe the nation's macho, anti-Western elite is less in touch with ordinary Russian people than it likes to think.)

Conchita Wurst's victory proved popular. In October, she gave a concert outside the European Parliament at the request of a group of MEPs. Several thousand people stood in pouring rain to watch the show. At a press conference in the Parliament she seemed uninterested in any controversy she had caused, and talked calmly about tolerance, respect and the need for people to agree to differ. A true modern European.

Second were the Netherlands' Common Linnets with the country-influenced 'Calm After The Storm'. This was a quiet, pleasant song that nobody really expected to get anywhere but which ended up selling more than the winner: a reward for one of Eurovision's most loyal participants (and, finally perhaps, forgiveness for 'Ding Dinge Dong').

Hungary's András Kállay-Saunders produced the darkest lyric of the evening. 'Running' is about child abuse. Kállay-Saunders based his song on the real experiences of a friend. Getting figures on the prevalence of such abuse in Europe is notoriously difficult. The European Commission website suggests that between 10 and 20 per cent of children suffer it – horrific if true. A survey carried out across Europe and published two months before the contest seemed to support this (though the sample, at 48,000, was rather small given Europe's population of 500 million). Ten per cent of the women questioned had experienced 'some form of sexual violence' before the age of fifteen. The report went on to talk of other kinds of violence in the home, against adult women. It came up with shocking statistics here, too, with one in three respondents reporting some kind of physical or sexual violence.

Even more scary perhaps, levels of reported violence were higher in 'progressive' countries like Scandinavia, the UK and France. Some people say this shows that violence is under-reported in other countries – but are they right? In defence of Europeans, the survey made no distinction between a one-off minor incident and the systematic, day-in-day-out cruelty that Kállay-Saunders is singing about. But the figures are still unsettling. 'Running' raised a deep and troubling issue for our supposedly liberal continent.

Less deep was Poland's entry, which featured a large-breasted lady doing an erotic dance with a washboard. The composers of 'My Słowianie' (We Are Slavic) claimed the piece was an ironic comment on sexual stereotyping. The song was the most popular with televoters in the UK, which either shows that that country's voters have an especially strong understanding of irony or that they don't take Eurovision very seriously. Irony-spotting televoters round Europe rated the song fifth, while juries placed it twenty-third.

Some commentators would link the last two paragraphs: do performances like 'We Are Slavic' demean women (if you miss the irony) and thus create a climate where sexual violence is more likely? The debate continues. When hemlines were rising in the late 1960s, the argument was the exact opposite. It was repression of matters sexual that created violence, and the more sexuality was 'out there', the less violence there would be. Eurovision's liking for good-natured vulgarity sits more easily with the latter approach.

Poland's washboard wasn't the only prop on show that year. The 2014 contest went to town on them. There was a circular keyboard from Romania, Greek singers bouncing on a trampoline, a trapeze artist from Azerbaijan (distracting attention from a rather beautiful song, Dilara Kazimova's 'Start A Fire'), a seesaw from Russia, and a man doing tricks in a giant hamster wheel behind Ukraine's Mariya Yaremchuk (distracting attention from a rather ordinary song). Old Europe was more restrained, though Switzerland's Sebalter (Sebastiano Paù-Lessi) sang, played the fiddle, beat a drum and whistled in his catchy 'Hunter Of Stars'.

Apart from the booing, Eurovision 2014 was a great show with a genuinely serious edge. Perfect!

On 7 January 2015, Eurostat, the EU's official provider of statistics, announced that the price of goods and services in the Eurozone had fallen by 0.2 per cent between December 2013 and December 2014. Deflation had arrived. Some historians were quick to remind us of the last major deflationary period, the Great Depression of the 1930s – though more optimistic ones pointed out that there had been brief periods of deflation in the 1950s, and that these had done nothing to harm the German *Wirtschaftswunder* or France's *trente glorieuses*. Others pointed to modern Japan, heavily in debt and with virtually no growth, but not suffering like the PIIGS countries – it still has a functioning economy and very low unemployment.

On the very same day as the Eurostat announcement, two terrorists from Al Qaeda in Yemen burst into the office of *Charlie Hebdo*, a Parisian satirical magazine that had published cartoons of the Prophet Muhammad, and killed eleven people: eight members of the team responsible for the magazine, a building worker and two policemen, one of whom, Ahmed Merabet, was a Muslim. Four people in a Jewish supermarket were also murdered.

Eurovision!

Around the continent people took to the streets to express their revulsion. On 11 January, up to two million demonstrators joined French president François Hollande and other world leaders in a march through the capital. 'Je suis Charlie' became a global slogan of solidarity; others added 'Je suis Ahmed'. From the point of view of this book, the most interesting thing about French reaction was that the attack was seen as an assault on France and French values. Europe wasn't really mentioned, except as an afterthought. In moments of pain and crisis, even core 'Lugano 1956' Europeans still revert to national identity.

2015

Date of the final: 23 May
Venue: Wiener Stadthalle, Vienna, Austria
Debut: Australia
Winner: Måns Zelmerlöw, Sweden
Winning Song: 'Heroes'

Eurovision 2015 was a close-run contest, with juries and public voters disagreeing (the public preferred Italy's operatic 'Grande Amore') and Sweden's winner only pulling ahead from Russia, its nearest rival in the actual live voting, towards the end. At least part of the reason for the victory of 'Heroes' were the stunning graphics, where the singer seems to interact with the background – yet another technical first for Eurovision. Måns' win was another 'soft power' coup for his nation.

Russia's 'A Million Voices' had reverted to the let's-all-be-nice-to-each-other theme of that country's 2013 entry. Singer Polina Gagarina appeared to mean it. She posted a picture of herself with Conchita Wurst on the net, in clear defiance of conservatives back home. Sadly, this didn't entirely silence the booing of her results, despite both the pleas of Conchita and the installation of Orwellian-sounding 'anti-booing technology' in the hall. Eurovision, as this book has argued, does not exist in a political and moral bubble – quite the opposite. So Russian artists will probably have to get used to this, as long as their homeland pursues its current policies on eastern Ukraine and LGBT freedom of expression. Gagarina did the best thing she could. She sang well and appreciated the applause she got from most of the crowd. She made more friends than enemies in Europe on 23 May.

More specifically political was Armenia's 'Face The Shadow'. The hook line is 'Don't deny', which had been the song's original title before the EBU insisted on a change. This was an obvious reference to the genocide of 1915 and Turkey's continuing refusal to accept the truth about the event. Historians continue to debate the death toll, but figures vary from half a million to two million people killed.

Romania's lovely 'De La Capăt' (All Over Again) dealt with that nation's diaspora. The song is sung by an émigré worker father to his son back home. It is estimated that around three million people have left the country (which has a current population of below 20 million) since 2002. This was Eurovision at its best, a postcard from the heart of a nation at a particular moment in its story.

Ireland did not make it to Saturday, but on the Friday between the last semi and the final held a referendum on gay marriage. A 'yes' vote was expected – commentators found few people under forty in favour of keeping the old ban – but the scale of the victory, by 62 per cent to 38 per cent, surprised many.

If one anglophone nation was absent from the final, a new one was present: Australia. The country has long had many Eurovision fans, and the EBU agreed to let it participate as a special guest for the sixtieth contest. Guy Sebastian did Oz proud, providing an outstanding vocal for 'Tonight Again' and coming fifth.

The UK, by contrast, struggled to get any votes at all. 'Still In Love With You' was a chirpy novelty song that had little resonance with the modern contest, which has been about quality songwriting and emotionally moving performances since the 50/50 system was introduced in 2009. (Eurovision never was a novelty competition, anyway, despite the odd *ding* and the occasional *diggi-ley*.)

This was not what the nation's prime minister, David Cameron, just given an absolute majority by his electorate, needed as he set out on a tour of EU capitals. Concerned at the possible defection of his supporters to the anti-Europe UK Independence Party (UKIP), he had promised voters a referendum on continued membership of the EU if he won. Now he had won, he had little option but to fulfil that promise. Could he gain enough concessions from Brussels on key (to him) matters such as immigration control to keep his critics sweet?

Sadly for Cameron, Europe was not in a generous mood. He had already alienated the new Commission president, Luxembourg's Jean-Claude Juncker, by opposing his election to the post. And Europe had its mind on other matters. 2015 saw a rising tide of difficulties facing the continent.

The first was economic. Growth remained elusive, especially in Greece, where it was needed most. And debt still seemed to be piling up in Europe-level financial institutions, in national accounts and in privately owned banks, major and regional.

To the non-expert observer, this appears unsustainable. Ultimately, surely, the financial conjuring has to end and real money has to be found to pay off the debt. Where from? Growth is the traditional answer, but what if there isn't any? Inflation is another answer: just print the stuff and worry about the consequences later (Germany is unlikely to accept such a solution). Could it come from asset sales to China? If this route is taken, there will be a price to pay – one can hardly expect this once-poor country to hand money over to us like an indulgent parent paying off a teenager's debts and not expect something substantial back. Despite Mario Draghi's confidence in 2012, a sense remains that difficult financial issues are being avoided or not fully understood.

The second challenge to Europe was the refugee crisis. Migrants had been attempting to enter the prosperous continent for many years, but political meltdowns, first in Libya then in Syria, meant that the number began to grow exponentially in the new decade. Many tried to make the crossing by sea, across the Mediterranean or the Aegean, in inadequate boats provided by gangs of people-traffickers. Such voyages were, and still are, incredibly risky. In September 2015,

Europe was horrified by a picture of Aylan Kurdi, a three-year-old Syrian boy whose body had washed up on a beach near Bodrum in Turkey. Yet the EU seemed unable to stop such tragedies.

It seemed equally unable to cope with those who made it to Europe. In May 2015, the Commission announced a system of 'relocation quotas' based on a number of objective criteria such as a country's size and GDP. This would settle 40,000 migrants, largely now camped out in Greece, Hungary and Italy. In September, the number was quadrupled and 780 million euros made available to support the relocation. But not every nation accepted the new quotas. The four 'Visegrad'* countries – Poland, the Czech Republic, Hungary and Slovakia – were (and still are) opposed. Other countries accepted but were in no hurry to take up their allocated numbers.

By contrast, Sweden and Germany were particularly generous-spirited. But in November 2015 a tearful Swedish deputy prime minister, Åsa Romson, announced that Sweden was effectively full. 'We simply couldn't do any more,' she said.

In early 2016, Europe made a deal with Turkey. We would pay it three billion euros to do more to stop the trafficking and to take back migrants who didn't qualify for asylum in Europe. However, this deal seems in the process of unwinding. EU member nations were supposed to produce the money, but much of it has yet to materialize. And part of the deal was the promise of Schengen-area visas for Turkish citizens as long as certain liberalization conditions were met by their home nation. After a failed coup on 15 July 2016, Turkey looks unlikely to meet these.

The numbers in the above paragraphs may seem large, but they are dwarfed by the full scale of the problem. The civil war in Syria on its own had produced 4.9 million 'registered refugees' by the end

---

* The group gets its name from the Hungarian city where their leaders held a 'summit meeting' in 1991.

of 2015, around half of whom were in Turkey. At the time of writing, this conflict shows no sign of ending.

More broadly still, the UNHCR reports a sharply rising trend in the numbers of people displaced by war or environmental degradation (a growing problem in sub-Saharan Africa). Around the world, this now amounts to 65 million. The issue – the size of the figures makes it so easy to forget that each 'unit' is a human being, an Aylan Kurdi – won't go away.

A third problem was terrorism. As this book shows, it's a phenomenon that has been part of European life since the early 1970s, but the threat is currently intensifying. On 13 November, a set of attacks took place in Paris that was even more horrific than the January *Charlie Hebdo* murders. In various outrages, 130 people were killed, including 89 music fans at a gig at the Bataclan theatre – the terrorists seemed to have a particular hatred for young people expressing their freedom to enjoy themselves (in other words, being modern Europeans). Bastille Day 2016 saw another mass murder, this time in Nice. Further such atrocities seem inevitable.

Terrorism, unlike the two other problems, does at least unite us in resistance to it. But it feeds into Islamophobia, which in turn divides Europe and hinders attempts to settle Syrian (and other) refugees. This is a particularly unfortunate vicious circle.

Terrorism has also led to the quiet erosion of previously solid European ideals. The dissolution of national borders, exemplified in the 1985 Schengen Agreement, is now under threat. Freedom is under threat, too. Governments are 'snooping' ever more on private communications. Most Europeans seem to feel that, in both cases, the loss is worth the security gain.

Given these challenges, it was small wonder that Mr Cameron's requests for concessions seemed a sideshow to his friends – and a godsend to his enemies.

2016

Date of the final: 14 May
Venue: Ericsson Globe, Stockholm, Sweden
Winner: Jamala, Ukraine
Winning Song: '1944'

2016 was another vintage Eurovision. It began and ended with controversy, featured some great songs and was hosted superbly, as we expected, by Sweden.

The opening controversy was about flags: which ones could be waved by fans and which couldn't. The EBU tried to keep the matter non-political, insisting that only the flags of UN-recognized countries could be flown (along with that of the EU and rainbow ones), but had to backpedal when it was pointed out that Welsh and Sami artists were performing. Then Armenia's Iveta Mukuchyan was filmed waving a Nagorno-Karabach flag in the Green Room at the semifinal. Cue protests from Azerbaijan, and a wonderfully Eurovision reply from Mukuchyan: 'I want peace everywhere.'

The closing controversy . . . well, I'll come to that later. In between we had (as expected) a stunning show from the Swedish hosts. Måns Zelmerlöw and Petra Mede were sharp, enthusiastic and funny compères. Their 'model' Eurovision song, 'Love Love Peace Peace', skewered the clichés of the contest (with some help from Alexander Rybak, Lordi and Loreen) – but did so with huge affection.

Several fine songs followed. France upped its game with Amir, the product of a TV talent contest, and his co-written 'J'ai Cherché' (I've Been Searching). Austria's Zoë also chose to sing in French, with the catchy, appealing 'Loin d'Ici' (Far From Here). Both songs did well. Even the UK had revamped its selection procedure to something more open and public. A much better song, 'You're Not Alone', resulted, but, sadly, no real improvement in the eventual ranking. The nation, a powerhouse in the global pop industry, needs to put its best foot fully forward in the contest and field current stars. Your country needs you, Adele!

By contrast Australia, who had done so well on their one-off guest appearance in 2015 that they simply had to be asked back, fielded a singer with a national number one single and platinum album to her name. After Korean-born Dami Im had sung 'Sound Of Silence', fans were left seriously pondering what would happen if it was Australia's turn to host the contest.

Australia looks set to become a permanent participant, which raises the question of who else can join in the fun. Oz has a huge fan base, and personally I welcome its participation, as long as it keeps sending acts as good as Guy Sebastian and Dami Im (in other words, as long as it treats the contest with traditional peripheral-nation respect). If other countries build large fan bases, and do so for a long time, the way Australia has, I don't see why they shouldn't join in, too. Maybe there should be some limit to the number of guest slots, but this is very much a problem for the future.

Russia was the pre-contest favourite. All the stops were pulled out for Sergei Lazarev's 'You Are The Only One'. Too many stops? Lazarev sprouted eagle's wings, then climbed over an obstacle course, then began hovering in mid-air ... Russia has now established an intriguing love-hate relationship with Eurovision. It looks at Sweden's soft power, and wants to do as well (in the 2010s, the two nations have become the contest's two superpowers*). But it has a lot of baggage: Ukraine, gay rights.

Ukraine itself followed three songs later. '1944' had been controversial from the start. Ostensibly about Stalin's deportation of

---

* Sweden's last six placings have been 3, 1, 14, 3, 1, 5. Russia's are 16, 2, 5, 7, 2, 3. Nowhere else comes near.

Eurovision!

240,000 Crimean Tatars in that year, the song was read by many people as also being a comment on Russia's much more recent annexation of Crimea and its treatment of the Tatar minority since then. Complaints were made, especially from Moscow, but the EBU concluded there was no mention of current events in the song so it passed the 'non-political' test. Jamala's performance was heartfelt (her own great-grandmother had been part of the forced exodus, along with her five daughters, one of whom died on the journey). So, one feels, was her 'Thank you, Europe' at the end. Despite its problems, Europe is still a beacon of liberalism and decency in much of the world.

A complex new system for announcing votes led to a much more exciting finish than in those years where one nation pulls ahead and vanishes into the distance. In the end, it was between Australia, Russia, Ukraine and possibly Bulgaria, with Jamala eventually winning (no doubt politics played a role in this, but '1944' was a relevant, powerful song sung with passion by its writer: a good Eurovision recipe). An Australian born in Korea, Russia, Ukraine, Bulgaria – this was a sign of how big the contest now is, and how it reaches across the world with its essentially positive message.

By contrast, Britain was preparing to vote on its continued membership of the EU. The campaign was not an elevating one. The leave campaigners were charismatic, passionate, street-smart – and deceitful. Their brightly coloured battle bus (deliberately painted red to attract disillusioned Labour voters) claimed that Britain gave £350 million a week to the EU, when the real figure was £163 million,[*] and implied that all that money would go into funding Britain's

---

[*] The EU has a formula for working out how much each nation should pay in. According to this, Britain should contribute £18 billion a year (which does equate to £350 million a week). However, Margaret Thatcher's annual rebate lops off £5 billion, taking the weekly figure down to £250 million. We also get £4.5 billion back from the EU in grants, meaning that our net annual contribution is £8.5 billion, or £163 million a week.

National Health Service, which it couldn't. They could also descend into xenophobia: UKIP leader Nigel Farage posed in front of a poster showing a line of refugees photographed in Slovenia in 2015 with the slogan 'Breaking Point'.

The remainers, by contrast, were simply boring. Their campaign was hijacked by the political parties, which essentially meant the ruling Conservatives (or those of them who weren't Eurosceptics), as the other two main parties were largely invisible. The remainers refused to deal with the emotive issues that were being stirred up – immigration, national sovereignty – and instead droned on about the economic benefits of membership, even though they had no hard facts to use: they fell back on citing a theoretical estimate of how much money Britons would lose from leaving, which nobody took seriously.

Things got really nasty on 16 June, when Jo Cox, a young Labour MP who had, unlike her leadership, been campaigning vigorously, was murdered by a far-right fantasist.

In the days before the vote, the pro-Brexit press became ever more shrill. Newsagents felt less like shops and more like those stalls you get outside fringe political rallies. Some thinkers claim that print media mean ever less in post-modern, wired Europe. The 'Brexit' campaign seems to disprove that.

Britain went to the polls on 23 June. It wasn't a crushing defeat for 'Remain', 48.1 per cent to 51.9 per cent. But it was enough. Europe's third biggest economy is now planning its exit from the EU. By the time you read this, it will probably have triggered Article 50.*

Precise analysis of who voted which way is difficult, but trends seem clear. Scotland wanted 'in', prompting more calls for independence

---

* The UK will, of course, remain eligible for Eurovision – though it remains to be seen how popular with Europe's televoters it will be. Arguably Britain was pretty unpopular before, so maybe it won't make much difference. Or will the many other Europeans who are sceptical about the EU rally round and vote for us?

(after which, one assumes, it would have its own slot in Eurovision). In the rest of the UK, age was one factor, with older people tending to vote for exit, but the biggest determinant seems to have been class. It was poorer people who voted to leave – people who felt no ownership of the European project, people who felt that they had been ignored by the elite (British and European) for too long.

This alienation is, of course, not just a UK phenomenon. That day, 23 June 2016, was Britain's answer to Italy's *Vaffanculo* Day. In other European countries, populist parties are growing. A few weeks before the Brexit vote, Norbert Hofer, the candidate of the Freedom Party, won 49.7 per cent of the votes in the Austrian presidential election. Marine le Pen continues to make threatening noises in France, and Geert Wilders to do the same in the Netherlands.

Britain, however, seems to have been particularly poisoned by its referendum. Hate crimes rose by 30 per cent in the six weeks after the vote. They have since receded a bit, though they are still (at time of writing) around 15 per cent higher than corresponding figures for the previous year. UK resident non-nationals to whom I speak report a new sense of distance between themselves and local people. Not hate – things haven't got that bad – but still unsettling. And whenever anyone dares question Brexit, they are savaged by the popular press with unprecedented viciousness. There is a new nastiness in the nation's life.

South of the olive line, much of the populism is left-wing, not right (Italy's Five Star is an interesting mix of both, aligning itself with UKIP in the European Parliament but supporting environmentalism and greater, internet-driven democracy. Spain's *Podemos* is more conventionally left of centre, as is Greece's SYRIZA). This feels much more benign than the far right, but history shows that the left can be just as totalitarian as the right once it has too much power.

Ironically, one thing that both sets of populists have in common is dislike of the EU. In the north, it is seen as a threat to national identity and a drain on national resources: people in countries like the Netherlands feel they are bankrolling a less industrious south. But the south is suffering, too, with its economies locked by the euro into 'internal devaluation', in other words massive unemployment. It's hard to be 'industrious' when you can't get a job.*

It's reasonable to ask where all the bailout money has gone. The answer seems largely to be to financial institutions. One recent study – from a German business school, not a group of radical anti-debt activists – showed that less than 5 per cent of the Greek bailouts 'directly contributed' to that nation's budget.

All over the continent, Europe-level government is seen as distant and arrogant. This reputation is probably deserved in part, but in another part is just a side effect of a more general anger against elites of all kinds – an anger that, given the result of the US presidential election, seems to have possessed the entire western world.

What would Jean Monnet and Marcel Bezençon make of all this? For them, European unity was an antidote to nationalism, but now seems to be stirring it up. It was supposed to be a guarantor of prosperity, but now seems to be standing in its way.

What has gone wrong? What can we do?

Maybe Eurovision can help us.

---

* According to an OECD survey, if you have a job in Greece, you actually work longer hours than anyone else in Europe (on average, of course). Fellow PIIGS nation Portugal comes second in this table.

Conclusion

I can't promise *that* much. 'Watch a couple of contests and you will immediately know how to stop the rise of the far right, help 4.9 million refugees, regenerate European economic growth and halt terrorism.' Would that were true . . . But I do believe that Eurovision has important messages for Europe – all of Europe, including Britain – at this difficult time.

First, I'd like to look at Europe-level government. This may seem irrelevant to British readers, post 23 June 2016, but I believe it still matters. Mainland Europe's history is our history and its future is our future – to think otherwise was a catastrophic mistake in 1914 and in 1938, and is still a mistake today. The EU is still the UK's biggest trading partner,* and looks set to be so for a long time. And maybe in the future, we will get the chance to design a better European system. Maybe.

The modern EU is suffering a crisis of legitimacy. This is partly its own fault, partly the result of a deeper sense of disconnect between Europe's citizens and its governments at all levels. In the long run, reconnection is essential. What can Eurovision show it about how to achieve that?

The contest is *transparent*: people understand how it works and what the rules are. Yes, the new results-announcement system is a bit puzzling, but the underlying system, the 50/50 split between televoters and jury, remains clear. 2016 also showed the rules to be a bit fuzzy round the edges – on flags, on political content – but only a bit. Basically, we know how Eurovision works.

---

* About 44 per cent of Britain's exports of goods and services went to other EU countries in 2015. Our next biggest export market was the USA, who took 17 per cent.

European government, by contrast, often seems incomprehensible, with its legalistic language and confusing institutions. Take, for example, the welter of EU presidents. All seven formal EU institutions have one, which leaves no clear figure as the leader, and thus no place where one can say, as US president Harry Truman did with a sign on his desk, 'The Buck Stops Here'. Arguably, the buck should stop with the president of the European Council, but the Commission president often takes more limelight. He (it has always been a 'he' so far*) gives the annual speech to the Parliament on the 'State of the Union', for example. It reminds me of Eurovision 1969, its four winners and the confusion and sense of bathos that the outcome produced.

The contest is *democratic without being demotic.* The 50/50 voting system is a nice example of balancing expert and popular opinion. However much the juries of music-industry professionals like a song, if the public don't vote for it, it won't win Eurovision. Democracy is the same. It isn't a system for giving the majority whatever they want the moment they want it. It accepts that in a complex world, experts sometimes do know best and we have to let them get on with the job. But in the end, it makes them accountable.

There seems to be insufficient accountability in Europe-level government. Its defenders will point to the European Parliament – if voters don't like what Brussels is up to, we can return different MEPs. But we don't. Turnout in European elections has been falling since they began. Whether for this reason or for others, the European Parliament has ended up failing to reflect the balance of opinion in Europe. Both its main parties, centre-left and centre-right, are in favour of the continuing transfer of power from national to Europe-level government. Europe's citizens do not share this enthusiasm.

---

* And a 'he' from core Europe. There have been twelve Commission presidents, and ten have come from countries that took to the Eurovision stage in Lugano in 1956 – including three from Luxembourg, whose population is 0.1 per cent of that of the EU.

Eurovision!

A really effective parliament should reflect both the shared values of its voters and the split of opinions among them. The European Parliament, despite having many able and honourable members, does not do this at the moment.

Eurovision's answer to this is 'get more *popular*'. Popular, not populist. Ultimately, Europe-wide political institutions will only have true legitimacy if the people of Europe embrace them, argue about them, start cheering and booing, and even vote en bloc – bloc votes are better than no votes (more on this later). Europe needs continent-wide political parties, more colourful candidates – more 'Theater' – and a sense that the European Parliament really does reflect the diversity of opinion across the continent's hundreds of millions of voters, the way the best Eurovision contests draw in musical styles from all corners of the continent (and beyond).

Eurovision is *flexible*. Look how much it has changed since 1956. If an issue becomes pressing, creative solutions are sought and implemented both quickly and with an understanding that they are provisional and remain open to change. Sorry to go on about it, but the 50/50 rule is a perfect example.

By contrast European government seems unresponsive and incapable of self-criticism, clinging to its existing rulebook, the *acquis communautaire*, like a child with a safety blanket. Surrounded by national governments making painful austerity cuts, the EU has done little to prune its own expenditure. For example, it still wastes 114 million euros a year on the Parliament's 'travelling circus' between Brussels and Strasbourg (members go to the Alsatian city for four days' debating a month).

Eurovision *respects national identity*. It has no truck with vicious, intolerant nationalism. The federalist project was begun in the shadow of what can happen when nationalism gets hideously distorted. Its founders hoped that Europeans would look back at the horrors of Fascism and decide to move on to a broader sense of

European identity. But we didn't. We didn't all turn into Fascists, either, just (by and large) nice people who like our countries.

Given the current rise of the far right, the above paragraph could be considered naïve. But I don't think so. Eurovision-style gentle nationalism is a friendly outlet for natural feelings of belonging. It is about mutual respect – plus a bit of fun-poking – and has nothing to do with any kind of hate. I believe that most of the contest's 200 million viewers feel the same way.

Europe-level government can even learn from Eurovision's tendency for countries to *vote in blocs*. Has it missed out an administrative tier? Should there be (let's say) a Balkan council, a Visegrad-countries council, a Nordic council, a Latin/Southern European council, a North-west European council?* In other words, was the Grand Design of Henry of Navarre and the Duc du Sully a better plan for Europe than the one we currently have? Eurovision suggests that it was.

I'd like to move on to some thoughts about European culture. Is there such a thing? Or, more subtly, of course there's such a thing, but how strong is it relative to national cultures, and what is it exactly?

This is an essential question to anyone interested in any European political project. Nations work, essentially, because they share a culture (or share it enough, anyway). The same is true of transnational institutions like the EU. No shared culture; no serious political entity.

Even if you are not interested in such projects, either by inclination or because your country is in the process of quitting one, the question remains important. Britain is still a European nation, and will be even when it quits the EU: much as some people might like to do so, we can't attach the UK to a tug and tow it out into the Atlantic.

---

* The Euro could then be scrapped and monetary union trialled in each of these areas separately (if they want it)? Just a thought . . .

Eurovision!

To use Eurovision as a tool for examining culture might grate on some readers. Culture, surely, is Schiller and Beethoven . . . But most Europeans don't read Schiller or listen to much Beethoven. Maybe we should, but we don't. Lots of us watch Eurovision, however.

So here is 'Europe', as I see it in the contest.

The contest is technologically savvy. Production is state-of-the-art. Behind this is a culture of meritocracy. Things are done well at Eurovision because the best people are brought in to do them. Ideological or religious purity, or family connection to influential elites, are no substitute for application and professionalism. (At the same time, we have enough humour to enjoy it when the mask slips a tiny bit. But not too much: for many of us, Eurovision 1991's presentation started off funny but ended up embarrassing.)

The contest is democratic, as we have seen, with its millions of televoters, even though their views are moderated by judges. It is participatory: we're encouraged to vote on national selections, comment on social media and generally be part of the fun.

Eurovision promotes political liberalism. When artists like Loreen meet protesters in places like Azerbaijan or Belarus, they send a clear message about the European model of a society where people are allowed to say what they think and get to vote on who rules them.

It fosters gentle nationalism. To be European, Eurovision-style, is to have more than one identity and to be at ease with, and curious about, other people's. I believe that this gentleness runs deep – Europe has learnt the hard way that political violence breeds violence. Eurovision's 2016 anthem 'Love Love Peace Peace' was a send-up – but accurate and witty because many Eurovision songs do have that message.

Eurovision is an intriguing mixture of state and market. The participating broadcasters are largely state institutions, but the contest flourishes in the now highly commercial world of media. Host broadcasters don't just use in-house employees but hire in the best freelance designers and technicians from the marketplace out there.

The nations of Europe strike this balance, too – but according to different traditions.* Their diversity is valuable, and it would be a shame to see it steamrollered by the one-size-fits-all logic of the single currency and some eventual political union. What suits Germany might not suit Spain or Sweden. Imagine a Eurovision with only one type of song . . .

Above all, I feel, Eurovision flies the flag, loud and proud, for a Europe-wide openness and tolerance, for the power and value of personal authenticity. Conchita Wurst's 2014 victory was seen in some parts of the world as a sign of moral weakness, but for modern Europe it was a sign of moral strength. Be who you are, and don't let anyone tell you different! This book has charted the rise of such values.

So here is the Europe that we see reflected in our song contest. It is technologically advanced and competent: we believe it matters to do things well. It is democratic, politically liberal and *gently* nationalistic (a mixture of diverse nations, enjoying that diversity). It does not see violence as a solution to problems. It understands that modern states balance the state and the market, though it comes up with variations on that balance in line with regional traditions. Most of all it is open and tolerant, believing both that human beings have a profound right to 'be who they are' and that such authenticity releases creative energy which benefits society as a whole.

I genuinely believe in this Europe. But looking around, I also see another Europe. What about those figures on domestic violence cited earlier? There's no point in eschewing political violence if all you do is hide it in the home. What about the xenophobia that is being stirred up by the refugee crisis? Or the lingering sense that black Europeans are still under-represented in Eurovision? Or, let's be honest, the continuing strain of arrogance in Europe's elites?

---

* Shown, of course, in our bloc voting at Eurovision.

Eurovision!

Europe, as a political project but also as a moral and cultural one, remains a work in progress. It always will be – there is no ultimate end in politics or philosophy. Events are bigger than any of these things, always evolving, always presenting new challenges. Right now, the challenges seem particularly pressing. Our values are there to help us meet them with imaginative new solutions.

As Eurovision enters its seventh decade, its quirky, tolerant, heartfelt humanity is needed more than ever. It reminds us – all of us Europeans, EU members or not – of who we are and where we have come from. It may even keep us going in the right direction.

Appendix A:
Five Steps to Heaven (or is it Hell?)

There are five generally accepted steps that nations take from being separate entities to becoming parts of a 'United States of X'. The idea was first mooted by émigré Hungarian economist Béla Belassa in 1961.

The first step is for them to join together in a **Free Trade Area**, where the tariffs (taxes on imports) that countries usually charge one another are removed, and goods move freely from one member state to another.

A **Customs Union** is the second: here, not only do area members charge each other no import duties, but they charge outsiders a common tariff. This was what was suggested for The Six in the 1956 Spaak Report.

The next step is a **Common Market**, within which there is free movement not just of goods but of labour, capital and services. Standards, regulations and qualifications are harmonized to remove 'hidden' barriers to trade. The 1957 Treaty of Rome, while setting up a Customs Union, expressed a desire to proceed to this stage, as a result of which the EEC became known as the 'Common Market'. Arguably a true Common Market did not come to Europe until 1993, with the formal introduction of the European Single Market (and arguably not even then, as Europe's legislators are still working on aspects of it).

Then it gets controversial.

Belassa argued that Step Four was **Monetary Union**, a shared currency – the euro, at time of writing in use in twenty-three European countries (this figure includes Andorra, San Marino, the Vatican and Monaco) – and that Step Five was Political Union, where there is a new, single nation like the United States of America. History, however, both ancient and modern, seems to show that these last two steps are not clear or distinct or even that they necessarily take place in this order. It tells us that a high level of political union needs to be in place before monetary union will work.

Maybe there should be six steps.

Step Four would be **Partial Political Union**, to the extent where there is an 'Optimal Currency Area', with a high level of political and cultural unity – where, for example, the richer parts accept the necessity of supporting the poorer parts.

Step Five: **Monetary Union**.

Step Six: **Completed Political Union**. A United States of Europe.

Appendix B:
Glossary and Acronyms

Here are a few more terms from Euro-debate and Euro-acronyms.

Terms of debate

Euro-cautious. Because the word **Eurosceptic** has come to mean anti-EU, I've coined my own word for someone who accepts the need for European institutions and understands that such institutions must evolve over time (as they did, for example, in the USA), but doesn't think the moment is right for federalism and dislikes some of the more self-serving Euro-talk that comes out of the Brussels bubble.

Europhile. Admirer of Europe-level political institutions, but not with the passion of full-on **federalists**. Can also just mean someone who likes European culture, travel, food, people – and song contests.

Europhobe. This term has largely been edged out by **Eurosceptic**. But let's keep it for people who don't just argue rationally against Brussels and the EU, but have a kind of irrational, visceral loathing of them. The classic example is that bloke in the pub who goes on and on about 'the dictatorship in Brussels'.

Eurosceptics oppose any kind of Europe-level government. It's an unfortunate term: all EU citizens should be 'Eurosceptics' in the proper sense of the word, meaning that they keep a close, critical eye on Brussels and do their best to ensure that it doesn't waste money or arrogate too much power to itself. The term Eurosceptic, however, now means firmly anti-EU.

Federalists want a United States of Europe (or at least to work towards that as a long-term goal). Classic federalists are Jean Monnet, Walter Hallstein, Jacques Delors and Eurovision's founder, Marcel Bezençon.

Intergovernmentalists approve of Europe-wide institutions but do not want them to have too much power. To them, such institutions should be mechanisms for helping sovereign governments work together on areas of mutual interest, such as free trade, crime and climate change. Classic intergovernmentalists are Ludwig Erhard, Charles de Gaulle and Margaret Thatcher.

Subsidiarity is the principle that decisions in European government should be made at as local a level as possible. **Intergovernmentalists** are keen on subsidiarity; **federalists** distrust it as back-door nationalism.

Acronyms used in the text

CAP	Common Agricultural Policy
CERN	Conseil Européen pour la Recherche Nucléaire (European Organization for Nuclear Research)
EBU	European Broadcasting Union
ECB	European Central Bank
ECSC	European Coal and Steel Community
EEC	European Economic Community
EFTA	European Free Trade Area. Rival to EEC, founded in 1960
ETA	Euskadi Ta Askatasuna, Basque terrorist organization
EU	European Union
GDR	'German Democratic Republic'. Communist East Germany, 1949–89
GDP	Gross Domestic Product. The value of the goods and services that a nation produces, usually measured annually
IRA	Irish Republican Army

Eurovision!

KLA   Kosovo Liberation Army
MEP   Member of the European Parliament
NATO   North Atlantic Treaty Organization
OCA   Optimal Currency Area
PIIGS   Portugal, Italy, Ireland, Greece and Spain, the countries most affected by the euro crisis
RAF   Red Army Faction, West German 1970s terrorist organization
RTÉ   Raidió Teilifís Éireann, Irish public service broadcaster
SYRIZA   Synaspismós Rizospastikís Aristerás, Greek anti-austerity party
UKIP   UK Independence Party
UNHCR   UN High Commission for Refugees
VRS   Vojska Republike Srpske, Bosnian Serb Army

Appendix C:
'Fifty Years of Celebration'

A poll was carried out online in 2005 to find voters' all-time Eurovision faves. The method would have graced the most complex Brussels directive. First, respondents chose their favourites from each decade of the contest. The top two from each decade went on to the list. Then four songs were added by the EBU. There were then two rounds of voting on the fourteen songs chosen. The end result was . . .

1   Abba, 'Waterloo'
2   Domenico Modugno, 'Volare'*
3   Johnny Logan, 'Hold Me Now'
4   Brotherhood of Man, 'Save All Your Kisses for Me'
5   Helena Paparizou, 'My Number One'
6   Olsen Brothers, 'Fly On The Wings Of Love'
7   Nicole, 'Ein Bisschen Frieden'
8   Cliff Richard, 'Congratulations'*
9   Sertab Erener, 'Everyway That I Can'
10 Céline Dion, 'Ne Partez Pas Sans Moi'
11 Mocedades, 'Eres Tù'*
12 Johnny Logan, 'What's Another Year?'
13 Dana International, 'Diva'
14 France Gall, 'Poupée De Cire, Poupée De Son'

Songs marked * didn't even win the contest they featured in.
What's your Top Fourteen? (Or Top Twenty. Or Top Seventeen. Or Top 103. It's Eurovision – choose your own number!)

Another, arguably even more enjoyable exercise is to produce a list of personal Eurovision favourites that do *not* include the classics above. Most fans will put 'Waterloo' and 'Volare' among their faves, but when these disappear, a list can get a lot more idiosyncratic and interesting. One of the many pleasures of Eurovision is seeing how different these lists are. Almost every one will include at least one song that leaves most other people scratching their heads wondering why the hell that individual saw fit to include it. But that just shows how tastes differ, which in turn is a part of the subversive appeal of the contest.

Here's my 'bubbling under' Top Twenty. I have also excluded the two most obvious candidates for the decade (and a bit) 2005 to 2016, 'Fairytale' (2009) and 'Euphoria' (2012).

Floaty New Age, Best of British, spine-tingling *chanson*, tribal trance, belted-out ballads, cabaret camp, more ballads, songs in made-up languages, plus Euro-anthems, wistful *sevdah*, a song nobody else likes – they're all here.

1   'Nocturne' (Norway, 1995)
2   'Love Shine A Light' (UK, 1997)
3   'Un Premier Amour' (France, 1962)
4   'Water' (Bulgaria, 2007)
5   'Quédate Conmigo' (Spain, 2012)
6   'Theater' (Germany, 1980)
7   'Su Canción' (Spain, 1979)
8   'Sanomi' (Belgium, 2003)
9   'Insieme: 1992' (Italy, 1990)
10 'Un Banc, Un Arbre, Une Rue' (Monaco, 1971)
11 'Lane Moje' (Serbia and Montenegro, 2004)
12 'Je Suis l'Enfant Soleil' (France, 1979)
13 'Tornerò' (Romania, 2006)
14 'Dansevise' (Denmark, 1963)
15 'Rise Like A Phoenix' (Austria, 2014)

16 'Lejla' (Bosnia-Herzegovina, 2006)

17 'La Source' (France, 1968)

18 'To Dream Again' (Malta, 2003)

19 'I Feed You My Love' (Norway, 2013)

20 'De La Capat' (Romania, 2015)

Apologies to near-misses 'For Din Skyld' (Denmark, 1965), 'Inter Er Nytt Under Solen' (Norway, 1966), 'Judy, Min Vän' (Sweden, 1969), 'Mikado' (Switzerland, 1976), 'Libera' (Italy, 1977), 'Não Sejas Mau Para Mim' (Portugal, 1986), 'Why Me?' (Ireland, 1992), 'To Nie Ja' (Poland, 1994), 'Never Ever Let You Go' (Denmark, 2001), 'Madness Of Love' (Italy, 2011), 'Lăutar' (Moldova, 2012), 'Ég Á Líf' (Iceland, 2013), 'Heroes' (Sweden, 2015), and . . .

Please feel free to email me your own list.

References

The 1950s

Church attendance:
http://econ.hevra.haifa.ac.il/~todd/seminars/papers09-10/franck_
iannaccone_religiosity.pdf

Sex education in 1950s:
http://www.open.edu/openlearn/body-mind/health/health-studies/
brief-history-sex-education

Change in Jewish population of Netherlands during the war:
https://en.wikipedia.org/wiki/History_of_the_Jews_in_the_Netherlands

Switzerland win first contest by one vote:
www.songwriter.co.uk/eurovision.html

Growth of TV ownership:
http://unesdoc.unesco.org/images/0003/000337/033739eo.pdf

Negotiations leading up to the Treaty of Rome:
http://www.cvce.eu/obj/how_the_common_market_was_born_in_
the_chateau_of_val_duchesse_from_communaute_europeenne_
march_1967-en-8e98b764-9cf6-4215-85ea-e62ae1aca8c4.html

De Gaulle quote from Julian Jackson, *de Gaulle* (Haus Publishing, 2003), p. 99

The 1960s

Tito and Stalin:
http://dalje.com/en-croatia/tito-threatened-to-assassinate-stalin/151090

EFTA and EEC:
http://www.funfront.net/hist/europe/econ-coop.htm

Nuclear weapons in 1962:
http://en.wikipedia.org/wiki/Nuclear_weapons_testing

Introduction of colour TV:
http://en.wikipedia.org/wiki/Timeline_of_the_introduction_of_color_television_in_countries
The CAP budget:
Pinder and Underwood, *The European Union, a Very Short Introduction* (OUP, 2013)
Figures on Spanish tourism numbers from Stephen Page, *Tourism Management* (Routledge, 2014)
Death toll in 1968 Prague invasion:
http://www.upi.com/Archives/1990/07/24/Death-toll-in-Prague-Spring-invasion-revealed/3068648792000/
Material on Olof Palme:
http://nome.unak.is/nm-marzo-2012/6-1x/24-articles61/77-olof-palme-one-life-many-readings

The 1970s
Julio Iglesias' record sales:
http://www.boomsbeat.com/articles/22220/20150903/50-things-julio-iglesias-sold-more-300-million-copies-80.htm
Viewing figures for ESC 1971:
J.K. O'Connor, *The Official History of the Eurovision Song Contest* (Carlton Books, 2010)
Security at 1973 contest:
http://josefoshea.blogspot.co.uk/2014/04/the-strange-history-of-eurovision-war.html
Who broadcast *E Depois Do Adeus?* Different sources claim different stations. My preferred source is *Foi Assim* (*How It Was*), the autobiography of Communist turned Social Democrat politician Zita Seabra, who lived through the events.
Material on social change in the early 1970s from Hartmut Kaelble, *A Social History of Europe 1945–2000* (Berghahn Books, 2013) and Colin Crouch, *Social Change in Western Europe* (OUP, 2004)

Karel Gott and the charter protests:
https://www.private-prague-guide.com/article/karel-gott-an-
international-singing-sensation/
Soviet funding for terrorists:
https://www.ncjrs.gov/app/abstractdb/AbstractDBDetails.
aspx?id=85273
Alla Pugacheva:
http://esctoday.com/8943/alla_pugacheva_launches_her_own_
radio_station/

The 1980s

The history of the Sami people:
http://saamiassimilation.blogspot.co.uk/2011/03/history-of-sami.html
The long-term effects of AIDS awareness campaigns (or of the lack
of such campaigns):
http://www.bbc.co.uk/news/magazine-15886670
German identity and the forests – for a discussion, see *Nature in
German History*, ed. Christof Mauch (Berghahn Books, 2004).
Levels of nuclear weapons in early 1980s:
http://www.bbc.co.uk/news/magazine-17026538
Abortion levels in Europe and elsewhere:
https://www.guttmacher.org/pubs/journals/25s3099.html
The worst *nul pointe*r ever?:
See http://www.sechuk.com/TheBigZeroResult.htm

The 1990s

For the Eurobarometer surveys, go to
http://ec.europa.eu/COMMFrontOffice/PublicOpinion/index.cfm/
Archive/index
and click on 'A chronological guide to Eurobarometer surveys'.

Yugoslavia, material from the Index on Censorship site:
http://i-scoop.org/scoop/blog/2010/02/25/political-use-of-the-eurovision-song-contest/
For info on the historical background to the Yugoslav conflict, see Keith Lowe's chilling book *Savage Continent* (Penguin, 2013) and Misha Glenny, *The Balkans, 1804–1999* (Granta Books, 2000)
'Club Med' objections to EU enlargement:
www.rferl.org/content/article/1096579.html
The Irish boom:
http://socialistparty.ie/2013/10/the-rise-a-fall-of-the-celtic-tiger/
Decline of organized religion: info from Callum Brown, *The Death of Christian Britain* (Routledge, 2000) and Colin Crouch, *Social Change in Western Europe* (OUP, 2000)
Centre countries accused of fudging economic data:
http://www.economist.com/node/159467
Number of Muslims, Jews and Hindus in Europe in 1990 from various sources, especially PEW Research
Dutch responses to Srebrenica massacre:
https://www.ft.com/content/d5ff149a-a1f7-11e0-b485-00144feabdc0
Number of cybercafés in Paris:
http://iml.jou.ufl.edu/carlson/1995s.shtml#1995
Levels of smoking in Europe: source, UK Office for National Statistics
Survey on attitudes to same-sex relationships:
http://www.bsa-30.natcen.ac.uk/read-the-report/personal-relationships/homosexuality.aspx
Figures for amount of space given to news vs celeb coverage from Howard Altman, 'Celebrity Culture', in *Issues for Debate in Sociology* (Sage Publications, 2010)
Levels of internet use: I estimated my figures from information on http://www.internetworldstats.com/emarketing.htm, which shows world-wide internet use around 200 million around the time of Eurovision 1999, and another site,

Eurovision!

http://royal.pingdom.com/2010/10/22/incredible-growth-of-the-internet-since-2000/, which shows use split about three ways, equally: Asia/USA/Europe

Bloc voting – does it exist? As well as Derek Gatherer's piece, I use http://www.euronews.com/2012/05/21/eurovision-the-great-voting-conspiracy/

Euro election turnout:
http://www.ukpolitical.info/european-parliament-election-turnout.htm

James Blount and his role in events at Pristina airport:
http://www.theguardian.com/music/2010/nov/15/james-blunt-world-war-three

The 2000s

Milošević role in Stambolić murder:
http://www.independent.co.uk/news/world/europe/death-squad-leader-guilty-of-killing-serbian-president-300063.html

Estonia celebrates its win:
http://www.escinsight.com/2011/01/19/the-eurovision-rise-and-fall-of-estonia-the-baltic-tiger/

Global survey on racism:
https://www.washingtonpost.com/news/worldviews/wp/2013/05/15/a-fascinating-map-of-the-worlds-most-and-least-racially-tolerant-countries/

Bush, Chirac and the book of Ezekiel:
http://www.theguardian.com/commentisfree/andrewbrown/2009/aug/10/religion-george-bush

Habermas on Iraq:
http://platypus1917.org/wp-content/uploads/archive/rgroups/2006-chicago/habermasderrida_europe.pdf

Kok Report on the failure of the Lisbon Strategy:
http://aei.pitt.edu/9308/1/Lisbon-Strategy-TZKH.pdf

Split electorate in Ukraine:
http://en.wikipedia.org/wiki/Ukrainian_parliamentary_election,_
2007#mediaviewer/File:Ukrainian_parliamentary_election,_2007_(first_
place_results).PNG
Global phone ownership:
Wikipedia entry on Mobile Telephony
Nokia market share:
https://www.statista.com/statistics/263438/market-share-held-by-
nokia-smartphones-since-2007/
Finnish GDP:
http://www.google.co.uk/publicdata/explore?ds=d5bncppjof8f9_
&met_y=ny_gdp_pcap_cd&idim=country:FIN:SWE:NOR&hl=en&d
l=en
Nokia turnover from Company Report and Accounts
Europe's ageing population: statistics from the Population Research
Bureau, a respected global NGO based in New York
Prime minister Zapatero on Wall Street:
http://www.realinstitutoelcano.org/wps/portal/web/rielcano_en/
contenido?WCM_GLOBAL_CONTEXT=/elcano/elcano_in/zonas_
in/ari11-2014-chislett-spain-banking-crisis-light-in-the-tunnel#.
VMjy5p1FD1I

The 2010s
Austerity and 2010 Eurovision:
http://www.theguardian.com/commentisfree/2010/may/20/
eurovision-spending-costs
A8 immigration and consequences:
http://www.theguardian.com/news/datablog/2010/apr/29/
eastern-european-immigration-uk-general-election
http://www.independent.co.uk/news/uk/home-news/
uk-migration-six-myths-about-immigration-debunked-as-latest-
figures-show-fall-in-non-eu-arrivals-a6895341.html

Eurovision!

Cost of Eurovision in Azerbaijan:
http://www.tol.org/client/article/23107-in-eurovision-spending-azerbaijan-is-a-clear-winner.html
Albania's pyramid schemes:
http://www.independent.co.uk/news/world/albanian-financiers-fail-to-play-the-game-1277155.html
Youth unemployment in Europe 2012:
http://one-europe.info/-lighting-of-the-fire-fighting-youth-unemployment
and
http://en.protothema.gr/the-ecs-youth-guarantee-to-the-rescue-for-the-eus-young-educated-and-unemployed/
Death toll in *Euromaidan* confrontation, February 2014:
http://www.bbc.co.uk/news/magazine-31359021
EU Commission on child abuse:
http://ec.europa.eu/dgs/home-affairs/what-we-do/policies/organized-crime-and-human-trafficking/child-sexual-abuse/index_en.htm
Survey on domestic violence:
http://www.bbc.co.uk/news/world-26444655
Deflation in UK:
https://docs.google.com/spreadsheet/ccc?key=0Asiju4DoCDhScFhNRlEzZTRhRlkxMW9Ra1RfN0ZoWmc#gid=0
Size of Romanian diaspora:
Various sources, including the promo video of 'De La Capat'
Number of Syrian refugees by end of 2015:
http://www.unhcr.org/global-trends-2015.html
EU Commission resettlement plan:
http://europa.eu/rapid/press-release_MEMO-15-5698_en.htm
General piece on refugee crisis 2015–16:
https://foreignpolicy.com/2016/10/18/europe-wishes-to-inform-you-that-the-refugee-crisis-is-over/

UK monetary contribution to EU:
https://fullfact.org/europe/our-eu-membership-fee-55-million/
(Other sources, including the Eurosceptic *Daily Telegraph*, come
up with similar figures)
Rise in hate crime in post-referendum Britain:
https://www.theguardian.com/society/2016/sep/07/hate-surged-
after-eu-referendum-police-figures-show
Where does the bailout money go?:
https://www.esmt.org/where-did-greek-bailout-money-go
Hours worked in Greece and Portugal:
https://www.weforum.org/agenda/2016/06/which-european-
countries-work-the-longest-hours/

Conclusion

UK export markets:
Office for National Statistics, http://visual.ons.gov.uk/uk-
perspectives-2016-trade-with-the-eu-and-beyond/
Cost of European Parliament 'travelling circus':
https://www.euractiv.com/section/future-eu/news/auditors-put-
price-tag-on-eu-parliament-travelling-circus/

Further Reading

On Eurovision, you can't beat John Kennedy O'Connor's *The Eurovision Song Contest: The Official History* (Carlton Books, 2010) for info, stats and pictures. There is also the wonderful Diggiloo Thrush website (www.digiloo.net).

Academic work is now being done on the contest and its deeper meaning. A good example is *A Song for Europe* (Routledge, 2007), a collection of essays edited by Ivan Raykoff and Robert Deam Tobin.

The video *The Secret History of Eurovision* is also recommended. Tim Moore's book *Nul Points* (Vintage, 2007) is a witty, very British look at some classic losers.

On the history side, there isn't really a standard volume on 'Europe since 1956' (which is one of the reasons why I decided to write this book). There are many good works on aspects of the story, however. Here are a few.

Academic/specialist texts first. Barry Eichengreen's *The European Economy since 1945* (Princeton, 2008) takes the (neo-liberal) economist's perspective, telling the story up to the mid-2000s. The baton is then taken up by Martin Wolf's *The Shifts and the Shocks* (Allen Lane, 2014), especially chapters 2, 5 and 9. Hartmut Kaelble's *A Social History of Europe 1945–2000* (Berghahn Books, 2013) looks (unsurprisingly) at social history.

On political Europe, sociologist Neil Fligstein's *Euroclash* (OUP, 2009) asks tough questions about who we Europeans think we are and where our project is going – not easy reading but very rewarding. The book seems to be becoming ever more prescient. Chris Bickerton's more recent *The European Union: A Citizen's Guide* (Pelican, 2016) includes an excellent brief history and is delightfully readable.

Chris West

Andrew Moravcsik's *The Choice for Europe* (Routledge, 1998) and Craig Parsons' *A Certain Idea of Europe* (Cornell UP, 2006) consider European political decision-making. Parsons argues that you can't make sense of European history since 1956 without taking into account the European ideal. Moravcsik disagrees: in his view, what appear to be 'European' motives disappear under closer scrutiny and turn out to be expressions of national interest.

For more general readers, Hugo Young's *This Blessed Plot* (Macmillan, 1999) berates the British political establishment for not getting involved in Europe earlier (sometimes, in my view, glossing over how difficult this was). Stephen Wall's *A Stranger in Europe* (OUP, 2008) is a British Brussels insider's view of UK/Europe relations from 1982 to 2004. Johan van Overtveldt tells the story of the euro (and predicts its demise) in *The End of the Euro* (Agate, 2011). The video on Estonia's Singing Revolution is very moving. Tim Judah's *The Serbs* (Yale University Press, 2009) throws fascinating light on Yugoslavia, and makes Maria Šerifović's win and the emerging modern European Serbia appear all the more impressive.

If you have any favourite books on the era or its major players – or the contest – please email me at chris@chriswest.info. I'm always eager to read more.

And as the Credits Roll . . .

Finally, I'd like to thank my lovely wife Rayna for helping make the writing of this book so enjoyable, for our many discussions about the contest we both enjoy so much and for putting up with my snarky comments about the Netherlands' 1975 winner.

Thanks to Stephen Wall, a true UK European, to Dean Vuletic, Sally Jones, Maddy Savage, Fernando Pacheco, Georgina Godwin, and the ever-helpful Dave Goodman at the EBU.

Thanks to the marvellous people who set up the Diggiloo Thrush website, which has been a goldmine. There are some really rather good lyrics in among the dings and dongs, and I'd never have got to know them without this site.

Thanks to Nikki Griffiths and Dennis Johnson at Melville House for spotting the book and believing in it, and to Nikki and to Steve Gove for their editorial input. It's lovely to be with a small publisher that takes time over authors and books.

Also please email me (chris@chriswest.info) with any comments – it's always good to hear from readers, even if it's just to let me know I've misspelt the Luxembourg entry from 1959 . . .

About the author

Chris West watched Sandie Shaw winning in 1967, and has been hooked on Eurovision ever since. As a teenager, he co-wrote a song for the contest, but it didn't get selected. After a short spell as a professional musician and a longer spell in some 'proper jobs', he became a professional writer. His books include *Journey to the Middle Kingdom*, *Death of a Blue Lantern* (a whodunnit set in 1990s China), *The Beermat Entrepreneur*, *The Hillwalker* and *First Class: A History of Britain in 36 Postage Stamps*. He lives in Hertfordshire with his wife and daughter.

Index

of notable politicians, thinkers, institutions, events and ESC participants